THE FUNDAMENTALS OF EXTREMISM

THE CHRISTIAN RIGHT IN AMERICA

Edited by Kimberly Blaker

New Boston Books, Inc.
Michigan

Copyright © 2003 by New Boston Books Inc.

All rights reserved

This edition published by New Boston Books, Inc.,
P.O. Box 195, New Boston, Michigan 48164

Printed and bound in the United States

Cover design by George Foster

Permissions acknowledgments for previously published
material can be found on pages 271.

Library of Congress Control Number: 2002095474

The Fundamentals of Extremism: the Christian Right in America

1. Fundamentalism—Controversial literature. I. Title.
2. Christianity—Controversial literature.
2. Christianity and politics.
3. Conservatism—United States—Controversial literature.
4. Evangelism—United States—Controversial literature.
5. Women—United States—Social Conditions.
6. Family Violence
7. Child Abuse

BR526.B   261.8

ISBN: 0-9725496-0-9 (Cloth)
ISBN: 0-9725496-1-7 (Paper)

To Cassandra and Caleb,

For your patience and understanding.

May you grow to possess
The liberties we hold and treasure today,
In a democracy that is flexible yet strong,
With the freedom to believe
In many gods
Or none at all
And to live according to the dictates
Of your own conscience.

To Donnie,

For your support and encouragement
And for believing in me,
In every endeavor I pursue

Contents

Foreword

Finally, here is a well-documented book about the dangers of Christian fundamentalism, both Protestant and Catholic. Mind control, including a strong relationship between fundamentalism and prejudice, discrimination, intolerance, and hate crimes are exposed with fact and credible evidence. Women, especially, suffer not only in fundamentalist homes, but also from the political results of fundamentalism.

Kimberly Blaker's book demonstrates not only the relationship between fundamentalism and far-right organizations—such as Dobson's Focus on the Family, and those of Jerry Falwell and Pat Robertson—it also reveals the funding by right-wing foundations and their corporate sponsors. It is not surprising that religious fundamentalists support private school vouchers and home schooling rather than public schools where students are taught to think for themselves.

This book also demonstrates the opposition of fundamentalism to sex education in the schools and the consequent result that teen pregnancy is higher in the United States than six other developed countries.

In fact, this is the most careful and devastating evaluation of the impact of fundamentalism on American society, politics, and customs ever produced in the United States.

Although Kimberly Blaker, a woman, is the chief author and creator of this exploration of the perils of fundamentalism, she has wisely included chapters from several men, including a medical doctor, who reinforce with their own research the basic thesis and ideas she has advanced so well.

I have seldom, if ever, reviewed a book so cogent, factually accurate, and enlightening as this one. It opens a new vista of knowledge and insight that will make a significant contribution to American parents, educators, and thoughtful religious and humanist leaders.

John M. Swomley
Professor emeritus of Social Ethics, Saint Paul School of Theology
President of The Churchman Co., Inc.
Author of *Religious Liberty and the Secular State*

Acknowledgments

This book has come to fruition because many people worked together to make it happen. It has been shaped not only by its authors, but also by those who have so graciously lent their assistance and expertise. I offer special thanks to all who have assisted. My coauthors Ed Buckner, Edwin Kagin, Bobbie Kirkhart, Herb Silverman, and John Suarez have shared both personal experiences and expertise in their chapters, shedding added light to issues that affect us all.

I cannot begin to express my gratitude to Richard Dawkins, Gerald A. Larue, John Shelby Spong, Nadine Strossen, and John M. Swomley, all of who eagerly agreed to read my manuscript without prior familiarity with me. Each of their wonderful endorsements to this book was a thrill I never anticipated. Their kind advice was appreciated as well.

My cover designer, George Foster, has done an outstanding job and given this book the cover it deserves. Jay Van Dyke has offered ongoing assistance and advice, and has been a dream to work with. I want to thank TeriLynn Hinkle for photographing me and making the most of a non-photogenic subject.

Much credit also goes to those who reviewed and critiqued the manuscripts, offered editorial suggestions, assisted with documentation and indexing, provided source materials, and/or provided interviews, all for merely a "thank you." For these services, we owe special thanks to Cassie Blaker, Ken Bonnell, Diane Buckner, Jack Censer, Amanda Chesworth, Larry Darby, Jan C. Fox, Sharon Fratepietro, Pat Harris, Jim Heldberg, Dillard Henderson, Helen Kagin, Paul Kurtz, William Martin, Jon Nelson, Paul O'Brien, Fran Prevas, Marjie C. Swomley, and Dr. Harvey Tippit. Maxine Parshall deserves credit for reviewing the complete book and offering extensive editing recommendations without compensation. I thank Timothy Dillon for copyediting and ensuring our manuscript is as free from error as possible.

Finally, I thank Margaret O'Kelley for allowing me the opportunity to hone my writing skills as a reporter for *The Huron River Weekly*. I also acknowledge the terrific impact my college instructors Timothy Dillon, Dr. John Holladay, and Ann Orwin had on this project. Without their outstanding teaching skills and high expectations, I never would have come to realize my ability to attack this project and discover my love of writing.

CHAPTER 1

INTRODUCTION:

THE PERILS OF FUNDAMENTALISM
AND THE IMPERILMENT OF DEMOCRACY

by Kimberly Blaker

Those who control what young people are taught, and what they experience—what they see, hear, think, and believe—will determine the future course for the nation.[1]

James Dobson

Who could say it better than Dr. James Dobson, former Professor of Pediatrics and founder of Focus on the Family? He is known to Christian conservatives as America's foremost parenting authority and is the calm voice parents across the country turn to daily on more than 2,000 radio stations. From Dobson, they seek answers to questions regarding marriage, relationships, and childrearing.

To others, Dobson is known for his strong web of ties to the Christian Right. In fact, his ability to wield power over the Republican Party suggests he is the Christian Right. Dobson, an evangelical, a patriarch, and an advocate of corporal punishment is an opponent of reproductive choice, homosexual rights, free speech, liberal sex education, and the right to die with dignity. Yet, he has a remarkable ability to manipulate unsuspecting Americans who otherwise might not agree with his views. His sly maneuvering through the political arena unseen and unheard—except by those whose chains he pulls—has been a key to his power and success. Dobson's pronouncement, however, which opens this work, is a revelation into the evangelical and fundamentalist mentality. It displays a hunger for mind control of youth, scarcely different from Pakistan and Afghanistan's Islamic fundamentalists.

7

Many Pakistani children are raised in such a controlling environment. Pakistani Muslim boys as young as six, mostly from poor families, are often given over to madrasahs, or religious schools, where they spend their youth learning an extreme form of Islam. In the madrasahs, boys are given little opportunity to socialize, spending most of their first three years memorizing the Qur'an in Arabic, a language they do not even understand. They are taught no science or math, and the only history they will ever learn is of the Muslim world. It is the graduates of these madrasahs who "swell[ed] the ranks of the Taliban" in the mid-1990s.[2] The Taliban continues to gain adherents through the training of children, from an early age, to think dogmatically—as do the Taliban leaders.

Similarly, Christian fundamentalists frequently home school their children or send them to ultra-conservative Christian schools in an effort to limit socialization that would otherwise open doors to critical thought. The key concept of fundamentalist education is controlling what children learn. As do those funding and running Pakistan's madrasahs in preparation for the Jihad, Dobson realizes, "If the salvation of our children is really that vital to us, then our spiritual training should begin before children can even comprehend what it is all about."[3] Dobson further reveals:

> I firmly believe in acquainting children with God's judgment and wrath while they are young. Nowhere in the Bible are we instructed to skip over the unpleasant scriptures in our teaching. The wages of sin is death, and children have the right to understand that fact.[4]

Christian fundamentalist schooling is known for indoctrinating children through recitation and memorization of Bible verses and prayers, reinforced with hellfire and brimstone lectures. Moreover, these children are taught from textbooks that distort scientific and historic facts. As you will learn in Chapter 3, these children learn only what neatly fits into the myopic views of their parents and teachers. In math, they are taught only mechanics and absolutes. New math that teaches problem solving skills is abhorred because it reveals that everything is not black and white.

Fundamentalists know too well that children who learn to think on their own may someday stray from their indoctrination. The ideology of children in fundamentalist families is predetermined. Mind control, therefore, is the mode by which fundamentalists, whether Christian, Islamic, Jewish, or any other group, gain adherents. Authoritarian in nature, their interpretation of sacred texts calls on them to dominate society and to "determine the future course for the nation," as Dobson suggests. If fundamentalists do not guard against children learning to think on their own, they risk turning out adults who will choose a path inharmonious or even opposed to their own. For many fundamentalists, this path is simple, to serve God by bringing him loyal servants. However, a large proportion works to raise leaders and followers who will bring about political change and build a society ruled by an ideology not conducive to democracy. Equally troublesome, some fundamentalists intend to raise an army of puppets who will kill—and even die—for their predetermined cause.

America's new war on terrorism, resulting from the staggering death toll of the September 11, 2001 attacks, has made one thing clear. Those who threaten our lives and security, even those who stand in the way of capturing terrorists will be wiped out for the good of the world—that is, providing they are neither Christian nor American. There has been a disturbing double standard in the United States' way of dealing with extremist factions. The Bush administration's objective to exterminate terrorism abroad neglects to recognize and address the dangers we face from within our own nation. In fact, President George W. Bush has called for more of what contributed to such an atrocity in the first place—the intrusion of religion into government.

America is not immune from breeding such extremism, as was seen when Christians Terry Nichols and Timothy McVeigh bombed the Alfred P. Murrah Building in Oklahoma City. Nichols and McVeigh were influenced by the extremist Christian Identity movement. The bombing was McVeigh's way of speaking out against the government invasion of the Waco Branch Davidians, a Christian sect. It was also in retaliation of the shooting deaths of the white supremacist Weaver family at Ruby Ridge, followers of the Christian Identity faith.

Terrorists of the Christian kind

It would be unjust to place all fundamentalists in the same category as terrorists. Yet, there is undoubtedly a strong relationship between fundamentalism and violence. And there are those who will stop at nothing to reign terror and destruction on whomever they perceive as their enemies. One such group, the small but radical Army of God, has targeted abortion clinics and been involved in kidnappings, bombings, and shooting deaths. According to many reports, they have even been linked to the 280 anthrax threats that hit abortion clinics in October following the September

11, 2001 attacks.

The poisonous mentality of this group was demonstrated when Army of God supporters met on January 21, 2001, in Bowie, Maryland, for its fifth White Rose Banquet. "During the event, numerous speakers called for violence against abortion clinics, approved of murdering abortion providers, and made jokes about killing homosexuals,"[5] reported *Church & State*. Chuck Spingola complained, "Now, these people [gays] are vile folks. . . . If you deal with these people long enough, you understand the wisdom of God when he says they should be put to death."[6] Reverend Michael Bray, who served a six-year sentence for his involvement in abortion clinic bombings, was also awarded the title of "chaplain" during the event.[7]

Catholic fundamentalists are no less extreme. Reverend David C. Trosch wrote to Congress on July 16, 1994:

> In the not too distant future, it is anticipated that we will be faced with a civil war . . . It is murder to take human life at any time following conception . . . a very bloody civil insurrection shall begin . . . first shot was fired in Pensacola early this year . . . Dr. Gunn was a practicing murderer . . . it took World War II to stop the slaughter of millions of innocent people . . . God will hold them [the faithful] accountable for not taking direct action to prevent this evil . . . [When] the normal constraints of pacifism, which pervades throughout this country, is overcome . . . the killing, in protection of the innocent, will begin to spill over into the killing of the police and military who attempt to protect them. Thereafter, it will begin to affect those who direct them to protect abortion providers. . . . American Civil Liberties Union will [be] place[ed] high on the target list . . . . National Organization of [sic] Women, members of Planned Parenthood and other pro-abortion/choice organizations . . . terminated as vermin are terminated . . . Participation in the destruction of evil would soon become understood as a meritorious action, as a prerequisite for entrance into eternal life . . . hoped that this will be sufficient for the Congress of the United States to reverse [US Supreme Court decisions] 'Roe vs. Wade' [sic] and 'Doe vs. Bolton' [sic]. . . . religious beliefs take precedence over civil laws when they are in conflict . . . socialism is a creeping evil. . . . National health care is a part of this creeping socialism. . . . no human force able to stop this movement once it has begun in earnest. . . . Lives of all who

speak in favor of abortion will be at grave risk. Perhaps, even probably, the lives of those politicians who fail to strongly oppose abortion will be at risk . . . No personal threat is intended. . . . Sincerely in Christ, fr. David C. Trosch.[8]

Two weeks later, Paul Hill, a former minister, drove to The Ladies Center, an abortion clinic in Pensacola, Florida, and shot to death Dr. John Bayard Britton and James Barrett, the doctor's escort. That same year, bullets were mailed to clinics in Montana with doctors' names inscribed on them. Clinics across the nation received death threats by mail and phone, and on August 9, a bomb was found outside a Planned Parenthood clinic. Despite the fact that Trosch had been advocating the murder of pro-choice doctors and adherents for years, only after these murders did the Catholic Church decide to disassociate Trosch from the Church.

The U.S. downplay of its own extremist factions has grown increasingly apparent. While focusing its war on terrorism halfway around the globe, there has been little, if any mention of the many Christian-based militias and training camps based across the U.S. and the many extreme Christian sects. Nonetheless, when the parallels between Christian and Islamic fundamentalism fully come to life, the reality will become something we can no longer ignore. The need for Americans and our government to recognize the threats posed by those living next door is imperative to our safety. Terrorism is terrorism no matter under what religion it is cloaked. It needs to be dealt with to assure every American's safety, not just safety in numbers, while at the same time preserving our democracy.

Our lives, their lives, and the media

Although one of the gravest dangers stemming from Christian fundamentalism, terrorism is only one of a multitude of problems posed by such extreme beliefs. As will be developed in later chapters, not only do children in fundamentalist homes often lack an adequate and appropriate education, they are at high risk for physical abuse and incest. And regardless of fundamentalists' opposition to premarital sex, they are at high risk for teen pregnancy. When these teens become sexually active, they are less likely to use contraceptives. Other children are affected as well by censorship that makes adequate sex education programs in public schools extremely difficult. They are also affected by censorship of literature and even textbooks. Furthermore, fundamentalist children, especially girls, are at risk for lower educational attainment.

Women are affected whether they come from fundamentalist homes or not. Lack of reproductive choice, educational and career opportunities, spousal abuse, rape, sexual and mental disorders, and welfare dependency are all highly related to Christian fundamentalism. Fundamentalist beliefs in the home contribute not only to these problems, but also to social stereotypes and political action, or inaction, resulting from Christian Right views. Men are no less affected as will be revealed throughout the following chapters. The negative impact on men is most often demonstrated by their treatment of women and children, through their political actions, and sometimes through acts of violence and terrorism.

Christian fundamentalism also creates a host of other problems. First, there is a strong relationship between fundamentalism and prejudice. This leads to discrimination, intolerance, and hate crimes often directed at gays, other races or religions, and women. Also problematic is the Christian Right's blocking of legislation that would otherwise give people options to reduce or end their pain and suffering. It opposes medicinal marijuana for the terminally ill and calls for prosecuting doctors who euthanize terminally ill patients at the patients' requests.

Fundamentalists also lack concern for the environment based on their belief in man's God-given dominion over all things, as is described in Genesis. They look to the Second Coming of Christ in the not-so-distant future, therefore, eliminating the need for the planet to sustain life for hundreds of millions more years.

In addition, fundamentalists misinterpret the United States Constitution, most specifically the First Amendment and its Separation Clause, and they rewrite history to fit their Christian Nation theme. In recent years, the political power of the Christian Right has seen significant gains by taking an alarming number of seats at all levels of government. In the upcoming chapters, the magnitude of the problems resulting from Christian fundamentalism will be fully uncovered. Fundamentalism affects our lives in a preponderance of ways, and it will be revealed how fundamentalists leave few groups of people and few social and political issues untouched.

But of more immediate interest is how this can be so unapparent to so many. The answer lies, in part, in the illusions the Christian Right strives to create. As Barbara M. Jones, author of *Libraries, Access, and Intellectual Freedom: Developing Policies for Public and Academic Libraries*, points out, "The religious right has become a particularly important interest group in shaping public opinion."[9] The Christian Right accomplishes this in several ways. In addition to its ownership of many media outlets, Christian organizations and denominations such as the Southern Baptist Convention and Catholic League for Religious and Civil Rights have come to be known for their control of the media. They threaten lawsuits and public embarrassment and participate in letter writing campaigns. In addition, they boycott companies that sponsor programs or publications to which the Christian Right is opposed. Through such actions they are able to silence negative publicity and most programming critical of religion or in direct conflict with their views.

I saw the reality of the media control firsthand when I unexpectedly encountered the Catholic League—an organization whose purpose is to prevent and eliminate all criticism of Catholicism and its leadership. On September 20, 2001, the *San Francisco Examiner* published a commentary I wrote identifying the similarities between Islamic extremists and their Christian counterparts. I revealed the Catholic League's use of intimidation to keep opponents and the media in line, as follows:

> While less violent in nature, The Catholic League for Religious and Civil Rights, a contradiction in itself, exists for the purpose of Canon Law 1369, which states: 'A person is to be punished with a just penalty, who . . . utters blasphemy, or gravely harms public morals, or rails at or excites hatred of or contempt for religion or the Church.' [10]

Furthermore, I pointed out:

> at a prayer breakfast during the 2000 Republican Convention, Father Frank Provone of Priests for Life claimed, 'The church does not dictate the policies of the nation. The Church proclaims the truth of God to which all these [public] policies must conform.'[11]

The Catholic Church is one of the main organizers and supporters behind the Christian Right. However, it has kept its identity concealed by calling on Baptists and other Christian sects to do its bidding. In a concerted effort, a wide range of Christian Right groups are working to break down the wall between church and state.[12]

Following the publication of my opinion editorial, William Donahue, president of the Catholic League, immediately telephoned Editorial Page Editor Michael Stoll at the *Examiner*. Donahue charged that I had libeled "millions of Christians."[13] According to Donahue's account, he requested the *Examiner* "provide [him] with evidence, drawn from criminal records, that the Catholic League is a violent organization."[14] Stoll responded that while his criticisms may have been valid, my comment, "while less violent in nature," was no more than a "rhetorical flourish,"[15] as was obvious, and my own "opinion"[16] to which I was entitled. Donahue then retorted, "And it is my opinion that she be fired for making patently reckless, and arguably libelous, accusations against the Catholic League."[17] Anyone reading the full opinion piece would have easily recognized the metaphor for what it was. I made no claim the League had acted in violence. Rather, I indicated the nature of the organization, while not as extreme as those I had previously discussed, was still, based on the wording of Canon Law 1369, a dangerous organization to be reckoned with.

Following Donahue's call, the League issued a news release on its website[18] that later appeared in its print edition of the *Catalyst,* as well. Both of these are outlets dedicated to the harassment of all who dare speak out publicly against the abuses of the Catholic Church and its political agenda. Those who offend Catholics in any way are candidates for severe censure. Using my words out of context and misleading its own members, the League then persuaded, "We urge members to write to Michael Stoll, *San Francisco Examiner* . . . and ask why the newspaper still hasn't dropped Blaker."

Intimidation is the League's means to an end. Opinion that does not paint religion or Catholicism in a positive light is libelous according to Donahue and his attractors, despite laws to the contrary. Donahue's ludicrous call for the firing of a freelance writer was a further attempt at bullying the *Examiner* into compliance and silencing me.

Following the posting of the Catholic League's news release, the *Examiner* was bombarded with more than a hundred letters coming from states other than California. Nearly all of them demanded I be fired from a publication with which I had never been employed. And, not only had I been elevated to a "staff" member, many of the League's letter writers took it to higher levels and were "enraged" over the fact I was a "reporter" who had opined in the "news."

That, however, was just the beginning. Most letters to the *Examiner* had included words like "libel" and "slander." Many went so far as to hope the League would sue the newspaper. One woman wrote requesting that the *Examiner* supply her with "proof" the League is a threat to liberty. Stoll responded:

I would note that many people of many political and philosophical persuasions consider a wide variety of institutions, people and ways of thinking a 'threat to liberty.' It is a statement that is pure opinion, and in my estimation does not require proof. Nor can it be proven or disproven. That is precisely why it appeared on the opinion page.[19]

Little did this woman realize her own allies were busy stating my case for me. From Louisiana came a letter calling on the *Examiner* "to do the right thing" because "the Supreme Court [sic] of the United States has affirmed that the United States is a Christian nation. . . ." While the statement itself is false, this was, in fact, the exact threat in which I described in my opinion editorial—an attempt to create a religiously based government. Additional proof of the League's threat to liberty came from an Oregonian who requested the *Examiner* "take a more critical view of such articles and *censor* [emphasis added] such blatantly biased writers." It would seem the Catholic League's membership unknowingly contradicts the League's stated purpose, which is to defend "religious and civil rights." Apparently, free speech, at least for the nonreligious, does not fall into that category.

A couple of League members even wrote that the *Examiner* should have automatically turned away my submission because I was "a known atheist." A Nevada woman also insisted an editor's note should have appeared underneath the commentary specifying, "that she is a noted atheist," even though opinions expressed by believers hardly ever have an editorial note identifying the author's religion.

The actions of Donahue and these members of the Catholic League indicate they are defending Catholic religious civil rights, not the religious and civil rights of all. What also became apparent is whether something negative said against Christianity or Catholicism is "libelous" or pure fact is not important. What matters is that public criticism of Catholicism takes place at all. This was evidenced by several League members. A Massachusetts man argued that his relative who is a priest has done good works. Therefore, he reasoned, "What right does she [Blaker] have to criticize people who have given up a comfortable life to do this type of work?" In the eyes of many fundamentalists, Christian or Catholic, any good works should eliminate all criticism.

But, what makes the Catholic League's members so apt to participate in these letter-writing campaigns? In addition to believing all criticism of religion should be suppressed, many are also convinced the Church and Catholics, in general, have become targets of a widespread contempt for

Catholicism. A New Yorker shared this typical belief described in many letters from Catholic League members. His grievance was, "Anti-Catholicism in America today exceeds acts of bias against any other ethnic, racial or religious group," even though this is patently untrue. Regardless, the member pointed out, "Page after page of the *Catalyst* newsletter is evidence of the hostility and intolerance the Catholic Church is subjected to in America."

The League exploits its membership by crying foul and riling it up for every minor offense against the Church. Yet, rarely does it exhibit evidence of discriminatory practices or hate crimes against Catholics. This is despite numerous documented cases of discrimination toward African-Americans, homosexuals, Jews, Muslims, atheists, and other minority groups in this country. The "bias" these Catholics denounce is most often criticism of Catholic beliefs imposed on its adherents and the beliefs it attempts to impose on the world, including Americans. Regardless of criticism, no one obstructs the practice of Catholic beliefs. And although they may say otherwise, today there is little discrimination against them.

Ironically, in December (2001), a freelance production assistant contacted the *Examiner* to discuss the fracas. While I was following up with the production assistant a couple of days later, he explained that a video magazine, *American Catholic*, had been asked to do a segment on Catholic bashing. However, the journalistic investigation quickly took a turn. According to the freelancer, in his attempt to uncover these injustices, he instead unmasked much to the contrary. What he found was the Catholic League wielding its power against anyone who exposed the Church or the League. [20] It appeared that the program would instead develop into an expose of the intimidation tactics used by the Catholic League in its efforts to keep negative publicity under wraps. As would be expected, the segment never materialized. [21]

Not long after, the *Palm Beach Post* became a target of the Catholic League when it published a cartoon by Don Wright, which also appeared in the *New York Times* and the *Sacramento Bee*. The cartoon depicted a contemplative woman who says:

> For women, sexual conduct is always closely monitored. The Catholic Church tells me what I can or cannot do with my body. Truly unforgiving. Absolutely no compromises. Unless, of course, you're a pedophile.

At Donahue's command, the League's director of communications, Patrick Scully, telephoned the editorial page editor of the *Palm Beach*

Post demanding an apology. Randy Schultz responded, "There will be no apology because there is nothing to apologize for." Schultz pointed out to Scully the cartoon was merely a "critique" of the Church's "policies." But to the League, it was no less "vicious" than my own criticism and deserving of another letter writing campaign. This was regardless of the cartoon's factual basis and that the League could not even misconstrue "libel." The League urged in its *Catalyst*, "Now it's time that Schultz heard from you."

The address to the *Palm Beach Post* was published with a request to, "Tell him [Schultz] that he and his boy Don Wright are doing such a good job that we've decided to honor them with an entry in next year's Annual Report on Anti-Catholicism."[22] As it turns out, I was honored in that report, as well.[23] Similar to Schultz's response to the Catholic control-mongers, the *Examiner's* Stoll informed me, "None of the letters convinced me of anything other than that there are hundreds of people around the country who are defensive and intolerant of criticism."[24]

In these two instances, the Catholic League's bully tactics did not pay off. As Stoll pointed out, "It was more of an annoyance than anything." But, the *Catalyst* contains many reports of victories in which businesses have capitulated to the League's demands; if for no other reason then to avoid the hassle as was described by Stoll. These threats are often effective. To many businesses and corporations, the time and costs involved in a legal suit are not worth the hassle. This is so, even when the company being threatened would ultimately win the case. In the end, the League plays a crucial role in the formation of public opinion as it latches its restraints on every form of media.

Fomenters of mass hysteria

At the same time, as Jones points out, the media also plays a crucial role in shaping public opinion because Americans accept the "spin" the media places on issues before critically evaluating the information and messages they are receiving.[25] The Christian Right uses this to its advantage as well. It knows the hunger of the media and the media's tendency to sensationalize. So, the Christian Right feeds it with misinformation and half-truths about anything to which fundamentalists are opposed. In this way, fundamentalists can easily meet their objectives and gain the upper hand. This is effective because of the controversy created, which leads to full-scale national debate. Such scare tactics lead the public to political action and voting booths as nothing else could. And it is exactly what has happened with the recent controversy over the diagnosis of attention-deficit/hyperactivity disorder (AD/HD) and its preferred treatment, Ritalin, a case in point.

AD/HD is "characterized by developmentally inappropriate impulsivity, inattention, and in some cases, hyperactivity."[26] The U.S. Surgeon General, the Centers for Disease Control and Prevention, the National Institutes of Mental Health (NIMH), the American Psychiatric Association, the American Academy of Pediatrics, and the American Medical Association have all recognized AD/HD as a real neurobiological disorder. And the American Academy of Pediatrics, NIMH, and U.S. Surgeon General, among others, recommend treatment that may include prescription, such as stimulant, medication. These include Adderall, Dexedrine, and Ritalin, which have each been found to have a seventy-five percent response rate in treating children with AD/HD.[27]

The ability of the Christian Right to shape public opinion has played a crucial role in this debate. Most troubling is not only the stigma that has emerged for those with AD/HD, but that at least twenty-nine states have proposed far-reaching bills in a period of less than two years. State legislation has been drafted to regulate psychotropic drug use in schools, which could ultimately give the state the authority to deny a child the right to take his or her prescribed and necessary psychotropic medications during the school day. Yet, other prescribed and medically necessary drugs are regulated only by the federal Food and Drug Administration, where such regulation should remain. Other legislation would censor educators' communications with parents and would ultimately undermine the detection of AD/HD—all aimed at curbing Ritalin use. In several states, radical proposals have already been drafted to ban the use of Ritalin in school settings altogether, and such measures are likely to be seen elsewhere. Such policies are likely to become a part of school law, because some Ritalin opponents repeatedly misuse statistics and take information out of context to support their cause.

Most parents are concerned with unnecessarily medicating their children. Yet, if fully and accurately informed about an illness, disease, or disorder and its treatment, most parents will opt to medicate when it is the best known treatment for the particular ailment and necessary to the child's welfare. Unfortunately, because of the hype over the issue, much of the public still misunderstands the reality and effective treatments for AD/HD and fails to recognize the disorder is not benign. Therefore, a large segment of the AD/HD population either has gone untreated or uses ineffective or minimally effective options.

The grave impact of this misinformation campaign can be demonstrated in a preponderance of ways. While only an estimated three to five percent of the population has AD/HD, a Utah study found twenty-four percent of its male prison inmates were classic AD/HD cases. The Medical Director of Buena Vista Correctional Facility and Assistant Chief Medical Officer of the Colorado Department of Corrections, T. Dwaine McCallon, M.D., shares his knowledge. He pointed out that experience, as well as studies he has conducted "have led us to believe that upwards of forty percent of our residents in a medium security prison have the findings along the Tourette/AD[/H]D spectrum." McCallon adds, "If you separate out the nonviolent, impulsive criminals (who I term my basic, charming, and even lovable car thieves and traffic offenders), the percentage [with AD/HD] is much greater."[28]

Other sobering statistics are that thirty-two to forty percent of those with AD/HD will drop out of school, fifty to seventy percent "have few or no friends," forty to fifty percent will show antisocial behaviors, seventy to eighty percent will perform poorly at work, forty percent of AD/HD girls will become pregnant in their teens[29]—and this is only a tip of the iceberg.

Yet, who are the major opponents of Ritalin and AD/HD and what are their motives? In recent years, several special interest groups have targeted AD/HD and Ritalin. The Church of Scientology, a nonChristian cult, has been at the forefront of the campaign. Still, few Americans, even those affected with the disorder, are aware of some of the groups and motives behind the crusade. Only by delving into an investigation of the Michigan-based Mackinac Center for Public Policy was I able to uncover other roots of this sham. The Christian Right's ties to this campaign now unravel—and their motives to halt Ritalin or stimulant use become clearer.

The Mackinac Center holds, "The best way to make a lasting impact on public policy is to change public opinion. When you change the beliefs of people, politicians and political parties change with them."[30] The Center, with an annual budget of about one million, is a sizable player in the formation of public opinion. In this case, along with its communications specialist, Samuel Walker, it appears to be on a publicity campaign to create public concern and hysteria over the diagnosis, or misdiagnosis, and treatment of AD/HD. Walker and the Center have published many articles appearing in newspapers across Michigan, contradicting scientific facts and causing mass public confusion.

The Mackinac Center, a right-wing think tank operating under a façade of a "nonpartisan research and educational organization,"[31] has been criticized repeatedly by Detroit's *Metro Times*,[32] James Ferency of the Mackinac Center for Public Policy Watch,[33] and many others. The reason for such criticism stems from the Center's disguised radical-right agenda to privatize schools, employ a school voucher system, and to create a free market. Under this economic system, businesses operate completely free from government regulation with no protections for public interest or the national economy.

Still, how does the Christian Right fit into this scheme? First, for many Christian fundamentalists, the reality of neurobiological disorders that can affect behavior is disowned. Pastor Terry L. Coomer of the Elwood Bible Baptist Church in Indiana exemplifies this view:

> As a Pastor, I have been greatly concerned to see and hear of many Christian parents putting their children on drugs such as Ritalin for behavior. I believe this is an epidemic of disastrous proportions to the children of America. It also shows the lack of spiritual training the parents are receiving in the church to rear their children spiritually as the Bible commands. Proverbs 22:6, 'Train up a child in the way he should go: and when he is old, he will not depart from it.'[34]

To fundamentalists, it is a "spare the rod, spoil the child" mentality all the way. It matters not that brain chemistry is malfunctioning and that those affected have little or no control. To fundamentalists, it is merely a matter of "good" and "evil" and breaking the will of the child. Nonetheless, there are fundamentalists who seem to recognize the reality of AD/HD and do not propose such severe discipline measures for children with the diagnosis. Yet, they still oppose psychotropic drug treatment.

Therefore, another reason for the Christian Right's involvement is that, like the Mackinac Center, one of the Christian Right's major objectives is a voucher system and school privatization, or Christian-based schools. Unlike some groups favoring school choice and private school opportunities, one of the objectives of fundamentalists and their counterparts is the total destruction of the public schools. As you will learn in Chapters 3 and 7, the religious right has discovered its road to victory. It can be achieved by attacking public education, misusing statistics, spreading misinformation, and overstating the issue of student failure in an effort to gain support for vouchers and school privatization. Fundamentalists believe it is their God-given duty to convert all American children to an extreme brand of Christianity. The fastest way for the Mackinac Center and the Christian Right to achieve their goals is dismantling the public education system.

Yet, what do Ritalin and AD/HD have to do with all of this? The devastating effects of untreated AD/HD are well established. Therefore, if

Ritalin use is reduced, more students would fail and drop out of school, educational assessment test scores would drop, and behavior problems and drug use would be on the rise—leading to an increase in school suspension and expulsion rates. All of this would create an illusion that public schools have failed, thereby strengthening support for vouchers and school privatization.

To the Christian Right's advantage, in private schools this problem would go unrealized. That's because private schools can select their students and remove troublemakers (often children with AD/HD) who are then disproportionately enrolled in public institutions. This increases the appearance of public schools' rate of failure if these children are forced to go untreated or inadequately treated for AD/HD. Although such a tactic alone might not be effective in meeting the Christian Right's objective, combined with other maneuvers it could be a final breaking point for the public school system.

Nonetheless, the Christian Right has escaped implication in this campaign because of its well-devised tactics of hiding behind and coordinating with others to meet its objectives. In this case, the Mackinac Center, among other organizations, has been the perfect cover. Rather than being at the front of the publicity campaign, Christian Right organizations fund the Mackinac Center and let it do its bidding. Twenty percent of the Center's funding comes from big corporations such as Dow Chemical; while another fifty percent comes from foundations, many with Christian Right ties—including the Prince and Merillat Foundations.[35]

Of course, these ties were not easy to untangle. The Mackinac Center refuses to divulge where its funding comes from. It has only been through investigations and figures disclosed by the National Education Association and author Russ Bellant in *The Religious Right in Michigan Politics* that this information has been uncovered.

Another major donor of the Mackinac Center is the Richard and Helen DeVos Foundation, founder of Amway.[36] The DeVos family, known for its Christian Right ties, also invested more than $4 million in 2000 in an attempt "to persuade Michigan voters to divert funds from public schools into private-school vouchers."[37] The DeVos Foundation also donated nearly a third of its $95.1 million from 1991 to 1997 to "organizations that espouse Christian values."[38] Furthermore, DeVos is a member of the Council for National Policy (CNP), a far-right organization with ties to the Church of Scientology. It has been noted for its secrecy, including its membership of the nation's most influential and dangerous religious right leaders like Paul Weyrich, Pat Robertson, Jerry Falwell, Bill Bright, Phyllis Schlafly, James Dobson, D. James Kennedy, Oliver North, and the late R.J. Rushdoony.[39]

Most telling of the Christian Right's involvement in the Ritalin scare is revealed by Scientology's Citizen's Commission on Human Rights (CCHR), an organization opposing the use of any form of psychiatric drugs or treatment. In 1995, a united front representing 40 million people met in Washington, D.C. to sign a compact. It stated, among other things, "We pledge to eliminate . . . all dangerous and invasive psychiatric/psychologically-based programs, assessments, and tests from our schools, and funding thereof."[40] Scientologists did not act on this alone. Signers of this pledge included Christian Right organizations such as Phyllis Schlafly's Eagle Forum, Gary Bauer's Family Research Council, The Rutherford Institute, Beverly LaHaye's Concerned Women for America, and many others.[41]

It should be noted, it is recognized that such groups as herbalists and New Agers may also personally oppose the use of nonorganic treatments. The difference is that they are generally not associated with political action to block access for others.

What has also gone unnoticed in this campaign are Christian Right and fundamentalist websites including Phyllis Schlafly's Eagle Forum. Some have become an avenue to discredit the reality of AD/HD, its devastating impact, and/or the effective use of stimulant medication especially when in combination with behavior modification. These sites post articles contradicting medical facts and induce guilt in parents who treat their children with stimulants or psychotropic drugs in general. A typical example is distorting and downplaying the reasons for diagnosis of AD/HD and the need for treatment with psychotropic drugs. In *Policy Review*, the publication of the Heritage Foundation, Mary Eberstadt insists:

> The most obvious reason millions of Americans, most of them children, are now taking Ritalin can be summarized in a single word that crops up everywhere in the dry-bones literature on add and its drug of choice: compliance. One day at a time, the drug continues to make children do what their parents and teachers either will not or cannot get them to do without it: Sit down, shut up, keep still, pay attention.[42]

Such accusations make concerned parents question the reality of the situation and overlook the severity of their child's symptoms. No parent wants to be perceived as lazy and unwilling or lacking in the ability to manage his or her children. By suggesting such parents and teachers would rather not be bothered by the everyday disobedience, more are apt to cave to the pressure of the anti-Ritalin campaign. In reality, AD/HD children are often severely disobedient (not necessarily intentionally) and lack control of their emotions. School failure due to hyperactivity, inattentiveness, and a host of other lifelong problems, as indicated in the studies above, also result.

In addition to the tactics employed by the Christian Right and the media to form public opinion, the hidden agenda is, for the most part, what has made this misinformation campaign such a success. Without understanding the motives behind this debate, it has been difficult for the medical and scientific community to get through to the public on this issue and for the public to see through the rhetoric.

Much of the AD/HD population has remained confused because of the anti-Ritalin and anti-AD/HD hype and, therefore, has not undergone adequate or appropriate treatment. No parent wants to medicate his or her child unnecessarily. Those who do not have access to all the information are easily won over to the, "I'm not going to drug my child" side. Those behind the campaign and even innocent bystanders caught up in it instill guilt in well-meaning parents who otherwise would opt for the often-necessary treatment. This is a well-devised tactic to institute ideological practices throughout all of society and to reduce Ritalin use until the public education system is dismantled.

Unfortunately, many Americans have innocently fallen prey to the spread of misinformation in this campaign and are now unwittingly fueling the fire—exactly as Scientologists and the Christian Right anticipated. It is therefore, the perfect example of the Christian Right's ability to manipulate the media and the public in ways we are only beginning to recognize. In this case, the consequence is that millions of children and adults with AD/HD and their families are the ones to suffer. And as revealed by statistics relating to the AD/HD population, society as a whole is dramatically affected by this Christian Right and Scientology campaign.

While it is not one of the Christian Right's most pertinent issues of the day, it is nonetheless a clear example of how the movement remains hidden from radar for most of society. Recognizing even the less monumental ways in which society is affected by fundamentalism is necessary to combating and minimizing the damage.

* * * * * *

In spite of all the dangers and frustrations posed by Christian fundamentalism, the writers of this book recognize that most fundamentalists and those with similar characteristics are good people. In many ways fundamentalists are no different from you and me; and we wish no harm to those who adhere to such beliefs. What we do hope comes out of this book is an understanding of the causes of fundamentalism, as you will discover in Chapter 2, and greater awareness of how fundamentalist beliefs and practices harm its adherents, its detractors, and everyone in between.

Recognition alone, however, is not enough. Knowing the ramifications of allowing this movement to slowly infiltrate all arenas, from public schools and local governments to Congress and even the presidency, hastens the need for Americans to find ways to protect against this invasion. What we hope is that readers will come away after reading about solutions to the growing danger (Chapter 8) with insight into ways to alleviate the problems posed by fundamentalism. In addition, it is hoped this book will create a desire to take action to protect ourselves and our democracy—without impeding the rights of or harming those we are up against.

CHAPTER 2

THE GATHERING STORM

by Edwin F. Kagin

I want you to just let a wave of intolerance wash over you. I want you to let a wave of hatred wash over you. Yes, hate is good . . . Our goal is a Christian nation. We have a Biblical duty; we are called by God, to conquer this country. We don't want equal time. We don't want pluralism.[43]

Randall Terry, founder of the
anti-abortion organization, Operation Rescue

Fundamentalism has been increasing around the world, including the United States, among Christians, Muslims, Hindus, and Jews.[44] This has been seen in the growth of born-again or evangelical Christians, which rose from thirty-two percent to thirty-seven percent from 1986 to 1990 alone. And in 1993, the fastest growing church in America was the Church of God in Christ, a fundamentalist Protestant denomination.[45] According to a 1993 Gallup Poll, the majority of Americans at that time held traditional beliefs. In spite of a drop in religious interest during the 1960s and 1970s, fundamentalism has since continued to increase.[46] Many Christians with characteristics similar or identical to fundamentalists do not consider themselves such. Still, about fifty percent of the sixty million born-again Christians in the United States claim the fundamentalist identity. At the same time, mainstream Protestant denominations are declining.[47]

Christian fundamentalism has seen similar growth in other parts of the world, as people are rapidly converting to evangelical and fundamentalist churches in the Philippines, Africa, Latin America, and elsewhere.[48] More alarming is that fundamentalist Islam has succeeded in the goal of imposing theocratic restrictions on members of many societies.[49] This is a fact that has dominated the media since September 11, 2001, offering a glimpse of fundamentalism's strength and extremity.

Yet, what exactly is Christian fundamentalism? To begin, it is an inflexible, absolutist worldview. Until recently, only the 1611 King James Version of the Bible was accepted by fundamentalists. This revered version, however, has recently come into some disfavor because fundamentalists have discovered what many historians have claimed all along: King James was a homosexual. To many fundamentalists, King James' homosexuality disqualifies the translation from acceptability. Gary Bauer from northern Kentucky is former president of the Family Research Council (FRC) a Christian fundamentalist "pro family" organization, a former domestic policy advisor to President Ronald Reagan, and a Republican candidate for the 2002 Presidential campaign. It has been widely circulated that Bauer concluded that nothing touched by a homosexual could be good for good Christians:

> I feel uncomfortable that good Christians all over America, and indeed the world, are using a document commissioned by a homosexual. Anything that has been commissioned by a homosexual has obviously been tainted in some way.[50]

This originated as parody, but so accurately fits Bauer's views, that it has been frequently cited by fundamentalists.

As a result of King James sexual orientation, fundamentalists have produced other translations, and, better still, "paraphrases" of the Bible. In doing so they have benefited their cause. They have managed to "clean up" certain stories, alter phrases, and clarify meanings. Such passages, otherwise, might prove problematic for a work held to be free of error and suitable for reading in schools. Unsettling uncertainty must arise, as fundamentalists no longer have a definitive translation of an ancient collection of writings declared sacred and the inerrant word of God. Regardless, people sharing the fundamentalist mindset generally believe all religious and secular laws and practices must conform to their belief system. Simply put, Christian fundamentalists, known politically as the Christian Right, want to control our laws and our lives. They have a fixed certainty that they are right about what God wants, and that what God wants is for them to be in power. This leads them to use a variety of tactics to achieve that end.

God's word, to them, is the final authority by which every aspect of our laws and our lives should be controlled. Any view of the Bible outside of an inerrant and literalist understanding is perceived, and denounced, as "modernism." Fundamentalists determine what is God's word, for truth has been revealed unto them alone, the ones favored by God who are to be raptured into heaven. Sinners are those who have rejected the fundamentalist vision of truth, version of righteousness, and view of the beginning, meaning, and end of life. They are to be "left behind" to suffer justly deserved eternal punishment.

To be sure, Christian fundamentalism is not unique in its, "we are right, and you are wrong" mentality and its insistence upon a literal reading of invented histories framed in legend and allegory. There is little difference in essence between Christian fundamentalism and Islamic fundamentalism. Nor is there much difference in any other system that believes the entire body of an ancient mythical system, frozen in time, is rendered holy by antiquity, and is made more worthy of belief by faith and hope than by merit and proof. All religious fundamentalists, however called, are much the same under the skin. They may be highly dissimilar in methods and goals, and their words may be different, but their tune is the same. God is on their side, and therefore, their beliefs are true and should be involuntarily enforced on all members of society.

In its broadest sense, "fundamentalism," or its claim to the adherence to the "traditional," the "old ways," the "orthodox," has probably been around as long as there have been religions. Although in many instances, it is not "tradition" to which fundamentalists cling. They hold fast to recent or newly created ways benefiting their cause. Still, a religious tradition may have been established once some primitive people, led by some primitive priest, decided good things would happen to the tribe if they stuck a bone into the left eye socket of a cave bear skull. Religious schisms probably resulted when some religious reformer or reform group announced a different way of doing something. To the outrage and dismay of the traditionalists, it may have been suggested religious purpose could henceforth be better served if a bone were to be placed in the right eye socket. More apostate, reformers could have recommended separate bones be entered into each eyehole of the skull. Religious war and denominations may have followed.

A fundamentalist priesthood can control kingdoms. Egyptian pharaoh Akhenaten may have been murdered by traditionalists, by the fundamentalist priests of Amon-Re. The heretic monarch sought to replace his religion with his personal sun god, the Aten.[51] For centuries, the rulers of Egypt had acknowledged the supremacy of the deity Amon-Re. A politically-powerful and wealthy priesthood had arisen around the religion, and the religious duties associated with that god. Akhenaten appears to have attempted to single-handedly change the traditional, or fundamentalist, view of religion.

Similarly, Christian reformers have attempted to modify traditional or fundamental Christian interpretations, based on new knowledge or expanded insight and vision. Akhenaten's new vision of religion, his modernism, was rejected by the fundamentalist priests. It was also dismissed by the people who felt safety lay in the familiar and traditional much as today's fundamentalists believe. Fundamentalism, in one form or another, has been around for some time. It may always be with us, because of what we have come to understand as "human nature." Hopefully, recognition and understanding of fundamentalism will broaden appropriate and effective ways to address the problems and such will be undertaken. This will assure our democracy's survival.

On the positive side, fundamentalism does attempt to address real problems. As Richard Swift in "Fundamentalism: Reaching for Certainty" notes, the difficulty is problems are handled obsessively and incompletely.[52] These attempts at coping are too often done in backwards, unlawful, and ineffective ways. Sometimes the problems are addressed in a manner that heightens, rather than reduces the problem. Therefore, the fundamentalist becomes part of the problem, rather than part of the solution. This can be seen with such crucial issues as teen pregnancy and child abuse.

America got the Puritans

Religious conservatism has been a force in American society since the early nineteenth century, if not before, according to Michael Lienesch of *Redeeming America: Piety & Politics in the New Christian Right*. This group, more recently known as the religious right, is not always visible to the public eye. Yet, it has been able to stand on its own and adjust to changing times and is always close by—whether we realize it or not.[53] That is because, as has been wittily observed, Australia got the convicts, and America got the Puritans. It has been more darkly mused Australia must have gotten first choice.

Many different types of people came to these shores for many different reasons. The Puritans came from England and elsewhere to practice their religion without restraint away from those who did not want to be controlled by the Puritans. Those cute Pilgrims we honor in school Thanksgiving plays and on festive holiday paper plates were actually some of the most repressed and repressive religious types in the history of the world. While the Puritans controlled England under Oliver Cromwell, they had, among other repressive actions, closed the theaters and outlawed Christmas.[54] It has been said in derision a Puritan is one who is haunted by a lurking suspicion that somehow, someone, somewhere might still be happy.

To be sure, many of the virtues of the Puritans have helped to mold the American character in desirable ways. Among those qualities were their commitments to hard work, honesty, integrity, duty, education, and family. Ideas are not responsible for the people who support them. The mischief of the Puritan heritage is seen in the clearly-stated and understood intent of the Puritans to form a theocracy in the New World. The Mayflower Compact of 1620 is often cited by modern day fundamentalists as a blueprint for how America should be, governed by God's law and those divinely inspired by him. Because of the importance of this much-talked about, yet little-read historic document, it is set out in its entirety:

> In the name of God, Amen. We, whose names are underwritten, the Loyal Subjects of our dread Sovereign Lord, King James, by the Grace of God, of England, France and Ireland, King, Defender of the Faith, e& [etc.].

> Having undertaken for the Glory of God, and Advancement of the Christian Faith, and the Honor of our King and Country, a voyage to plant the first colony in the northern parts of Virginia; do by these presents, solemnly and mutually in the Presence of God and one of another, covenant and combine ourselves together into a civil Body Politick, for our better Ordering and Preservation, and Furtherance of the Ends aforesaid; And by Virtue hereof to enact, constitute, and frame, such just and equal Laws, Ordinances, Acts, Constitutions and Offices, from time to time, as shall be thought most meet and convenient for the General good of the Colony; unto which we promise all due submission and obedience.

> In Witness whereof we have hereunto subscribed our names at Cape Cod the eleventh of November, in the Reign of our Sovereign Lord, King James of England, France and Ireland, the eighteenth, and of Scotland the fifty-fourth. Anno Domini, 1620.[55]

Seldom noted is that the document was signed by only forty-one of the 102 passengers of the Mayflower, thirty-seven of whom were Separatists fleeing "religious persecution" in Europe.[56]

Our nation was established on principles that deliberately and expressly rejected the forced state-sanctioned religiosity that was attempted by fundamentalists who put together the "Mayflower Compact." Yet the seeds the Puritans sowed fell on rich and fertile soil in the heartland of America. While much is different, much abides. Today's fundamentalists are the intellectual descendents of the Puritans. They offer America a theocracy that differs little from what the Puritans intended. For some fundamentalists, however, it is not an offer, but an imposition that must be accepted.

Despite the claims of the modern fundamentalist movement, the Mayflower Compact forms no part of the laws of the United States. There was no United States of America at the time, nor was there such a country until the ratification of the Constitution of the United States. It was adopted in 1787 and completed in 1788, 168 years after the signing of the Mayflower Compact. Whereas the Mayflower Compact was, "undertaken for the Glory of God and Advancement of the Christian Faith . . . ," the Preamble to the Constitution of the United States sets out a far different purpose:

> We the People of the United States, in Order to form a more perfect Union, establish Justice, insure domestic Tranquility, provide for the common defense, promote the general Welfare, and secure the Blessings of Liberty to ourselves and our Posterity, do ordain and establish this Constitution for the United States of America.[57]

There is no mention of God in the Preamble or anywhere in the Constitution. This was conscious and deliberate. The Constitution intended to establish the United States as a secular state, rejecting all attempts to make it otherwise. This fact did not escape the notice of the fundamentalists of the day, who denounced the Constitution as a "Godless document." Indeed, to make unmistakably clear the wholly secular nature of the new government being created, Article VI, Clause 3 of our Constitution states:

> The Senators and Representatives before mentioned, and the Members of the several State Legislatures, and all executive and judicial Officers, both of the United States and of the several States, shall be bound by Oath or Affirmation, to support this Constitution; but no religious Test shall ever be required as a

Qualification to any Office or public Trust under the United States.[58]

Fundamentalists did not like that American truth then, nor do they like it today. They still maintain America was established as a "Christian nation." They insist there is no "wall of separation" between church and state created by our Constitution, as President Thomas Jefferson assured the Danbury, Connecticut, Baptists there was. They wanted separation of church and state at that time in our history because they were the outsiders then, the ones facing religious harassment by the fundamentalists du jour.

There are many safeguards and guarantees to ensure our nation remains forever free of any form of religious control. Despite this, some fundamentalists, throughout history, have continued in their attempts to make the United States a nation controlled by their religion and, therefore, by them. It is overwhelmingly obvious and documented that our nation was set up to forever keep separate the business of the state from the dogma of a given religion or religion in general. So, one might well consider this a betrayal of our Constitution and democracy. Fundamentalists who share the views of those who lost out in the great religious debates at the time of our founding are with us still—and are more virulent than ever.

The fundamentalism that arose in the United States has a rather clear history, at least as to certain watershed events shaping its direction. A century following the arrival of the Puritans, writes historian Alan Brinkley in *American History: A Survey, Volume I: To 1877*, colonists came to the conclusion, "religious piety was in decline, and opportunities for spiritual regeneration were dwindling."[59] This led to "the first great American revival," now known as the Great Awakening,[60] which began in New Jersey in the 1730s. The movement spread throughout the colonies, but had its greatest manifestations in New England.[61] There, colonists heard the preaching of the British evangelist George Whitefield and of the Connecticut-born and Yale-educated New England Congregationalist preacher Jonathon Edwards.[62]

One of Edwards's dark sermons with which he stirred adherents became the emblem of the Great Awakening. "Sinners in the Hands of an Angry God"[63] is a classic diatribe. It is a bitter, abusive denunciation of those who do not share the preacher's views and what God's wrath will do to them:

> The devil stands ready to fall upon them, and seize them as his own, at what moment God shall permit him. They belong to him;

he has their souls in his possession, and under his dominion. The scripture represents them as his goods, Luke 11:12. The devils watch them; they are ever by them at their right hand; they stand waiting for them, like greedy hungry lions that see their prey, and expect to have it, but are for the present kept back. If God should withdraw his hand, by which they are restrained, in one moment they would fly upon their poor souls. The old serpent is gaping for them; hell opens its mouth wide to receive them; and if God should permit it, they would be hastily swallowed up and lost . . . Thus it will be with you that are in an unconverted state, if you continue in it; the infinite might, and majesty, and terribleness of the omnipotent God shall be magnified upon you, in the ineffable strength of your torments. You shall be tormented in the presence of the holy angels, and in the presence of the Lamb; and when you shall be in this state of suffering, the glorious inhabitants of heaven shall go forth and look on the awful spectacle, that they may see what the wrath and fierceness of the Almighty is; and when they have seen it, they will fall down and adore that great power and majesty.

Recently, this rant has been rescued from well-deserved obscurity. It is now held up as a work of great worth to many God-fearing people in the modern Christian fundamentalist movement. Preaching that is simple, direct, absolutist, and condemning of others has come to be favored among many fundamentalist churches.

In addition to the dwindling religious atmosphere, the revival was also spurred by social tensions and a strong desire among the people "for an intense religious experience."[64] Thus, it "spread over the colonies like a religious epidemic."[65] However, it reached a climax in the 1740s.[66] The revival lost much of its strength and momentum because many colonists, including many who would become the founders of the United States, held more rationalistic views. Thus, their age was titled, "The Enlightenment."[67] Regardless, Edwards and Whitefield brought about lasting changes. Revivalist churches took the form of rousing and appealing to congregations. To their credit, these churches also came to be run in a democratic manner.[68] But, the fear of hellfire and the power of conversion proved to have little staying power. It was little different from the passing of the Puritan zeal in England and other situations where rabid faith faded like mist with the passing of a frightening contemporary threat or leader.

For several decades, it appeared religion in America was a weak and dying force. But, after the American Revolution, at the turn of the century, religion gained a new wind in the "Second Great Awakening."[69] According to William Martin, the Harry and Hazel Chavanne Professor of Religion and Public Policy in the Department of Sociology at Rice University and author of *With God on Our Side: The Rise of the Religious Right in America*:

> The first phase of this revival, the southern and western camp meetings, turned the American South into perhaps the most distinctively and self-consciously religious region in Christendom. The second phase came remarkably close to achieving the evangelical dream of making America a Christian nation.[70]

This time the revivalist denominations were not interested in restoring the religious institutions of the past. Instead, they promoted acceptance of many different denominations and sects as being "committed to essentially the same Christian faith." They were serving the purpose of creating social stability and order in communities that did not yet have an identity.[71] Millennial expectations were again roused. Most importantly, there came a theological emphasis and preoccupation with living sinless lives, known as "sanctification." Fornication, profanity, alcohol, gambling, and dishonesty were of utmost concern for personal piety. This emphasis on personal perfection seemed to relieve fundamentalists of any political, economic, or social duty. The Second Great Awakening, according to Martin, had its strongest impact on the South where revivals, Biblical inerrancy, and piety and purity permeated the culture.[72]

But, when Charles Finney, a Presbyterian lawyer, was persuaded to join the Association of Gentlemen, a group of wealthy millenarians that later came to characterize evangelical Christianity, Finney started the movement on a political course. He urged: "The great business of the church is to reform the world—to put away every kind of sin,"[73] and he preached it was the duty of true Christians to procure legislation according to God's law.[74] He began preaching at revivals in upstate New York following an experience of "a mighty baptism of the Holy Ghost" during the time of the "Second Awakening."[75]

Because of this revival, Martin says America became the most Christianized nation of all time. By the mid-1800s, evangelism was the dominant Christian force. The movement was a success because of the business know-how of its practitioners, from fund raising and advertising to teaching unchurched children, entertaining, and using effective revivals.[76] Such techniques have not been lost on their modern successors. In the North during the first half of the nineteenth century, evangelical Christians zealously campaigned to eliminate war, poverty, slavery, profanity, subjugation of women, and much more. They believed their goal for a perfect society would bring the second coming of Christ.[77]

In the South, the Ku Klux Klan became a clearinghouse for the cause of fundamentalist Protestantism. This new Puritanism was dedicated to preserving the old ways that benefited its cause against the press of modernity. Denominational disputes over slavery, as well as the impact of the Civil War and Reconstruction eventually divided and weakened the evangelicals. The combination of urbanization, immigration, and industrialization also substantially changed the face of America and eventually further weakened the control Protestants had over America.[78]

By the mid-nineteenth century, science also continued to further influence religion and faith. Biblical criticism and the realization that the books of the Bible were written by many authors at different times throughout history, led to a struggle dividing Protestants into two groups. Modernists accepted Biblical criticism, while fundamentalists held to their beliefs of Biblical inerrancy.[79]

The 1859 publication of *The Origin of Species* by Charles Darwin challenged Biblical literalism, the belief that every word of the Bible was dictated by God and that the book is inerrant, to its very foundations. The creation myth of Genesis in the Bible and the findings of science that life had evolved without a supernatural creation were not seen as compatible. If the evidence Darwin advanced that life had evolved over millions of years were true, then Genesis could not be literally true. Darwin recognized this and understood just what his findings implied and how people would react. Indeed, he did not mention human evolution in *The Origin of Species*.

The young man who had studied at Cambridge to become a cleric must have found the shock of this discovery and realization overwhelming. His intellectual honesty forced him to change his previously held belief in Biblical creation. But it took years before he would risk the publication of *The Descent of Man* (1871). In this, he argued humans, like finches, evolved from other and much different forms of living things. Then, just as today, fundamentalists viewed this science as a threat, as something devised by bad people to lead good Christians astray.

As is true with many things of uncertain or complex origin, there are wide ranging opinions as to just how modern fundamentalism evolved. However, the American movement that came to be known specifically as "Fundamentalism" began in the early twentieth century. In 1909, two

Christian laymen began publishing *The Fundamentals: A Testimony of Faith*, a series of booklets passed out to ministers, evangelists, and others. *The Fundamentals* "demand[ed] that Christians accept the Bible as 'revealed, inspired, infallible and inerrant.'"[80] If the discoveries of science contradicted any aspect of the Bible, fundamentalists' determination was the Bible was right and the claims of science wrong.

As *San Francisco Chronicle* religion writer Don Lattin pointed out, fundamentalism arose as a reaction against reading the Bible liberally. This is where Christians and scholars look at the Bible for its historical content, rather than just as the unquestionable, literal word of God.[81]

The Fundamentals pamphlet series (1910), introduced the Fundamentalist movement. It emphasizes five points Fundamentalism came to be associated with:

1. The verbal inspiration of the Bible
2. The virgin birth of Christ
3. The substitutionary atonement of Christ
4. The bodily resurrection of Christ, and
5. The second coming of Christ[82]

In 1942, Fundamentalism gave way to the formation of the National Association of Evangelicals. This somewhat less rigid outgrowth of Fundamentalism, in terms of Biblical interpretation, also came to be known as the "born-again" and "charismatic" movement.[83] The more puritanical members tended to maintain their identity with Fundamentalist sects. While their very similar, but more worldly, counterparts came to be associated with the evangelical sects and denominations, which are recognized for their emphasis on the personal experience of conversion.[84]

By their fruits ye shall know them

Not all ancient thought, religious or otherwise, is primitive, outdated, or wrong. But it becomes easier to recognize those who would rob us of our hard-won freedoms by identifying and understanding their commonly-held beliefs, many of which are outdated in light of the evolution of society and the arrival of the Information Age. There are certain features that are common to all Christian fundamentalists, according to Nancy Ammerman, Professor of Sociology and Religion at Hartford Seminary in Connecticut. She was also one of the scholars on the Fundamentalism Project. Fundamentalists, says Don Lattin, "believe that the Bible is literally true and without error, stress evangelism, emphasize the approaching 'end times' and the second coming of Christ and practice separation from nonbelievers."[85]

Other common characteristics are seen in fundamentalists' responses to the uncertainties in life. They become reactionary, oversimplify or deny realities, and do not allow their faith to be questioned.[86] In consequence, some fundamentalists, but not all, tend to avoid the secular world as they look to a world to come. They also tend to believe truth is theirs alone. It has been revealed to them by an all-controlling God that intervenes in all matters of this world, acting favorably toward those who do not question their faith. Fundamentalists are also most commonly identified with the political right.

Regardless of these and other common features, coming up with a clear profile of Christian fundamentalists has been virtually impossible. This is because, as Lattin agrees, fundamentalists come in many forms. Their variety of styles and beliefs can include such diverse denominations and movements as Baptists, Pentecostals, Protestant and Catholic evangelicals, and independent fundamentalist churches, among others.[87] Even certain branches of such denominations as Presbyterians have their fundamentalist congregations.

One of the key characteristics common to Christian fundamentalists is their view on Biblical literalism. This provides some interesting paradoxes. Evolution, according to this view, must be wrong. This is because evolutionary theory, along with physics, geology, astronomy, and all biological sciences, holds that the Earth is much older. Current evidence indicates the Earth is approximately 4.5 billion years old, that life first appeared about three billion years ago, and early humans evolved approximately one million years ago.[88] The Bible, in contrast, presents a creation myth in which the Earth and every living thing were created in six days. By counting the generations listed in the Bible from Adam to Jesus to determine the number of years B.C. (before Christ), the age of Earth could not exceed 6,000 to 10,000 years. When the facts don't fit the dogma, the literalists discard the facts.

Fundamentalists also want their belief system taught in schools because the Bible says it should be. Yet, they want prayer in public schools and arenas, even though public prayer is specifically forbidden by Jesus in the Sermon on the Mount (Matthew 6:6). This paradox reveals what is seen time and again by fundamentalists. They cling to Biblical inerrancy and a literal interpretation of the Bible. But such views are only adhered to when they support the fundamentalist purpose.

John Shelby Spong, an Episcopal bishop of Newark, fully and articulately addresses the problem posed by fundamentalists' literal and inerrant interpretation of the Bible. He points out the threat they pose to not only faith in thought but also to thoughtful faith. His book, *Rescuing the Bible from Fundamentalism: A Bishop Rethinks the Meaning of Scripture* is, or should be, a deathblow to the idea a literal interpretation of the Bible is "fundamental" to Christian faith. Indeed, there is certain urgency in his appeal for reason in a modern world. He warns, "If it continues to be viewed literally, the Bible, in my opinion, is doomed to be cast aside as both dated and irrelevant."[89]

Another common characteristic of fundamentalism is evangelizing, or the practice of saving people from sin and eternal hellfire by zealously preaching the gospel. This is seen in revival meetings, often held under tents or in large arenas and, most recently, on television. Evangelizing is predicated on a belief the end of the world is at hand and the second coming of Christ near, at which time the saved, or the "born-again," will enter into heaven. The business of evangelizing is saving souls.

Perhaps the best-known and most successful example of the modern evangelist is Billy Graham. He has been a counselor to several presidents of the United States. Seeing him in person several times, I can attest he is a world-class orator. The power he brings to the spoken word has an electric and magnetic effect on audiences. He paints a visual image of the joys of heaven that await the saved, and those who reject the free gift of salvation glimpse a colorful view of the horrors of hell. Graham's audiences number in the thousands. They answer his altar calls to come forward and be saved, while a magnificent choir repeats verses of the glorious Protestant hymn, "Just As I Am," by the hundreds. Millions of people have been saved, many on more than one occasion, by Billy Graham.

Authoritarianism, the practice of requiring blind obedience, has been widely recognized by scholars as another common feature among fundamentalists. One can certainly be fundamentalist without being authoritarian and vice versa. And it is uncertain whether authoritarians mask as fundamentalists or fundamentalism leads to an authoritarian personality. Regardless, there is a high incidence of the two traits combined. This is seen as women and children have few, if any rights in many fundamentalist homes, based on a literal reading of the Bible in which men have all authority. God, identified in the Bible as male, issues the laws, and men interpret and enforce them. All civilized societies recognize the need for rules. Yet, Christian fundamentalists believe the rules they impose have been handed down from God and obedience to such rules must be maintained. Their authoritarian personality helps explain why fundamentalists believe society must conform to their rigid views. At the same time, the nature of authoritarianism assists in understanding some of the personality traits common to fundamentalists.

Gary Leak and Brandy Randall in the Journal for the *Scientific Study of Religion* (1995) found that those who score high on the Rightwing Authoritarianism scale have several tendencies. They are likely "to aggress against unpopular or unconventional groups, feel morally superior and self-righteous," and "possess a mean-spiritedness that is coupled with vindictiveness."[90] They often take "'secret pleasure' when others experience misfortune and appear prejudiced toward out-groups."[91] These negative traits are commonly seen in fundamentalists and will be revealed in the following chapters. They can be better understood and more appropriately dealt with by recognizing this connection.

The Second Coming of Christ is also associated with fundamentalism and is most often seen in either pre-millennial or postmillennial beliefs. Under pre-millennialism there are several competing theories dealing with "the Rapture" and "the Tribulation." The Rapture is the time when true believers assume they will be lifted from the horrors of end-time destruction. It is "a mass migration of living and dead, born-again Christians . . . [who] will ascend through the air and meet Jesus Christ in the sky."[92] Rapture is derived from the Latin word "rapare" and "means to take away or to snatch out."[93] According to this view, "Pilots would disappear from planes, truck drivers from their trucks; [and] people from automobiles. . . ."[94]

The Tribulation is the belief the Antichrist will appear on Earth to begin a seven-year period of utter misery. According to pre-millennialists, the Second Coming of Christ will then occur in which he will rule for a period of 1,000 years, known as the Millennium. There is theological dispute over the timing of the Rapture. Some hold the Rapture occurs just before the Tribulation. Others say the faithful will be raptured after the horrors of the Tribulation. And others still, maintain the Rapture will take place midway, or forty-two months into it.[95]

Pre-millennialism has become the dominant of the end-time beliefs in many Pentecostal and fundamentalist churches.[96] Martin observes the pre-millennial doctrine holds the view, "bad news—political anarchy, religious apostasy, increased wickedness, earthquakes, plagues, and the like," are a sign of the Second Coming.[97] It is perhaps for this reason James Watt, the Secretary of the Interior under Reagan claimed, "We don't have to protect the environment, the Second Coming is at hand."[98]

Pre-millennialism generally fares better in bad times because it offers hope for those who believe.[99] The Rapture, in the eyes of the fundamentalist, is a glorious moment for the chosen because it secures eternal salvation. Believers in Pre-millennialism imagine an Earth filled with general mayhem, blood-filled rivers, nuclear war, and strange beasts stalking the land.[100] At the same time the righteous are transported to heaven to meet Christ, nonbelievers are to be eternally damned.[101] Mark Twain, in his posthumously published *Letters From the Earth*,[102] satirized this view. He described the saved inhabitants of heaven looking down into hell. These heavenly creatures took delight in watching the suffering of all of the unsaved children, particularly those of different religions than the blessed observers. Today, one can see bumper stickers proclaiming: "In the event of the Rapture, this car will be unoccupied."

The pre-millennial doctrine appears to contain an inherent flaw for the fundamentalist believer, however. Christ can only return when things are at their most horrendously sinful state. While many pre-millennialists look forward to this wholeheartedly, at the same time, according to ReligiousTolerance.org:

> they tend to be very outspoken and active in their opposition to abortion access, equal rights for homosexuals, pre-marital sex, adultery, sex education in schools, access to physician assisted suicide, the use of embryonic stem cells, etc. By their opposition to these "hot" religiously controversial topics, they are delaying Jesus' return to earth, the rapture and the 1,000-year millennium.[103]

Dr. Edward Hindson, Dean of the Institute of Biblical Studies at Liberty University, in "What Will It Be Like To Be Left Behind?" is a typical example of the pre-millennialist. He relies upon the Biblical book of Revelations in attacking the idea of a world at peace, a situation fundamentalists see as an anti-Christian "New World Order":

> While the desire for peace clings to the deepest crevice of the human heart, the prospects for global destruction are far greater than the prospects for global peace. Undoubtedly, men will continue to strive for peaceful solutions. But beyond the attempts at peace is the final holocaust. Those who are left behind after the Rapture will face a terrible future. . . . John's description of the trumpet judgments (Revelation 8:2-11:19) sounds very similar to a global holocaust. The entire planet will be affected by massive destruction, loss of life, and human suffering. The chaos that results will destabilize both the global economy and the world government predicted in chapter 13. . . . John the revelator paints a

picture of global devastation. He sees the vegetation burned up, a mountain of fire falling into the sea, stars falling from heaven and the darkening of the sun by a thickened atmosphere. It is no wonder that he hears an angel flying through heaven shouting, 'Woe, woe, woe, to the inhibiters of the earth' (8:13).[104]

This rhetoric is a common view among Christian fundamentalists today. The world will be destroyed, as they insist, because of the evil of secular humanists and those who do not conform to fundamentalism.

Modern Biblical scholarship and "form criticism," or understanding a text in terms of how and when it was created, might offer proof the book of Revelations is an allegory written to give comfort to early Christians suffering under Roman persecution. However, to the fundamentalist mindset the last book of the Bible is seen and interpreted as true prophesy that applies now, not to the time in which and to which it was written.

Postmillennialism, another commonly held end-time belief, is also known as "Kingdom Now Theology," "Dominion Theology," and "Christian Reconstruction." It holds the Second Coming of Christ cannot take place until the end of the millennium, a "glorious thousand-year period." Therefore, the Reconstructionist must transform society into the moral society cleansed of all sin.[105] Postmillennialism arose during the early nineteenth century through the belief people could achieve social perfection. It was thought massive religious revival, spiritual awakening, and purification would convert the entire human race, including Jews, to Christianity. It would be followed by a millennium of peace and righteousness. Only following this millennium would Jesus return. Christian Reconstructionists, such as the Chalcedon Foundation, disregard the Rapture and Tribulation and actively promote postmillennial doctrine.[106]

As these end-time beliefs indicate, superstitious thinking and belief in magical happenings is more comforting to fundamentalists than facts—but only religious magic. There is much fear among fundamentalists pertaining to the popular Harry Potter series. Fundamentalists are attempting to ban this series, just as a generation ago they attempted with *The Wizard of Oz*. This is because in the absence, or in their denial, of scientific explanations for aberrant behavior or unknown happenings, fundamentalists believe there really are demons, witches, wizards, and other mythical beings. These beings are capable of possessing people and of being purged from them by medieval practices such as exorcisms. To fundamentalists, the Harry Potter stories are not delightful fantasies but dangerous truths that should be kept from impressionable children, who might otherwise adopt them. Dorothy and Toto should be banned because their imaginary story might cause children to believe there can be good witches. This suggests the hysteria of 1692 and the Salem witch trials are not as far removed from our time as we might like to believe.

Lack of social responsibility is also frequently seen among fundamentalists as they avoid seeking useful solutions to social problems. They rely instead on ancient authority by looking to the Bible for passages to explain the problems at hand. In less "rational" times, a common practice of divination was to open the Bible at random and to find meaning in the passage the finger first touched or the eye first beheld. Imagination and creative symbolic interpretation would then find the answer. A similar method was used by the less religious, but classically educated, by opening the works of Virgil to find guidance for future planning or present frustration.

It is fundamentalists' belief in the rapture, of being protected from the end-time disasters, that leads some to cling to their separatist world and to avoid social responsibility.[107] Some keep to themselves in almost pious separation and isolation to avoid involvement with "the things of this world." They look to the world to come; and keep themselves, their children, and their activities apart from the affairs of politics and social action. To them, Earth is but a dwelling place, and all earthly activity is devoted toward leaving this world of flesh and getting to their heavenly home.

Another reason fundamentalists avoid social responsibility is, as Swift points out, they "hold the view 'God helps those who help themselves.' The rich do, and the poor don't."[108] Biblical literalists may justify this with the passage in 2 Thessalonians 3:10, which is occasionally quoted on bumper stickers: "this we commanded you, that if any would not work, neither should he eat." To the simplistic view of the fundamentalist, persons in need are generally lazy and deserving of their lot in life. To provide help would be to enable their laziness, as well as violate the Biblical command.

This view cannot be reconciled with other Biblical teachings lauding charity and the giving of alms to the poor. Yet, it is another of those seeming contradictions of which fundamentalists do not concern themselves. Charity may be permitted only from the church, not from the state. The same fundamentalist who helps give out Christmas baskets to the poor may well be opposed to any form of welfare or aid to the poor by the state. Secularization to fundamentalists is seen as an evil, as something referring to removing "religious control over social life" and the loss of "control over personal decision."[109] Of interest, is the fact fundamentalist groups appear most willing to take government grants for their charitable work, yet oppose the government bypassing them and aiding the poor directly.

Nevertheless, while some fundamentalist groups want nothing to do with this world, others want to control it and are known for taking political action in an effort to mandate a Christian-based society. These groups become politically active to the point of posing danger to individual rights and to all of democracy. This has grown increasingly apparent in recent years since fundamentalists have managed to commandeer the Republican Party. Among the key goals, issues, and aims of politically-active fundamentalist groups in America are opposition to abortion, gay rights, pornography, sex education, the teaching of evolution, gun control, equal rights for women, governmental regulation of environmental or industrial activities and practices, separation of state and church, and the First Amendment. They support prayer in public schools, the death penalty, governmental use and display of religious slogans, governmentally-funded "faith-based" charities, school "vouchers" for religious schools, teaching the Bible story of creation in science class, and public display of the Ten Commandments as a kind of magic talisman.

Many who are not religious fundamentalists may oppose or support one or more items on this list. And there are fundamentalists who may not oppose or support a particular issue as described. But as a rule, fundamentalists are the main defenders of these issues, as stated.

Fundamentalist yearnings: new wine into old bottles

The fundamentalist craze seen over the last decade, as Jeffrey S. Victor points out, is similar to times when there has been great social change.[110] The causes of fundamentalism, while complex, are most often seen as rooted in the failed promise of modernity. This can be understood as human progress that has taken place in recent centuries. The extreme change in pace, especially during this century, has left people with constant pressure to adapt their habits and beliefs. All of this confusion has created the perfect environment for fundamentalism to breed.[111]

The yearning for the simple worldview offered by fundamentalism is evidence of the strain that modernity, and what some have seen as the dehumanization associated with it, imposes on people. Much that is new, progressive, or contrary to tradition is distrusted and feared by fundamentalists. But regardless of their fears and their desires to return to the days of Ozzy and Harriett, fundamentalists still tend to make good use of technology. Over the last few decades, the use of the modern invention of television, a delicious paradox, has also been employed by fundamentalists. They use it to spread their message of the evils of modernity and the errors of the scientific method.

A wave of Televangelism began in the 1960s after an FCC ruling allowed television stations to air religious programs while still receiving "'credit' for public interest broadcasting." Televangelists associated themselves with fundamentalism, preaching Biblical literalism and "literal existence of the devil, hell, and the second coming."[112] Because many of their viewers became unhappy with evangelical ministers who tried to accommodate a somewhat more liberal society, these new televangelist-fundamentalists took a new approach. They believed it was their duty to uphold public morality.[113] Fundamentalists continue to do so with the latest in technology and often with great skill, such as their use of computers and the Internet for advancing messages condemning modern society.

A second cause of fundamentalism stems from a life crisis or struggles with life in general. Professor Elmer Towns, vice president of Liberty University in Lynchburg, Virginia, and also a Christian fundamentalist, "agrees that fundamentalism appeals to people who are experiencing a life crisis."[114] And as Strozier indicates, even at its worst, Christian fundamentalism provides hope to those who are at a disadvantage in society.[115] Fundamentalism offers certainty to a comfortable life after death. This was especially appealing to Americans, at one time, who had a life of "unrelieved hardship," explained Norman F. Furniss, in *The Fundamentalist Controversy, 1918-1931*.[116] The poor, the handicapped, the uneducated, and discriminated are likely to seek out fundamentalism. That is because it promises not only life after death, but also because in choosing fundamentalism, they become the chosen, the elite of God. This brings a sense of importance and hope to those who are struggling with an otherwise seemingly hopeless future. This could be seen in televangelism's early years as Southerners, the lesser educated, and the elderly took the most interest in televangelists.[117]

Not all fundamentalists come from the lower strata of society, however. A growing number of fundamentalists are wealthy business people, powerful corporate owners, and the elite. What draws them to fundamentalism is a psychological need for a "sense of identity, a sense of stability, and a sense of belonging within a like-minded community of purpose . . ."[118] Fundamentalism offers fellowship and an end to loneliness for affluent Americans who possess all the luxuries in our modern society, but have yet to achieve true happiness.[119]

Such was the state of President George W. Bush, who only found meaning in life when he became "born-again," a favorite phrase of the fundamentalist. He expeditiously gathered fellow fundamentalists to his aid in governing the country. U.S. Attorney General John Ashcroft, appointed by Bush, at taxpayer expense covered the exposed breast of the Statue of Justice in Washington, D.C. He is reported to be using his office, paid for by "We the People" to hold prayer and Bible study meetings. Chuck Colson, ex-Watergate conspirator under President Nixon, became a born-again Christian in prison. Apparently, prior to such rebirth he did not know it was wrong to lie, cheat, and steal. Present U.S. Representative Tom DeLay has credited Colson with motivating him to "get out of the church, and into the streets, and standing for [God's] worldview."[120]

Understanding the nature of religious denominations and fundamentalist sects offers insight into the reasons people often turn to certain groups, especially fundamentalist sects. Denominations are generally accepting of other religious beliefs and are comfortable with society. Sects, on the other hand, break away from society and claim to be the only true believers, or in this case, true Christians.[121] Denominations, because of their acceptance of diversity, do not generally search for new members. Sects abhor diversity and therefore, find recruitment necessary to convert society and gain conformity. Sects employ a variety of tactics to recruit new members. Focusing on the strong social needs of the human race, they hold friendly social functions as an attractive lure.[122] Another draw is charismatic leaders. Some sects are more accurately personality cults—sometimes leading to tragic and horrifying results. Consider the mass suicides at Jonestown and among the Branch Davidians of Waco, Texas, where followers adhered to the madness of their respective leaders, Jim Jones and David Koresh.

Another recruitment tactic often used by fundamentalist leaders is the use of oratory, similar to Jonathan Edwards who at one time "scared the hell" out of audiences. Such rhetoric induces people, especially those who are uncertain, afraid, and confused over the complexities of life, to leave more established denominations. They seek protection from eternal fire from a charismatic preacher.

A need for immediate and simple answers also can be a root cause of fundamentalism. Scott Appleby explains fundamentalists "want some simple truths for their personal lives."[123] They have difficulty with complexity and uncertainty, and a literal reading of the Bible gives them the immediate and simple answers they seek. As Appleby explains in "Fundamentalism and Its Motivation," "People feel out of control and vulnerable" when they don't have simple answers to life's questions.[124]

Unfortunately, as the Pontifical Biblical Commission states in *The Interpretation of the Bible in the Church*:

> The fundamentalist approach is dangerous, for it is attractive to people who look to the Bible for ready answers to the problems of life. It can deceive these people, offering them interpretations that are pious but illusory, instead of telling them that the Bible does not necessarily contain an immediate answer to each and every problem.[125]

There are, of course, many other reasons people may be drawn to fundamentalism as well. As Flo Conway and Jim Siegelman, authors of *Holy Terror: The Fundamentalist War on America's Freedoms in Religion, Politics and Our Private Lives* argue, this fervor has less to do with religion and more to do with power and control—and we are all targets.[126] This is a likely scenario for many fundamentalists. Further research has suggested right wing authoritarianism may manifest itself as religious fundamentalism. Fundamentalism, in turn, encourages and reinforces the right-wing authoritarian personality.[127]

Furthermore, as some scholars have argued, fundamentalist movements are patriarchists desperately "seeking to restore or secure [their] 'traditional' position of privilege."[128] Given the present situation, the potential for religious right-wing power and control of the American government becomes something beyond a matter of academic interest. Officials at the highest levels of government in the United States are actually attempting to advance fundamentalist causes. If religious authoritarians gain enough power, it may become a matter of survival.

In the shadow of the Puritans

Apart from the generalities discussed, attempting to define "Christian fundamentalism" is like attempting to lasso smoke. It has the broad generic characteristics that fit a number of conservative subgroups. Most Christian fundamentalists are not members of, nor do they share the beliefs and politics of, the more dangerous ultra-conservative groups. Those advocate and practice lawless, aberrant, and pathological violence. It would be as unfair to group all Christian fundamentalists with these criminals, as it would be to claim all who follow the faith of Islam share the vision of the murderous Taliban. All of the subgroups covered in the following chapters and many more, can be understood to be fundamentalists. Nonetheless, not all fundamentalists can be understood as being a part of all of those subgroups. Moreover, certain individuals can, and do, belong to more than one subgroup.

Fundamentalists do share the general characteristics of looking back to the old days and old ways as a model for a better life, a belief in the inerrant truth of the Bible, and the view they have been correctly informed by God. Yet, there is little the Amish communities share with the Army of God, a fanatical group dedicated to bombing abortion clinics and killing abortion providers. Members of the former make good friends and neighbors. Members of the latter belong in prisons, or in hospitals for the criminally insane. Many Christian fundamentalists are peaceful people who would be horrified by the true nature of some of their fellow travelers in faith. Regardless of those differences, for purposes of discussion, this broad group, which combined poses a number of dangers to American society, will be referred to as "fundamentalists."

The term "fundamentalist" was first used specifically to define the early 1900 movement that arose from the publication of *The Fundamentals*. But in recent years, the term has come to loosely encompass many Christian denominations and sects. Whether they choose the label or not, many have characteristics which closely resemble, or in some cases are identical, to those that adhere to the fundamentalist doctrine. The current usage of the term "fundamentalist" (not capitalized and used as an adjective or improper noun) has generally been accepted by scholars as a descriptive term. It is used to discuss adherents and sects that hold a number of similar characteristics to those that are defined by the proper noun, "Fundamentalist." Therefore, unless capitalized, the term "fundamentalist" throughout this book is used as a general descriptive to refer to any Christian who demonstrates most, if not all of the following characteristics:

- A belief in Biblical inerrancy or a literal interpretation of the Bible.
- Practices separation from nonbelievers or acts politically, specifically for imposing religion or Christian-based ideals on society.
- Attributes most or everything in life to divine intervention.
- Emphasizes end times and the Second Coming of Christ.
- Practices evangelism.
- Is authoritarian in nature and holds there are absolute truths to all issues, regardless of circumstance.

Politically active fundamentalists may also be referred to as the "New Right" or, as has become common in recent years, the "Christian Right" or "religious right." This consists of not only born-again Protestants, but also Catholics who are focused on traditional views.

The development, characteristics, and causes of fundamentalism, as described, offer an awareness necessary to understanding fundamentalism and the dangers it presents. Fundamentalists, perhaps more than most, fear death and feel insecure when confronted by departures from the old ways. Although fundamentalists are sure they know what is right and wrong in the world, they are very pessimistic because they live in a world where they have no control.[129] This poses problems as they come to "believe that the Bible provides unambiguous answers to all moral questions, and they contrast the purity within the church to the wickedness without."[130] They, therefore, reject situational morality and think certain moral absolutes apply in all situations and for all people at all times.

For this reason, fundamentalists desire the Ten Commandments to be posted in public places. Yet, many may not even know what the Commandments say or that they are found lacking for today's society. What fundamentalists know is that the Commandments are considered holy and they are, therefore, used not necessarily as a guide to behavior, but as a magic talisman to ward off evil. Such thinking creates a dangerous potential.

Regardless of modernization's effects on society, the pace is only going to increase. Therefore, the growth in fundamentalism is also likely to continue. As Strozier reveals, because fundamentalism touches on such ultimate issues, it is likely to resist being tamed and could quickly expand in the event of a crisis[131] such as what was seen on September 11, 2001. Since that day, there has been a resurgence in calls for organized prayer in public schools, posting of the Ten Commandments in public places, and a religious outpouring from public officials. America may have gotten the Puritans, but their vision for the country was not written into the U.S. Constitution.

Still, America is home to their spiritual descendents and secularists must unhesitatingly continue to remind them, as did our ancestors, of the wholly secular nature of our Constitution, and therefore, government. To do otherwise is to defile the graves of our martyrs.

CHAPTER 3

LITTLE ONES TO HIM BELONG

by Bobbie Kirkhart

*Our goal is not to make the schools better. . . . the goal is to hamper them,
so they cannot grow. . . . Our goal as God-fearing, uncompromised . . .
Christians is to shut down the public schools . . . step by step, school by
school, district by district.*[132]

Robert Thoburne in *The Children Trap*

"The rod and reproof give wisdom…"[133]

Larry Slack was a Chicago Transit Authority machinist, his wife, Constance, a nurse in a children's hospital. Most of all, the couple was devoutly religious. They headed a strict Jehovah's Witness family, protecting their six children from outside influences by home schooling them. The Slacks did not allow their children to play with others in their South Side neighborhood of Chicago. Neighbors reported seeing the family only on Sunday morning, as the Slacks headed to church. The Slacks' home, their marriage, their children were all dedicated to the service of their god.

On November 10, 2001, the family was getting ready to head out for dinner, a special Saturday night treat. However, Constance could not find her jacket where her wallet and credit cards had been left, so she and Larry told the children to look for it. The children were not trying very hard. So, Larry picked up a three-quarter inch cable, and gave the youngest, eight-year-old Lester, a few thumps on the buttocks and leg.

But, that didn't seem to help. The problem was that dirty clothes were scattered all over the house, and twelve-year-old Laree, who was responsible for the laundry, had not done her job. So, using the same cord, Larry gave Laree four or five hits, until she tried to squirm away. Then, Larry told the two teenage boys to tie her, face down, to a metal futon

48

frame. He gave her thirty-nine whacks to the back, counting, as he later explained, because he wanted to adhere to the Biblical edict of forty lashes minus one. He then handed the cord to Constance, who added twenty wallops.

Laree started to scream, so Larry ordered the boys to bring him a towel, and he stuffed it in her mouth. He tied a scarf around her head, securing the towel, and then tightened the scarf with a stick, as with a tourniquet. He removed her shirt, and told the other children to pull off her pants as he prepared to administer thirty-nine more strikes. Constance followed by adding twenty. But things just were not going right. Laree's back was bleeding; so Larry turned her over, and administered the final thirty-nine smacks. Laree died within an hour of being checked into the hospital.

Religious affiliation, according to a 1974 report in *American Sociological Review* by H. Erlanger, has been found to be a better predictor of violent behavior toward children than age, gender, social class, or size of residence.[134] Conservative religions are found the most violent. Indeed, the fundamentalist is correct in saying the Bible prescribes corporal punishment. Reasonable Christians and Jews, however, recognize a 5,000-year-old code of childrearing does not apply today. The Old Testament, after all, glorifies violence of all kinds, and worships a god who would kill children for making fun of a prophet.[135] It is a collection that includes both wisdom and poetry, but it is not an anthology modern humanity can read literally.

For those who do take it literally, a child is a beast to be tamed, not a person to be taught. Religious conservatives talk about the "problem" of willful children. To them, children need to learn obedience, not so much through trust as through fear. Proverbs 22:15 is consistent with the concept of original sin, the belief all children are born with the sin of Adam, as well as with other scripture. It proclaims, "Folly is bound up in the heart of a child, but the rod of discipline drives it far from him."[136]

The belief in male dominance is a Biblical tenet, and a fundamentalist conviction that is also closely related to child abuse. In *The Battered Child*, noted physicians and child-protection advocates, Ray E. Helfer and C. Henry Kempe are cited. They report, "the assault rate on children of parents who subscribe to the belief of male dominance is 136 percent higher than for couples not committed to male dominance."[137]

In addition, social psychologist Henry Danso, in "The Role of Parental Religious Fundamentalism and Right-wing Authoritarianism in Child-Rearing Goals and Practices," cites agreement with other research.[138] They agree that child discipline by corporal punishment is linked to religious conservatism.[139] Although this could be because of certain Biblical scriptures, they point out it can also be attributed to authoritarian personality types, a trait common among fundamentalists of all religions.

Harsh corporal punishment is not limited to the home, however. State law, which usually forbids teachers and school administrators from hitting public school students, often puts the religious institutions out of reach. This can be devastating to those most dependent on their caretakers. The *New York Times* reports "roughly" fifteen states have religious exemptions for daycare centers, or residential academies. Although some have virtually no regulation, "the exemptions are often fashioned in a more shaded manner. Religious groups agree to follow basic health and safety requirements in exchange for being allowed to teach, discipline, and hire as they please."[140]

Irwin Hyman of Temple University's National Center for the Study of Corporal Punishment and Alternatives says that although data are inexact, his perceptions are that spanking in educational institutions is decreasing, even among Catholic schools, which have been known to rely heavily on corporal punishment in the past. Still, "it is increasing in the Christian academies with a fundamentalist bent."[141]

Fundamentalist Christian schools, like the homes their students come from, are often unbending in their determination to keep to scriptural punishment. Pediatrician Dr. Eli Newberger recalls testifying in a South Carolina case. A nine-month old baby had been spanked to the point of bruising because he was crying. This happened during his first week in the church-run day-care center, a time when an infant would be expected to cry. The state offered to allow the center to remain open if it would stop corporal punishment, but the minister refused on Biblical grounds.[142]

In Arizona, parents gave permission to a religious school to subject their children to whippings. A teenager reported the principal stripped her, and beat her in her mother's presence, as the three of them prayed. The principal was arrested. In the investigation, it came out the principal had been charged with child abuse before, yet many parents still supported him.[143]

In rural Missouri, the Heartland Christian Academy used what the *New York Times* described as "old-time religion and old-fashioned discipline to try to save the lives and souls of its students." As was revealed, "The teachers do not spare the rod—here, it is a paddle—and they expect children to pray."[144] Paddling did not work for infractions such as not paying attention or talking back to their teachers. So, eleven teen-age students were taken to a nearby dairy farm and forced to stand in pits of cow dung.[145] In June of 2001, five staff members were charged with child abuse for that incident.

Later, four were charged with hitting a child with a board. In October of the same year, 115 children were removed after a runaway reported abuse in which a boy's eardrum was injured. Accounts of the incident varied, but the Heartland employee involved refused to talk with police, and the school would not fire him. The Heartland founder and director wrote to parents "local juvenile officials have undertaken a destructive campaign to destabilize this nurturing environment."[146]

Because no American law labels spanking by parents as abusive in itself, and because the privacy of the home often protects abusive parents from interference, less is known about the scope of parents hitting children in the home. While abuse that does not result in death may be prosecuted, it rarely becomes a matter of public discussion.

One exception, because it involved so many families, is the House of Prayer in Atlanta, Georgia. Originally, forty-nine children were removed from congregants' homes, but most were returned when parents, after some resistance, agreed to obey the judge's orders. This included promises not to allow the minister to spank the children or to take their underage daughters out of the state for marriage. Both of these had been practices of the church. Member David Wilson took issue with the judge's instructions to visit his children in their foster homes, and to take a parenting class. "We'll take the visitation," he told her, "but only if they bring her to our house." He added he and his wife did not need a parenting class because the Bible already instructed them in disciplining children.[147]

Although some fundamentalists advocate methods of corporal punishment which are, by any reasonable definition, child abuse, the best known emphasize some restraint in hitting children. Marvin Munyon of the religiously conservative Family Research Forum in Madison, Wisconsin, demonstrated the "proper" way to spank. He said, "You spank them right here in the gluteus maximus, which God made for that purpose." This quote was repeated on at least one sado-masochistic website,[148] but the Bible verses Munyon cited throughout his two and one-half hour lecture did not make the news reports.[149]

In more cautious fashion, James Dobson of Focus on the Family sounds moderate when he says:

> Spanking can be a valuable disciplinary tool—if it is administered appropriately. It is essential to always balance firmness with loving sensitivity. Indeed, spanking is not appropriate for every child or at every age, and is unnecessary in many situations. For

> example, willful disobedience or defiance of authority might warrant corporal punishment, while mere childish irresponsibility does not. When spankings are properly managed, there is no reason to fear they will produce harmful emotional or psychological effects in children.[150]

Dobson fails to add the considerable evidence, of which he must be aware, that the spanking he advocates is rarely effective in the long-run and frequently leads to harsher measures, developing into child abuse.

While it is clear fundamentalists are not alone among Americans who spank their children, they, unlike others, are not allowed to reexamine this method when its ineffectiveness becomes obvious. Fundamentalists are virtually alone in holding an explicit belief that the welfare of the child is secondary to the rule of Biblical discipline. For the most part, American society and government have forsaken the children of these zealots. It trusts in the scant mercies of the parents, who often hide their own misbehavior in their country's respect for the privacy of families.

More than sixty percent of Americans believe in spanking children,[151] in spite of the fact childrearing professionals and educators almost universally censure the practice. The American Academy of Pediatrics strongly condemns spanking. So do the American Psychiatric Association and the National Educational Association.[152] Punishment by hitting children is illegal in at least nine developed countries. Not many parents would espouse the philosophy "might makes right" to their children. Yet, many demonstrate that idea with a few painful swats on the buttocks.

Beyond the philosophical objections, spanking is both ineffective and dangerous, forewarning possible misbehavior of both parent and child. It is unlikely many mothers and fathers would hit their children if they understood what a risky habit it is, if they knew it often leads to disciplinary problems as the child grows, and is tied to serious emotional difficulties in adulthood.

In the United States, this information is available to only the most highly-educated families or those in the rare communities and school systems where adequate funds are allocated to parenting resources. At best, others think the concept is truly controversial. This is in part a result of the Christian Right's lobbying through such "educational" institutions as Focus on the Family. The organization offers advice on more than 3,000 North American radio stations. The professional community has offered official studies and reports but these are accessible to few, and the professional community has not been proactive in educating parents.

Perhaps it hesitates to confront directly anyone's sincerely-held religious beliefs.

Wendy Walsh in *Family Relations* magazine explored the sources of information people rely on in making the decision to spank or not to spank. She writes her most important finding overall points to the need for childcare professionals to increase their efforts to educate.

For this chapter, also significant was that mothers who spank were only slightly more likely to consider the advice of their religious leader important. Despite this, they were much more prone to cite their cleric as favoring spanking.[153] This suggests that perhaps religious beliefs are sometimes used to condone inappropriate behaviors that are difficult to change. In fact, some of the appeal of conservative religions is they insist the old ways of relating to each other are better.

Numerous studies link spanking to aggressive and antisocial behavior in childhood and adulthood. Murray Straus of the University of New Hampshire found that mothers who spanked even once during a one-week period, when questioned two years later, reported more antisocial behavior of their children than did those mothers who had not spanked.[154]

Repeated studies have shown when the spanking of children with serious behavior problems is discontinued, their antisocial behavior decreases. In addition, a 1999 Canadian study, the largest ever on spanking, showed adults who were spanked or hit as children are twice as likely to suffer from an anxiety disorder as their peers who were never spanked. Drug and alcohol abuse rates were also found to be high among those who had been spanked, as was depression.[155]

Correlation is not causation, however, and when care is taken to separate infrequent open-handed spanking of young children from frequent, severe, or abusive spanking, the effects are less clear. Psychologist Diana Baumrind concluded in her twelve-year study with colleague Elizabeth Owens the negative associations with spanking were few. She attributes them to other aspects in the parent-child relationship. Nevertheless, Dr. Baumrind does not endorse spanking, and Dr. Straus, while praising her study, added, "There is not absolutely conclusive evidence [that nonabusive spanking of young children is harmful], but there is very strong evidence, and there's strong evidence that other methods work just as well."[156]

Despite Dr. Baumrind's concerns, the research deals primarily with nonabusive spanking by loving parents. While it is possible some spankings were more malevolent than reported, there is no reason to doubt the vast majority of spankings were as innocent as they were portrayed. Our society does not consider frequent spanking or spanking of an older child abusive, although Dr. Baumrind excluded these practices from her study of benign spanking.

There is some evidence, however, spanking may also increase the aggressive behavior of the parent. Those who spank are four times more likely to physically abuse their children as those who do not.[157] Undoubtedly, some part of this statistical linkage can be attributed to the fact parents who abuse are more likely to spank. It also reflects the fact spanked children are more likely to misbehave, perhaps causing those parents who have meager disciplinary tools to snap.

Why, then, with all this information, do Americans believe in spanking? In addition to the fact the data are not generally available, there are several reasons loving parents may resist facing the facts about spanking. Attempts to change child-rearing patterns are always difficult. People usually want to raise their children the way they were raised. Perhaps more important, spanking is quick and easy, traits valued by today's typical American family that finds time in short supply. Corporal punishment often gets the desired short-term result. One thing is clear from the overwhelming evidence against spanking: No god of love prescribes hitting helpless children.

Lot's daughters

> 'Father Porter's coming, Father Porter's coming.' The warning flew down the quiet corridors of St. Mary's Grammar School whenever one of the girls saw the priest approaching. Then, as if on cue, dozens of girls in bobby socks and skirts that always covered their knees fled the center of the hallway for the walls, pressing their backs against the hard, cold tile. They knew that if you didn't turn your back from Porter, he couldn't [sic] sneak up and grab you from behind. If you didn't turn your back, he couldn't [sic] get his hands under your skirt. No one taught the polite parochial school girls these rules…[T]hey just knew. They learned from experience.[158]

Fundamentalist religion shows up as a risk factor for sexual abuse in many studies, most likely due to a number of characteristics of conservative religions. In addition, among the generally accepted risk factors for victimization of sexual abuse are two, independent of religion, which arguably, correlate with fundamentalist families: a high degree of isolation and a dysfunctional family. Such supposed correlations do not explain, however, the direct link between victimization and religion.

A 1988 study suggested three characteristics of families at high risk for sexual abuse. These directly correlate with fundamentalist ideals. First, fundamentalists often have a patriarchal family structure, with the man as owner of the family. Second, all sex may also be considered sinful, which confuses the distinction most make between acceptable and unacceptable sexual behavior. Third, sexual activity within families becomes hidden behind a curtain of secrecy no one wants to talk about.[159] In these associations, a cause-and-effect relationship seems virtually certain, though one could argue which is cause and which is effect.

Usually, when one mentions child sexual abuse in the context of religion, people immediately think of the Catholic problem with priestly pedophilia. This is a scandal of global proportions, which has resulted in an estimated $1 billion in settlements.[160] In the Boston archdiocese alone, between seventy and ninety priests were implicated. Because the horrible scope of the problem is well known, there is no need to offer additional detail here, but it should be noted this does indeed belong in a discussion of fundamentalist sexual abuse. Theologian James Seghers offers this definition:

> What is called Catholic Fundamentalism refers to those who would cite Conciliar documents, Papal encyclicals and the Catechism of the Catholic Church in a very literal sense to support authentic Catholic teaching and practices.[161]

While this definition does not include most American Catholics and does not apply to all Catholic clerics, it inarguably applies to the church itself. It is the authoritarian, closed, absolutist hierarchy that has allowed, and to a degree promoted, the disgrace the church faces today. Although neither the offending priests nor their victims are necessarily fundamentalists, the philosophy of the church certainly influences the tragedy of clerical molestation.

The church structure clings to each of the three risk factors, which enable and perhaps promote abuse. These factors include patriarchy, with the priest addressed as Father. All sex is sinful, with the vow of celibacy. And secrecy dominates the confessional and permeates much Catholic practice. This is in spite of the exceptions the Church has been forced to make.

For these reasons, priestly pedophilia deserves inclusion in any inventory of fundamentalist behavior. In their book, *A Gospel of Shame*, writers Frank Bruni and Elinor Burkett seem to agree. Citing a lack of flexibility within the hierarchy, they write, "Child sexual abuse has become a scandal within the Catholic Church . . . because it is embedded in the very structure of Roman Catholicism."[162] It should be noted the treatment of children by lay Catholics is not included in this chapter by virtue of their Catholicism. But, it may be included when the families meet other criteria for fundamentalism.

Among Christians, Catholics are not alone in clerical sexual misbehavior. Indeed, when all forms of sexual misconduct by clergy are considered—not just those with children—the denominations are about equal, and the incidence across the board is high. Still, psychotherapist Gary Schoener, who specializes in the field, notes mainline Protestants have been the quickest and most decisive in their response, while fundamentalists have been the slowest and least aggressive.[163]

The statistical connection between sexual abuse and fundamentalist Christians is dramatic. Jackie J. Hudson, author of *Characteristics of the Incestuous Family*, explains sexual abuse is normally higher among stepfathers than biological fathers. But in conservative Christian families, the incest rate is so high, the rate of sexual abuse by biological fathers is higher than by stepfathers in the general population.[164]

Hudson contends, "the religious right promotes attitudes toward women that allow for a tolerance of sexual abuse in our society today." She cites many studies offering reasons for this,[165] noting Cohen and Jehu, who say that fathers who molest their daughters generally see women and children as their property.[166] And according to several other sociologists,[167] explains Hudson, fundamentalist fathers believe "women and children should be subordinate to men and that children should be obedient to parents."[168]

The fundamentalist father expects unquestioning, automatic obedience, and such is usually motivated by fear. These father figures are usually autocratic, patriarchal, or dictatorial. Hudson notes the mothers of incest victims are generally women who are submissive[169] or subservient.[170]

Perhaps the study most relevant to this discussion is *Religiosity and Child Sexual Abuse: A risk factor assessment*, published in 1997. The authors surveyed 416 freshmen at a university in the southern part of the United States. Noting some theological difficulties with the term fundamentalist, they used the combined label evangelical/fundamentalist Protestant denomination. They asked not only about religious affiliation, but also about degree of family involvement in religious activities.[171]

The authors expected most people have had some sexual experience they might have found unpleasant. So, questionnaires were very specific as to whether the students had been victims of explicitly illegal sexual actions by adults. Status crimes, such as statutory rape of a willing participant by a slightly older boyfriend, were not included. In addition to religion, respondents were measured on a scale of the family's social isolation.[172]

The first look at the data showed an interesting paradox. The child's risk of sexual abuse increased as the family's denomination became more fundamentalist, but as religious activity increased, the risk of abuse decreased. A lower level of participation correlated with family isolation, an abuse risk factor found in several previous studies.[173] When separate graphs were made for victims of abuse within the family, and for victims of non-relatives, the pattern became much clearer. The correlation between denomination and victimization by a family member was pronounced and increased as the family's denomination became more conservative.

There was no correlation between degree of religious activity and incestuous victimization. The risk of victimization by a non-relative increased as the family's religious activity decreased. This was most likely because the decrease in religious activity correlates with isolation. [174] The authors make the point correlation does not prove cause and effect, and incestuous adults may be attracted to fundamental religions, rather than created by them.[175] It seems most people would agree.

The abuser likely believes the deviant sexual behavior to be an outgrowth of his or her religion, rather than the cause of it. Indeed, the need to molest children may be perceived as a commandment from God. One case involves the most infamous pattern of child abuse in recent decades, David Koresh and the Branch Davidians. Follower David Thibodeau's account may be suspect and is at odds with more objective accounts in several areas. Still, his description of the seduction of adolescent virgins, an act he clearly disapproved of, rings true, if not as an objective narrative of actions, as a subjective account of the way those involved perceived the events.

Koresh professed to have had a vision in Jerusalem, telling him to father a child with his wife's eleven-year-old sister. He claimed to be disturbed by this vision, to resist obeying it. His wife, of course, disapproved of the idea. They struggled internally and with each other for more than a year. Then David's wife had a dream threatening dire consequences if David did not follow his vision. [176] No one knows, of course, what really went on in this man's twisted mind, but it seems unlikely he looked in the mirror and said, "I think I can satisfy my craving for young girls if I say it is God's will." Still it does not seem unlikely, something beneath his conscious mind drew exactly that conclusion.

Perhaps it makes little difference how pedophiles rationalize their behavior, but it is clear from the data many have found in fundamentalist religions a safe structure to house their proclivities. While it would go beyond unfairness to paint all fundamentalists with this broad brush, there is enough information to hold the institutions accountable for their problems and to demand they find effective means, not just commandments and sermons, to combat this—their dirtiest open secret. Every state has laws requiring authority figures, such as doctors and teachers, to report suspected child abuse, but twenty-four states exempt the clergy from this obligation.[177]

Train up a child in the way he should go[178]

The new chancellor, in office less than three months, was a dynamo. Taking advantage of the emergency powers granted him, he was determined to restore a law-abiding and religious attitude to the country. On April 26, 1933, Adolph Hitler set up the Gestapo, but his speech concerned itself with the youth and, most likely, with his negotiations with the church, as he informed his countrymen:

> Secular schools can never be tolerated because such schools have no religious instruction, and a general moral instruction without a religious foundation is built on air; consequently all character training and religion must be derived from faith . . . we need believing people.[179]

Nothing frightens the perpetrator of a bad idea so much as education. And clearly, fundamentalists are against true education, particularly in its etymological meaning, "leading out." But, it is fair to say America's once-strong commitment to public education has changed because, as the religious right points out, public education has changed.

Some of the difference troubling much of our society has little or nothing to do with religion. *Brown v. Board of Education*, and subsequent rulings requiring equal education for all brought about more diverse, and therefore more challenging, classrooms. The cultural revolution of the 1960s not only brought into the school the history of minorities in this country; it also suggested pride in one's ethnic group. This opened the dominant culture and the traditional version of history to criticism, bringing controversy to the social studies class that had once taught only one version of events. Additionally, the feminist movement of the 1970s made high-quality, low-cost teaching virtually impossible to obtain, thereby raising the cost of quality education. However, to the fundamentalist parent, the definitive blow was the school prayer decision of 1963.

Conservative Christians have a point about the historical purpose of public education, which in this country had often meant Protestant education, from the Puritan schools on. Our great push to widespread public education in the latter part of the nineteenth century was a response to immigration. These new Americans were mostly Jews and Catholics, and we feared our culture was threatened if we did not instill Protestant values in the newcomers.

The famous *McGuffy's Readers* of the 1800s mentioned the word God, every third page on average,[180] proving religion was not forbidden in school; however, it was kept to the "right" kind. The Fourteenth Amendment had been passed, extending the guarantees of the Bill of Rights to cover state law. But interpretations of it remained very narrow, limited to the "due process" clause for decades to come. Not only was Protestant teaching allowed in public schools, it was encouraged.

Catholics responded to this by setting up their own schools to replace the public system, while, most Jews used the public system, adding their own after-school Hebrew classes to teach language and religion. Indeed, on matters of faith, general observations are that Catholics have maintained church loyalty to a much higher extent than Jews. This perhaps supports the fundamentalist idea that an education that does not support a religion undermines it.

Regardless, fundamentalist responses are largely divided into attempts to control their own children's education, and attempts to control *all* children's education. In the former, no group has been more successful than the Amish, who operate their own schools, where teachers typically have only an eighth-grade education. This is all the schooling the children are offered, as well. There is rarely homework because the children are required to do chores, typically farm labor, after school. Science is not even a curricular subject.

The Amish fund their own schools with little or no government subsidy and do not try to influence the public schools, so most Americans seem willing to overlook these practices. Yet, these would be considered gross instances of educational neglect and serious violations of child labor laws if they occurred outside a religious context. That the schools are designed to allow exploitation of child labor, and to ensure the child will not leave the community as an adult is no secret. In 1972, the Supreme Court decided to allow this practice. Justice Warren Burger wrote that a high school education is "irrelevant" to the lives of Amish children and would make it impossible for them to continue as Amish.[181]

One can hardly imagine a small urban ethnic cluster making this argument. Consider members of an ethnic group putting their children to work in their stores. Suppose they were to teach their children communally by an older child and take them from all instruction in the early teen years so that they are free to help with the demands of commerce. For some reason most Americans find the Amish charming, and few question the Amish's right to ensure their children will never be able to survive outside the closed community.

Other fundamentalist private schools are harder to generalize about. As in the comparisons with public schools, private schools tend to be lumped together. Although many seek outside accreditation, they do not accept the more rigorous standards of state oversight. Many states exempt private schools from teacher credentialing requirements, as well.

Religious schools are the largest portion of private schools, with Catholic schools making up thirty-two percent and "other" religious schools forty-seven percent. Twenty-one percent are secular. Approximately eleven percent of the total elementary and secondary school population is in private schools.[182]

The political push for vouchers would benefit religious schools, perhaps more than other private schools. In Cleveland, where its voucher system has been approved by Supreme Court, almost ninety-nine percent of the voucher students are in religious schools. In other voucher programs, the religious dominance is repeated, both in schools accepting vouchers, and in the schools of choice for parents who use vouchers. The majority of these schools are Catholic, but they include a large number of Christian fundamentalist schools, and a growing number of Muslim schools.

In fundamentalist schools, one can be sure sex education and biology courses are simplified, compared to the public school curricula. There is some reason to believe they usually do an adequate, although not exemplary, job of teaching the lower-level basic skills. Test scores reported by the National Assessment of Educational Progress show a comparison of public and private school students, when adjusted for parents' income, reflects no difference in student achievement. Yet, private schools have the ability to reject applicants, to require parental involvement, and to expel problem students. When one considers the other statistical advantages, this suggests most of the private schools are not doing the job they claim.

All states have reporting laws requiring professionals who work with children to report instances of neglect or abuse. Yet, there is anecdotal evidence that failure to report violations in the school is more likely in private schools of all kinds. This is because economic pressures may motivate administrators to avoid scandal at all cost. The fundamentalist philosophy that children have few, if any, rights, and that the school is for the glory of God may well add to the pressure to cover up scandal. It then seems more than likely reporting standards are not up to the usually-rigorous practice as in public schools.

Unfortunately, the exemptions many states offer to religious residential academies allow abusers to continue functioning, even after they have been identified. For example, Mountain Park Baptist Boarding Academy left Mississippi in 1987, due to problems with juvenile authorities. It moved to Missouri, and operated without difficulty until 1998, when a student was killed by a classmate.[183]

The fastest-growing alternative to public schools is the home schooling movement. This has gained wide acceptance in recent years. *USA Today* reported in 1985, sixteen percent of Americans approved of home schooling; as approval went upwards steadily, by 2001, forty-one percent approved.[184] Certainly home schoolers and their supporters are not all fundamentalists. In fact, there is an on-line e-group for atheist parents who home school.

Most of these join many other home schoolers in believing the highly-personalized methods are simply better educationally, although a common complaint among these atheists is the religion promulgated on their children in the public schools. Their anecdotes vary from the expected "under God" in the flag salute to the subjective, "the other kids are always proselytizing." Occasionally there is an outrageous reality, the teacher is ignoring the curriculum and teaching religion as fact.

Still, the typical home schooling parent is white, Protestant, with above-average income and education. When only one reason for home schooling is elicited, the most common reason for the decision is the importance home schooling parents put in religious education. One might expect virtually all home schooling parents include in their reasoning they believe they can provide a better education. Interestingly, in a 1999 survey, although this was the most popular reason cited, it was included by slightly fewer than half of the parents. This is in spite of more than one answer being allowed. Religion was a close second at thirty-eight percent, and undoubtedly overlapped the fifteen percent who chose character building and the twelve percent who objected to what the school teaches.[185]

While home schooling parents' education is usually above the average,[186] in only ten states are parents required to have a high school diploma or general equivalency diploma to home school. It has been found that almost nineteen percent of home schooling parents did not finish high school.[187]

There is no question home schooled children may do well academically. Home schooling proponents point to the large percentage of spelling bee and geography champions who have been home schooled. Unfettered by curriculum mandates, those parents whose ambition for their children lies in these subjects have a huge advantage in home schooling. It is more difficult to make sense of the "average," however. Proponents point to relatively high percentiles on SAT and ACT scores, and on various "norming" tests. Indeed, they are impressive, but they reflect a self-selected minority of home-schooled students.

On the other hand, by its nature, home schooling is nonconformist and individualized. So neither universal nor random samples are attainable. It should be noted that there is good evidence home schooling frequently offers above-average basic education: reading, arithmetic, traditional grammar, and such. Among educators and child development specialists, the biggest concern with home schooling is the lack of social experience, both inside and outside the classroom. Many home schoolers form collectives for providing enrichment activities, such as field trips, and enter their children in such things as group dance class or group sports. But the interaction provided is structured and controlled, lacking the diversity the child will face in the workforce and without even the limited freedom of speech and association present in the high school hallway.

Many home schooling parents see this as an advantage. But if it is an advantage, it is not one an adult can maintain and still enjoy the full mobility, cultural opportunity, and freedom our society has to offer. Educators point out peer interaction is a valuable and necessary component of a good academic lesson plan. Class discussion, oral reports, and cooperative learning assignments such as small group projects are important segments of the modern classroom day. Most teachers consider them vital to a total educational experience. Some of the reasons this is true may in fact be among fundamentalists' objections to public education. Peer interaction increases creativity and critical thinking skills. It is a teacher's job to tell the students what is required, so students may meet the expectations.

But when one is trying to please fellow students, there is no clear line, no "this is the answer they want" to seek. In class discussion, students have some social protection if they want to question the authority of the teacher's statement or the instructional materials. This is a practice good teachers encourage, as it forces the student to look critically at the issues and take ownership of his or her own ideas.

The time pressures home schooling puts on parents are enormous, particularly when one considers sixty-two percent of all home schoolers are from families of three or more children.[188] Imagine the baby is crying, the phone is ringing, lunch is cooking, and the dog is barking. Is the mother, who is most often the home schoolteacher, giving her full attention to the children studying at the kitchen table?

Home-teaching parents are often criticized as also lacking the depth of knowledge in a variety of areas to continue this practice into the high school area. This is a problem I am familiar with. For ten years, I taught in the Los Angeles school's Individualized Instruction Labs. I was responsible for as many as forty high school courses in all disciplines. Students had to complete a list of assignments at eighty percent or more to receive credit. No one claimed this was an ideal educational arrangement, but it was a way to meet the needs of some students within the tight budget of an urban public school district.

For the first several years, I was able to do little more in some subjects than help the student interpret written information in the books. This is not teaching! After years of using the resources of a large school district, I think I did an adequate job of teaching in every field. I consulted with specialists in the various fields, and gradually accumulated supplementary materials. Nevertheless, students suffered significantly in the social sciences and literature (where they did not have the advantage of group discussion), and in the sciences which are best taught with a fully equipped laboratory.

Typical fundamentalist home schooling parents have taken their children out of school as much to protect them from learning which they consider harmful, as to instill religious values. This greatly decreases what the parent needs to know. Certainly, in the field of biology, the debate is well known. Without evolution, any real understanding of DNA is not important. Teaching it in depth might lead the child to conclude the evolutionists are right.

The typical public high school literature class includes work encouraging students to think beyond the cliché, and to question traditional values. This is not as much to get students to change their values, but so that they will know why they hold them. To the fundamentalist, all values are prescribed in the Bible, as explained by some earthly authority. Questioning them is sacrilege. Neither William Shakespeare nor Toni Morrison fit in this scheme. Literature can go as far as oversimplified interpretations of Milton and Blake.[189]

Ancient history must be shaped to conform to Biblical accounts, and American history is distorted into an account of a struggle to establish and maintain a Christian religion. Any serious study of ancient India or of America's Founding Fathers calls these standards into question. Indeed, many fundamentalists claim the Founding Fathers were Christian, in spite of a clear record that the majority of the most prominent were not.

Other social sciences have to include the concepts homosexuality is a sin, anti-social behavior is inspired by Satan, and people who have not heard the word of Jesus are culturally deficient. This, then, excludes much of the traditional teaching of the courses that might call the entire belief system into question. Therefore, fundamentalist children are left with very primitive concepts of biology and physics, with—if the parent can teach it—some chemistry, though much organic chemistry is suspect.

Mathematics does present a real problem. Though its applications are often considered sinful, it is not philosophically excluded from the fundamentalist curriculum. New math, where children are taught to use critical thinking skills, rather than just the mechanics, is typically avoided. However, at the higher levels, the math is beyond most parents' abilities.

Health class, of course, excludes any in-depth study of the human reproductive system and certainly of birth control. It may also well omit common psychological issues, such as depression.

Finally, Bible study is important to the fundamentalist curriculum, but study here may be a misnomer. The fundamentalists' assertion they take the Bible literally, without need for interpretation, belies the internal contradictions within the collection. So, even Bible study, in addition to lacking any critical analysis, is inadequate in significant detail. Fundamentalists teach the story of Jesus' resurrection as history. Yet, they cannot teach the contradictory events and time lines of the various versions without adding explanations that defy both logic and Biblical scholarship.

It is no surprise fundamentalists are less likely than the general population to obtain a college education. Sociologists Alfred Darnell and Darren Sherkat reveal fundamentalists were found to "have significantly lower educational attainment in 1973 and 1982" than others. They are also less likely to take college preparatory classes and have lower educational aspirations.[190]

Fundamentalists are also often opposed to colleges, because they see Christians lose their faith with higher education. By not obtaining a higher education, fundamentalists never learn to think critically about religion, politics, and social issues. This leads to mental stagnation in many areas, and therefore, such problems cannot be resolved.[191]

After September 11, 2001, Americans were shocked to learn some Muslim schools in this country were indoctrinating children against the U.S.A. This came to the fore at a time when private schools were asking for, and receiving, more public subsidies. Moreover, some politicians, including President George W. Bush, were asking to further blur the line of separation between government and religion. This suggests Americans may be ready to discuss some oversight of private schools and home schooling.

Following the current trend may be disastrous. Arguing against Muslim secular education specifically, Azam Kamguian notes the problems parochial education has brought throughout the world:

> The dire riots in Oldham and Bradford last summer in England, and shocking scenes in Ardoyone with Catholic girls spat at by Protestant parents in the Northern Ireland, and the Islamic Madrasahs in Pakistan, has shown the ugly faces of religious schools . . .[192]

He points out that Islamic schools were very popular in the 1990's in Sweden. In these schools, he charges, children were beaten and threatened. Kamguian accuses such institutions of breeding fanaticism, sexual apartheid, and hatred.[193]

As long as there are math tests...

> Oh, be careful little hands what you do,
> Oh, be careful little hands what you do,
> There's a father up above
> And He's looking down in love
> So, be careful little hands what you do.

When I was very young, this was my favorite Sunday school song. My mother often led the singing, and she indulged my taste by including it almost every week. I rang out, loud, proud and off-key with each verse, admonishing myself, "Be careful little feet, where you go," and even "Be careful little mouth what you say"; until came the last verse. I wanted to understand it, to like it, to obey it. But it bothered me to sing it, to contemplate the idea: "Oh, be careful little mind what you think."

Evangelist Pat Robertson talks of adding Christianity to the public schools saying:

> [The] public education movement has also been an anti-Christian movement . . . . We can change education in America if you put Christian principles in and Christian pedagogy in. In three years, you would totally revolutionize education in America.[194]"

The issue is about including the Christian Right's point of view in the public educational standard. Yet, anyone who reads the newspaper knows the movement is as much about excluding ideas and materials, controlling young minds, and limiting options for all American children. Therefore, it is not simply the home schooled who are affected. If they succeed, all children will suffer the narrow education fundamentalist children now undergo in home schools.

To this end, Robert Simonds, author of *How to Elect Christians to Public Office,* (1985), heads the perhaps ironically-titled conservative group, Citizens for Excellence in Education (CEE). In his book, Simonds offers a stealth strategy for gaining control of school boards, which has been highly successful. In 1993, the CEE claimed to have successfully gained 7,153 school board seats. By 1995, 1,700 committees had been formed for electing Christian school board members.[195] The CEE has created a list for identifying the secular humanist enemy. Among the more than 300 words used by humanists are: academic freedom, analysis, career education, creative writing, human growth, identity, parenting, racism, worldview, and self-understanding.[196]

In *The Children Trap,* Robert Thoburne, an educator at Fairfax Christian School in Virginia, and a Christian Right advocate, states:

> I imagine every Christian would agree that we need to remove humanism from the public schools. There is only one way to accomplish this: to abolish the public schools. We need to get the government out of the education business. According to the Bible, education is a parental responsibility. It is not the place of the government to be running a school system.[197]

Agreeing with Simonds, Thoburne says the way to accomplish this is for Christian candidates, of the right wing of course, to keep their religious beliefs and motives hidden.[198]

On the CEE's agenda for public school curricula, the law may be clear, but the mind of the American public is not. Those who would return our schools to instruments of Protestant indoctrination would seem, at first blush, to have no chance. Though it may not always be practiced, diversity is a value most Americans espouse. This is particularly true when it is a matter of respecting individual rights. And compromise is widely accepted, even taught in our schools, as the preferable way to settle disputes.

Ironically, fundamentalists, who abhor diversity and who believe real compromise to be sinful, have perverted these values into weapons for their own use. The power of the call for "compromise" is evident in the attack on evolution. Many offer, 'If we teach evolution, why not teach 'scientific creationism' along side it, and let the kids judge?" Even as parents clamor for higher standards, they think this sounds reasonable. They rarely ask, "why not teach all the mythologies?" or "If we teach supposition in science class, how will the children understand what science is?"

In a 1997 Gallup Poll, sixty-eight percent of Americans said they believe creationism should be taught along with evolution in the public schools. Shockingly, a large minority of America's high school biology teachers—as many as forty-five percent in 1986—agreed. In 1988, a majority (fifty-three percent) of the nation's school board members held that belief.[199] Still, the vast majority of Americans, eighty-seven percent in a 2001 Gallup Poll, favor teaching evolution—though not exclusively.

Where evolution is not taught exclusively, however, it cannot be taught well, and teaching creationism or "intelligent design" alongside the science of evolution is the equivalent of teaching in math class that two plus two make four, except that it may also make three. The student may eventually figure out what two plus two is, but the system the student needs to learn is lost in the confusion.

A vital component of any science teaching is vigorous implementation of the scientific method. Science progresses. Although it is the nature of science to make all conclusions tentative, specific information that a student gets in a high school course will likely hold up as true throughout his lifetime. However, the line of inquiry may be so far extended in a decade the data learned in high school is irrelevant.

The scientific method is what students must learn, and it will serve them in adulthood. We live in a rapidly-advancing technological world. Therefore, the process of drawing conclusions from observation, testing those conclusions, and abandoning them if they do not work, is important not just to the scientist but to the layman. It is that, much more than the fact of evolution, terrifying the fundamentalist. And the concept of "equal time" for non-science in science class is exactly the formula for ensuring that only a few of the brightest students are prepared to cope with tomorrow's issues.

The unanimity of the scientific community that "creationism" by any name is not science has stymied the religious right in the courts. Therefore, fundamentalists have concentrated on influencing state standards, where they have been quite successful. A recent book, *Good Science, Bad Science* by Lawrence S. Lerner, Professor of Science and Science Education at California State University, Long Beach, was summarized in the *Scientific American*. It designated only ten states with very good to excellent state standards in science.

The twenty-one states, plus the District of Columbia, rated satisfactory do, indeed, teach evolution. But they include such states as Texas and Montana, where human evolution is not taught, and Nebraska, Massachusetts, and New York, where creationist jargon or ideas infuse the standards. The eighteen states that are rated poor are not necessarily in the Deep South. In fact, the Carolinas are rated excellent, and Louisiana is good. Alaska, North Dakota, Wisconsin, Illinois, Ohio, and Maine join the other southern and border states with unsatisfactory or useless standards. Iowa is the only state that does not mention evolution at all in its state standards.[200]

The other issue of well-known concern to fundamentalists is sex education. This matter resonates well with the mainstream community. Both evolution and culture protect the human race from the dangers of inbreeding by making them loathe looking upon their children as sexual beings. Unfortunately, this fact of nature and society seem to have made it difficult for many Americans to face reality.

The study, *Teenage Pregnancy in the United States*, reveals teen pregnancy is ranked highest in the United States over six other developed countries. Yet, the level of sexual experience among teenagers was equal among the United States and the other six countries. This reveals American teens are just not using contraceptives regularly.[201] In fact, the Alan Gutmacher Institute compares sexual activity among five developed western nations, Canada, France, Great Britain, Sweden, and the U.S. It finds the U.S. has not only the highest birthrate among girls aged fifteen to nineteen, but also the highest abortion rate in this age group. The birthrate of fifteen to seventeen-year-olds is higher than two percent in only two of the forty-six developed countries studied—the United States at 3.4% and Georgia at 3.5%.

The amount of teen sexual activity is similar in all developed countries, with the U.S. slightly above average in the activity of teenagers younger than fifteen, and slightly below average in teenagers older than eighteen.[202] This high rate of teen pregnancy in the United States can be linked to the lack of adequate sex and birth control education in public schools. It also stems from the deficiency of contraceptive availability to teens.

The argument that parents are responsible for sex education finds a lot of agreement throughout society, even with the best-informed audience. It reflects a family value almost all Americans hold. The problem with this attitude is when parents do not meet the obligation or do the job well, it is not only those parents who suffer. In 1989, the public cost of teen motherhood was in excess of $21 billion, approximately $77 per year for every person in the country. This figure does not include the indirect costs, many of which amass years after the child has reached maturity. Women who become mothers in their teens accrue a lifetime earning half that of women whose first child comes in their twenties.

Sixty percent of teen mothers who marry before age twenty divorce within five years, and seventy-five percent of teen mothers drop out of high school.[203] Much of this cost and the heartache creating it are preventable. This was revealed through a study at the John Hopkins School of Medicine, which offered free medical and contraceptive services at a school-based clinic. The results were a thirty percent reduction in teen pregnancy after only three years.[204]

In the mind of the fundamentalist, of course, teen pregnancy is not the problem; teen sex is. Certainly one does not have to hold to any religion to worry about sexual activity among our children. However, the fundamentalist assumes, contrary to all research, the sterile environment of the classroom can either encourage or deter sexual activity. Many espouse the idea the responsibility of an unwanted child or suffering from a sexually transmitted disease is a necessary punishment for sexual behavior. Such people are not moved by repeated data showing no correlation between information and promiscuity. In fact, those who use birth control are no more likely to be promiscuous than those who do not. Furthermore, some data suggest when birth control information is given with advice about delaying intercourse, it is quite effective in delaying sexual activity. It also reduces the number of partners an adolescent may have.[205] As Susan Motamed reports in *Condom Availability and Responsible Sexuality Education*, providing condoms in schools increases condom use among students who are already sexually active. But it has no impact on those who are not, neither in the amount of sexual activity nor in the number of partners.[206]

The curriculum of sex education classes is a hot potato to the politically-minded school boards. In spite of most people's favoring such classes, the issue is so emotional the minority who oppose it can strike fear in the hearts of anyone who aspires to further political office. Consequently in many districts, our children, whether they are the victims of their own passions, exploitation in their family, or a stranger's rape, are often denied the information or the tools to protect themselves.

Sex education and evolution are only the two best known of the curricula the fundamentalists wish to change. Their interference into curricula goes into every classroom and beyond. History is a problem to most fundamentalists, as it disagrees with their Bible and their prejudices. A "Bible as history" curriculum produced by the National Council on Bible Curriculum in the Public Schools illustrates the confused situation in some of the lower courts. The course, adopted in Lee County, Florida, taught Biblical events such as the resurrection of Jesus and the parting of the Red Sea as fact. The court allowed the Old Testament course to stand, with the parting of the Red Sea and all. But it did not allow the New Testament course, as the court ruled the Resurrection of Jesus was a doctrinal claim, not a historical fact.[207]

Fundamentalists are the largest censors of books not only in America's schools, but also in libraries, retail stores, and even youth organizations. One does not have to look to the Bible belt for an outrageous example. Most Americans have heard, and have likely shrugged off, the objections to the popular Harry Potter children's series as glorifying witchcraft. The Penryn, Pennsylvania, police department, however, did not take it so lightly. One of the area's most popular events is the triathlon, sponsored by the YMCA, which requires rerouting and directing traffic.[208] The eight-member local police force voted unanimously to boycott the September 2002 event because the YMCA had read Harry Potter stories to children in its after-school care program.

"I don't feel right taking our children's minds and teaching them [witchcraft]," Fire-Police Captain Robert Fichthorn told the Associated Press.[209]

Similarly Satanic in the eyes of fundamentalists is the reading series *Impressions*, an anthology of children's literature. Donna Harrington-Lueker, author of "Book Battles" from the *American School Board Journal*, reports controversy in many public schools throughout the United States. By using the threat of opposing upcoming school tax issues unless schools remove this "occult" literature, fundamentalists have been quite successful in eliminating it.[210]

Perhaps no such controversy is as confusing as the Reverend James Dobson's objection to the reading series *Quest*, which was accused of promoting New Age religion and secular humanism. When Dobson joined the religious opposition in the early 1990s, there was surprise because he had contributed to the original series. In response to questions, Dobson praised the program for consulting Christian psychologists, using Christian authors, and teaching values "compatible with the Christian perspective." Still, he could not endorse the books because they included the works of some secular humanists. He concluded the series could only be acceptable if taught by a Christian teacher.[211]

In our society, the appeal to diversity and individual rights is strong. Fundamentalists ask, "Don't our children have a right to pray in school?" They often follow with many anecdotes, mostly false, of teachers forbidding children to engage in private prayers on school property. Because most people see religion as a useful moral guide, or at worst, a benign exercise, these stories, even if only half believed, are powerful arguments. There is, of course, no judicial proclamation against the personal exercise of religion on school grounds. But when a student—often pushed by a parent or minister—tries to commandeer the classroom, that is a different issue.

The primary case forwarded on behalf of coercive school prayer certainly appeals to the Eden myth. This is not the one of the Bible, but the one taught in Sociology 101. It is the commonly held idea that there was a time when things were much better. Fundamentalists are firmly convinced the "good old days" ended in 1963 when atheist Madalyn Murray O'Hair got prayer and God kicked out of the schools. They exploit this idea and find sympathy in a culture that has always viewed its children with frightened ambivalence.

Did our society deteriorate after the ruling? In fact, the homicide rate went down slightly, but steadily in the years following the decision.[212] Some would argue the turmoil of the Vietnam protests showed degeneration; others would credit a new moral awareness of America's youth. In either event, these were children educated before the ruling. It was in the 1950s, not the 1960s, when the term "juvenile delinquency" was popularized, and fundamentalists were burning records and condemning Elvis Presley for corrupting America's youth. It seems religious conservatives did not recognize the redeeming power of mandated prayer until they lost it.

What of prayer in schools today? A study commissioned by the National Catholic Education Association, and partially funded by the National Institute on Drug Abuse, found illegal behavior is higher among seniors in Catholic schools, where prayer and religious instruction are daily occurrences, than in public schools.[213] Indeed, the lack of Catholic school moral superiority is well known to most adolescents. In Los Angeles, the hills of Los Feliz are home to Immaculate Heart High School, well respected by the adults of the community for a good academic record. L.A. teenagers refer to the school as "The Hill on the Pill"[214] because of the school's high rate of sexual activity.

National tragedies, such as the catastrophe of September 11, 2001, give proponents of religious indoctrination in the public schools an excuse to resume their efforts. While this does meet a fundamentalist goal, it does not necessarily come from the political right. Politician and minister Jesse Jackson's liberal politics contrast with his conservative religion. He led the students at Thomas Jefferson High School for Science and Technology in Alexandria, Virginia, in what could be mistaken for the prayers at an old-fashioned revival.[215] *Time* magazine reported:

> the gymnasium broke into a rousing call-and-response chant. It could have been a school pep rally, except that many of the students and teachers had their heads bowed, and they were calling out prayers for each other and peace on earth.[216]

A Hindu student asked, "Can he do that?" *Time* concluded in the months following the Trade Center attacks, he could. The magazine described other incidents of teachers praying with troubled students or giving religious messages over the public address system, and of a school auditorium turned into a sanctuary.[217]

What does American society and government have to say to that Hindu student? What about to the Christian who takes literally the admonishment, "When you pray, go into your room and shut the door, and pray to your Father in secret"?[218] How about the nonbeliever who has been taught to seek rational solutions to problems. Finally, consider the Muslim adolescent who is trying desperately to fit in. Does America care about these children?

The Alabama State Senate does not. In February of 2002, it passed a bill requiring the Ten Commandments to be posted in all schools. Imagine the abused child having to face everyday, "Honor your father and your mother, that your days may be long in the land which the Lord your God gives you." What about the Catholic, a small minority in most of Alabama, seeing the law, "You shall not make for yourself a graven image, or any likeness of anything that is in heaven above, or that is in the earth beneath, or that is in the water under the earth." This is what Protestants use to "prove" Catholics are not Christians.

Then there is the high school senior who is working to save for college, "Six days you shall labor, and do all your work; but the seventh day is a Sabbath to the LORD your God; in it you shall not do any work, you, or your son, or your daughter... ." Finally, what do you say to the third grader, trying to figure out what it means to "covet your neighbor's wife" or his ass.[219] Fortunately, this bill died in the House.

What's it all about?

When I was in high school, a classmate's parents were killed in a car wreck. The boy and his little sister were badly hurt, but were allowed to leave the hospital to attend the funeral. It was the Bible belt, and we were all religious, but the hellfire-and-brimstone fundamentalism of the preacher was shocking to any sensible person.

My friend's parents, you see, were going to hell for their evil ways. What their evil ways were, I never learned, and in such a small town, that suggests they were not unusually evil. I watched John and Lisa's faces as their minister damned the parents they had just lost. This "holy man" offered no mitigation, no qualification, and only stern warnings if we, the congregation, did not change our sinful habits, we would follow the deceased straight to hell. And the children sat stoic, denied the right even to hear a simple eulogy of the parents they had lost.

I knew about fundamentalists, of course, and thought their methods crude. But their theology was not very different from my own. It seemed possible, even likely, that my classmates' parents were going to hell. But I could not then, and cannot now understand any earthly or divine justification for asserting this to the children. I had no words of comfort for my friends. Like everyone, (except the minister, and a few of his loyal flock) I was speechless. It was the first time I had seen the callous, deliberate disregard for the well-being of children that is implicit and sometimes explicit in fundamentalist thought.

The above sections discuss specific issues of recognized public concern in the battle for the future of America. Nevertheless, there are issues that may have no place in public policy, but are of interest to anyone who cares about children. If Americans can do no more than protest many of the cruelties and bad judgment that belie the loud protestations of "family values," then they must speak out. When ideology rules over reality, people suffer, and the most vulnerable suffer most.

America is not ready, as a nation, to pass or even consider limits on family size, but the tendency to large families is perhaps the most widespread problem of fundamentalism. The National Incidence Study reports physical and educational neglect is three times more common in larger families than it is for single children. The report also found, "professionals in schools play a central and critical role in identifying children who are abused and neglected."[220]

Unfortunately, this resource was not available to the five home-schooled children of Andrea Yates. The interaction between her religious beliefs and her mental illness is too complex to attempt to unravel here, but one fact is extremely relevant. Years before she drowned her children in the family bathtub, the couple decided not to use birth control and to accept all the children their God gave them. Neither Rusty Yates, who claims no mental illness, nor Andrea reconsidered, even though they were warned by a psychologist what they should have known from experience, that Andrea was not up to the task.

Sadly, Andrea Yates' children did not grow to adulthood, but most fundamentalist children do, and they often find themselves pathetically ill-prepared. Children develop decision-making skills by making decisions, self-esteem by succeeding on their own, and empathy by contact with people who are quite different from themselves. In *Raising Kids Who Can*, therapists Betty Lou Bettner and Amy Lew point out, not only the individual's well-being, but also our country's well-being is at stake. "Children in a democracy must learn to think for themselves," the therapists say, in espousing democratic decision-making in family meetings.[221]

The traditional, authoritarian fundamentalist family does not provide such experiences. These young people enter adulthood as newly-released slaves, whose only knowledge about dealing with life's problems are the methods of slave or of master. The child who is raised to see himself as a sinner who needs to be controlled may well grow into that image. Educators H. Stephen Glenn and Jane Nelson cite that the major "obstacle to developing mature judgment" is having parents who:

> lecture, instruct, explain, moralize and ultimately make all judgments themselves . . . Such parents retard the development of judgmental maturity and critical thinking, inhibit the acquisition of wisdom, and replace them with threat and intimidation.[222]

Those researchers who find positive value in church activity, nevertheless, find problems with fundamentalism. In 1984, K.M. Brigman concluded family church participation created more stable, happier families. However, the "rigid doctrines that promote traditional sex roles or negative approaches to family planning were thought to be detrimental to family life."[223]

Many of this country's most infamous examples of child abuse appear to have grown out of such ill-prepared attempts to apply the absolute moral standard of Christian fundamentalism to a somewhat more complex world. One example is Mary Kay Latourneau. Hypocrisy is certainly not unique to fundamentalists, but it is inevitable in a value system framing everything in moral absolutes. It is difficult for a child to learn truly ethical behavior in such an environment.

John George Schmitz was an early "family values" conservative, a darling of the group leading the Reagan Revolution, a member of the U.S. House of Representatives from Orange County, California, and the patriarch of a fundamentalist Catholic family. His wife, Mary, was a self-proclaimed antifeminist who was active in the Right to Life League. Schmitz had a house full of kids who adored him. His favorite, and perhaps the one most admiring of him, was the one he called "Cake," Mary Kay.

Everything came crushing down when Schmitz's mistress, a former student of his, was legally charged with abuse of one of her two children fathered by Schmitz. To his credit, Schmitz acknowledged the relationship and his paternity. The mistress was found not guilty, but Schmitz's political career was over, and the family was devastated. Shortly thereafter, Mary Kay, barely out of childhood, met Steve Letourneau. When she became pregnant, they married and moved to Seattle, where they enlarged their family. Things were apparently normal. That is until Mary Kay, an elementary school teacher, "fell in love" with, and became pregnant by, her sixth-grade student.[224]

Through many talk shows and interviews, she pleaded for people to understand she meant to hurt no one, that theirs was true love, and she had to follow her heart. It really is not difficult to understand how she became confused about right and wrong in matters of the heart. She grew up in a world of simple "good" vs. "evil," only to learn that, by those definitions her mentor and hero was "evil." Certainly, sensible people are aghast the confusion could be this dreadful.

It would be ludicrous, of course, to suggest infamous adults who came from fundamentalist families commit their harmful acts solely because of their parents' religion. However, it would be a serious denial of reality to suggest the unrelenting, absolutist God of their fathers had nothing to do with their perverse behavior. The question, of course, is how many children are being raised today to disrespect human standards of decency in favor of some "higher law" that is as inflexible as it is unattainable.

If fundamentalists can call for compromise in things as basic as the definition of science, is it not appropriate to demand some compromise, some standards met in the education of their children? And what about some oversight in the physical discipline of defenseless babies?

America indulges fundamentalists' concepts of discipline and education, their absolute right to inflict violence, to insulate their children from the marketplace of ideas, and to protect them from a well-rounded education. Is this not abetting crimes against today's children, as well as the crimes their children may commit in the future? Certainly, freedom of religion is an American value that must be preserved, but it need not mean religion is an easy and acceptable disguise for physical, sexual, and intellectual abuse or neglect of children.

CHAPTER 4

ETERNAL SUBSERVIENCE
CREATED FROM MAN FOR MAN

by Kimberly Blaker

A wife is to submit graciously to the servant leadership of her husband, even as the Church willingly submits to the headship of Christ. She . . . has the God-given responsibility to respect her husband and to serve as his helper in managing the household and nurturing the next generation.[225]

The Baptist Faith and Message,
Article 18, of the Southern Baptist Convention

To many Americans today, this portrayal of woman's role reads like a line from a history textbook describing the station of women from decades, if not a century or two, past. Those of us in mainstream homes have been shielded from the reality of modern-day male domination. In the eyes of many, the only shred of first-hand evidence such roles once existed is seen in some of our grandparents and great-grandparents, generations that will soon pass. But, this command for a woman's submission to her husband is not centuries or even decades old. Neither is it part of a long-time document simply never erased. Eight thousand three hundred delegates of the Southern Baptist Convention (SBC), the largest Protestant denomination in the world, met in Salt Lake City for its annual convention on June 9, 1998. To the dismay of many moderate Baptists, Article 18 of the SBC's Baptist Faith and Message was approved.

The Baptist Faith and Message had gone unchanged for thirty-five years. The SBC, although conservative in its beliefs, had not previously so defined the role for women. The new Article 18 requires millions of Baptist women desiring to enter the workforce, or other equally pedestrian matters, at least in homes adhering to the Baptist Faith, to get permission from their husbands. This is something the Article's drafters have acknowledged.[226]

The implications of such growth in conservative Christian views and on woman's role are many, whether by fundamentalists or those just bordering such views. Christian fundamentalism not only affects women in fundamentalist homes but women throughout society. In fact, fundamentalist beliefs impact women more severely than any other group. First, women in fundamentalist homes may have little or no control over their own reproduction and are often unfamiliar with effective forms of birth control, should they opt for such a health convenience. Other women are affected by a government that fails to ensure teenagers are adequately educated on reproduction and contraception. Poor women, especially, are at risk. This is because contraceptives are expensive and the Christian Right has worked to prevent insurance policies from covering birth control and the social programs offering them.

Women are also affected in the way they are treated by their fathers and husbands. Many women in fundamentalist homes accept their position of servitude and obedience as the proper role for women. Whether they recognize and admit to it or not, they are treated as second-class citizens. The husband may control his wife's decision to work, to further her education, even to socialize. Such control often leads to spousal abuse, which, as will be seen, is not uncommon in Christian fundamentalist homes. Spousal abuse affects mainstream women as well if they marry men who learned this pattern of behavior from a fundamentalist or religiously conservative upbringing. Even when the man does not hold tightly to the religious views with which he was raised, such patterns have been instilled. These men often learn only one way to resolve marital conflict and discord—by physically enforcing their wives' obedience.

This treatment of women leads to serious implications for their physical, mental, and sexual health. Fundamentalist women often suffer from beliefs preventing them from obtaining appropriate medical treatment. Similarly, the health of mainstream women is affected by conservative religious views influencing the care they receive in Catholic-controlled hospitals. They are also affected by laws and the absence of laws, pertaining to women's reproductive health and choice.

Further, the mental health of fundamentalist women is compromised as they see themselves as loyal servants to their spouse, family, and church. They eventually accept that, as women, they are unworthy of a more satisfying life. Fundamentalist women may view pleasurable sex as evil. This ultimately leads to the development of any number of sexual dysfunctions and disorders. These stultifying views may affect the larger population of non-fundamentalist women. State laws have been proposed, and in one case enacted, prohibiting the sale of vibrators and other sexual devices vital in treating sexual dysfunction, among other privacy issues.

Patriarchal Beginnings

The origins of patriarchy are unclear. Some scholars believe it began to develop during the Paleolithic Age, when women were stolen from other bands. Others believe Indo-Europeans transformed what was once a matrifocal society into a patriarchal one.[227] Biologist Richard Dawkins points out that it likely dates back long before the Indo-Europeans and that "a case can be made that it goes way back in evolution."[228]

Regardless of when it first came to be practiced, it has been prevalent in different societies throughout history. In America, women were historically "ruled" by their fathers and husbands and often married into a life of servitude. This revolved solely around caring for and educating their children, keeping the home, working in the fields,[229] and catering to their husband's every need.

Coverture, a concept based on Anglo-American common law, which was gradually abandoned by the various states throughout the nineteenth century, defined the status of married women.[230] "Under the common law doctrine of coverture, a wife, like a slave, was civilly dead. A slave had no independent legal existence apart from his master, and husband and wife became 'one person,' the person of the husband," explains Carole Pateman,[231] a leading political theorist.

Only men were able to request divorces. Women could not write wills, sign contracts, or obtain loans. They had very limited property rights. Male authority was well established both within the home and in public. In most parts of the country, women could be raped or beaten by their husbands with no laws to protect them. Women also had little access to education, and although they did often help produce income for the family, they were limited to only certain types of work.[232]

By the nineteenth century, some women began to demand equality in the home. But contrary to what would be expected, industrialization in the mid part of the century brought more rather than fewer restrictions on women. They came to be seen as guardians of "domestic virtues." Men became the sole income producers, and the strictures on women's traditional roles became tighter.[233] Yet, at the same time, a distinctive female culture began to arise, and female relationships began to intensify. These social networks would ultimately lead to woman's reform.[234]

In 1848, the woman's movement was launched when Lucretia Mott and Elizabeth Cady Stanton called a women's rights convention, held in

Seneca Falls, New York. Its purpose was "to discuss the social, civil, and religious rights of women." Out of the convention came a "Declaration of Sentiments and Resolutions," stating "all men and women are created equal." The goals of the women's movement were defined.

In 1859, reliable condoms became available, and women gained the ability to limit their family size. This played a crucial role in gaining equality, as women were no longer forced into roles of lifelong childrearing. A Women's Suffrage Amendment was then introduced to the United States Congress in 1878. Still, women's rights progressed slowly and were fought tooth and nail, not only by men, but also by women.

In 1897, Susan B. Anthony predicted, "there never will be complete equality until women themselves help to make laws and elect lawmakers." She was right. Forty-two years after its introduction, the Nineteenth Amendment, which gave women the right to vote, was ratified in 1920. After that milestone, the pace toward women's equality gained momentum.[235]

Another major stepping stone toward women's equality was the wider availability of birth control and a greater variety of contraceptive options. In 1916, Margaret Sanger braved imprisonment to open the United States' first birth-control clinic in Brooklyn. In 1917, she founded the National Birth Control League that later became Planned Parenthood Federation of America. Her commitment to birth control and reproductive freedom for all came from her experiences as a nurse. She had seen the horrifying images of death and deformity caused by self-induced abortions.[236] Finally, in 1936, birth control devices such as condoms and diaphragms were ruled legal for preventing pregnancy. In 1960, the FDA approved oral contraceptives. Women finally gained complete control over their reproduction when in 1972, the landmark *Roe v. Wade* case established a woman's right to abortion.

The Equal Rights Amendment that had been proposed in 1923 to eliminate gender discrimination passed Congress that same year. The simple, straightforward amendment stated, "Equality of rights under the law shall not be denied or abridged by the United States or by any State on account of sex." Susan Faludi, author of the national bestseller *Backlash: The Undeclared War Against Women*, points out that within two years of these major accomplishments for women, all the New Right groups arose. They began a concerted effort to crush the ERA. The Conservative Caucus called it one of "the most destructive pieces of legislation to ever pass Congress." Feminists were demonized and held responsible for every societal and family ill.[237]

Again, as before, misogynists were not the only ones standing in the way of the ERA. Women of the religious right obstructed ERA ratification as much as the men.[238] Women had some legitimate concerns with ERA, such as whether it would lead to the removal of protections like alimony for women and the possible emergence of unisex restrooms. Yet, it also revealed the severity of mind control many women had been subject to in conservative Christian homes and churches.

The effectiveness of Phyllis Schlafly's Eagle Forum, established primarily to fight ratification of the ERA, was especially disheartening, as it proved just how effective the New Right would be. Polls revealed two-thirds of Americans favored the ERA, and it had been ratified by twenty-two states within its first year following Congressional approval. Nonetheless, ratification came to a screeching halt between 1975 and 1977, then began to reverse as "five states rescinded their previous approval."[239]

Still, the Christian Right's fight to block the ERA from ratification did not abate. In 1980, Reverend Jerry Falwell argued in *Listen, America!* "The Equal Rights Amendment strikes at the foundation of our entire social structure." According to Faludi, Falwell railed at the women's movement, which, he concluded, had wreaked havoc on America and the family. Typical of his irrational bombast, he went so far as to accuse feminists of launching a "satanic attack on the home." Then he promised to destroy the ERA, burying it "once and for all in a deep, dark grave."[240]

The following year, 1981, the New Right introduced the Family Protection Act drafted by Paul Weyrich, "Father of the New Right," and his advisers at the Heritage Foundation. The Act was "a blueprint for the New Right program"[241] and, as such, was far from what its title implied. The act was nothing more than a device to destroy women's rights.[242] As Faludi explained, among other things, "The act's proposals [would]: eliminate federal laws supporting equal education" and would "require marriage and motherhood to be taught as the proper career for girls."[243] The act also offered "tax incentives to induce married women to have babies and stay at home."[244]

Although the oppressive Act didn't pass, in 1982 the New Right won one if its greatest battles. The deadline for ratification of the ERA expired, and it was defeated falling three states short of ratification. Still, putting a halt to the ERA was not enough. The New Right wanted nothing short of a complete return to the patriarchal society. Over the next few years, it continued to make many legislative proposals under the guise of "family." These included a bill for censoring all birth control information from not only teens but adults as well, until marriage. Equally disturbing, a "chastity" bill was proposed.[245]

Regardless of the patriarchal push and the growth of Christian conservatism, by 1989 a survey of Christian women found only three percent went to their ministers for "moral guidance." Evangelical preachers felt threatened and began their battle cry from the pulpit by reciting, "The husband is the head of the wife, even as Christ is head of the church," (Ephesians 5:22-24) on a regular basis.[246]

Then in 1992, Pat Robertson wrote in a fundraising letter:

> The feminist agenda is not about equal rights for women. It is about a socialist, anti-family political movement that encourages women to leave their husbands, kill their children, practice witchcraft, destroy capitalism and become lesbians.[247]

Less than a decade later, the continued growth of the conservative movement was enough to lead the 15-million member Southern Baptist Convention to add Article 18 to its Baptist Faith and Message. This widespread growth of patriarchal views among Southern Baptists ultimately led to a division in the SBC in 2000. The moderate minority of the SBC had been adamantly opposed to the growing conservatism of the Church leadership, which insisted on Biblical literalism, wives' submission to their husbands, and the barring of women from the ministry.[248]

Lessons in sexism

The role of women in Christian fundamentalist homes is well defined and generally accepted without question. There is little doubt who will prepare dinner, wash the dishes, clean the house, and rear the children. These traditional tasks are viewed as woman's work and are assigned, if not by man, then by the church. Women are expected to serve their spouses dutifully and not question the authority of their husbands. They must seek permission for any activities outside the realm of what has traditionally been considered feminine, from taking a job to involvement in social activities. This is especially so where mainstream socializing might take place. In these patriarchal homes, when important decisions need to be made, women may be offered the opportunity to give their input, but ultimately decisions rest with men.

As David M. Scholer, Professor of New Testament at Fuller Theological Seminary points out, today's major proponents of male headship and female submission express their views quite clearly. Robert D. Culver, in his essay "A Traditional View: Let Your Women Keep Silence," relates the following after quoting Genesis 3:16 "he shall rule over thee." According to Culver:

> with occasional exceptions, this is the way it has always been and likely always will be . . . it is a statement of fact, which neither the Industrial Revolution nor the feminist movement is likely to overturn. . . . The radical feminists should give up and quit. Normal, universal female human nature is against them. Most women prefer things the way they are, at least wherever biblical norms have prevailed. . . . Male ascendancy in most affairs is not a legal ordinance to be obeyed; it is a fact to acknowledge. . . . Ordinarily the authority of adults over other adults ought to be by men and almost certainly will be. The scriptural standard for male leadership of churches is even stronger.[249]

The question many of us ponder is why so many women would accept this way of life. The answer is complex, but stems in part from childhood indoctrination, social isolation through home schooling, instilled guilt, and promises of gratification. The guilt that is thrust upon conservative Christian women is revealed in a tract written by the Church of God in Christ that prescribes:

> Woman's first duty is the making and keeping of her home. Many a modern woman chooses a career, hires a baby-sitter, and rushes her children through childhood so that she can be free to pursue her selfish interests. The Bible teaches that women are to be 'keepers at home' (Titus 2:5). This means a women [sic] is to be there, loving her husband, teaching and enjoying children, and applying the homemaking arts with joy in her heart.[250]

Inducing guilt in women for having needs and desires of their own by referring to these as "selfish" is one way in which Biblical literalists achieve control. At the same time and in contrast, the responsibilities charged to the woman are riddled with positive emotional language that impresses on women the feelings they should hold. These descriptive terms: "loving," "enjoying," "with joy in her heart," are used not only to induce these positive feelings about her roles, but to arouse a sense of guilt when negative feelings surface regarding her assigned station in life.

Instilling guilt in women is one of the best ways Christian sects gain women's full cooperation and support for the hierarchical marriage.

Should a woman still question how this role is to her benefit or why she should submit, she is likely to be informed, "A woman's submission to her husband liberates her from a multitude of frustrating problems, and her submission to God's order frees her from guilt. Submission is a blessing, not a curse!"[251] Here, the author even admits guilt, the crucial element to mind control, is a feeling these women likely hold. Then, after the woman has been pounded with guilt-inducing messages, the patriarch becomes the saint. He offers a way to relieve her shame, which he originally created. The woman's guilt is erased, then, by serving her husband, and thus she confuses his control for an act of love.

It is necessary to understanding the wide acceptance of these gender roles, to see how sexist attitudes develop and are maintained. A study conducted by sociologists Charles W. Peek, George D. Lowe, and L. Susan Williams (1991) found the level of sexism held by men and women in conservative Christian homes is about the same. Yet, the cause of these stereotypes varies by gender, especially for fundamentalists.[252] For males, affiliation with fundamentalist groups is what lends to greater sexism. But, for women it is not the groups to which they belong but instead, their belief in Biblical literalism that lends to their sexist attitudes. Thus, as these sociologists point out, "Women who take the word of God with a grain of salt are less sexist."[253]

This would explain the significance of groups such as the Promise Keepers (PK), which was founded in 1990 by Bill McCartney, a former University of Colorado football coach, in shaping sexist views. Men are inclined to form their opinions based on group beliefs. Those who participate, even if truly with the intent of becoming a better husband and father, are more likely to come out more patriarchal instead. This is because the PK leadership promotes male headship. While many bystanders have failed to see this connection, and the PK has insisted its purpose is for the betterment of marriages, nothing could be further from reality. Those who become involved in the PK receive a strong message not conducive to marital harmony. As Tracey Ann Martin, former newsletter editor for the Western Wayne County, Michigan Chapter NOW points out:

> True: there are those Seven Promises of Promise Keepers. And, for the most part, they are high-minded enough. Integrity, Honesty . . . but they sum up to a promise to control you. And Promise Keepers does promise what they preach. A family unit in which

the husband serves as domestic shepherd and women and children . . . are completely subordinated to his blessed, God-ordained shepherding. Men who infuse themselves into the all-male Promise Keepers paradise must be willing to accept this verity wholly and agree, within their cell groups each headed by a leader man, to a mutual accountability for its implementation. Then they are expected to subsume themselves as well into a male chain of command leading from all directions back to Boulder, Colorado.[254]

Tony Evans, among other PK leaders, has made this loud and clear by exhorting, "I am not suggesting that you ask for your role back [in the marriage], I am urging you to take it back. There can be no compromise here."[255] What messages are these men receiving whose sexism stems mainly from male relationships? They are urged to "take" rather than to "ask," which implies force. As most of us well know, a good marriage is built on compromise, yet Evans throws compromise out the door. How forceful will many of these men become to uphold their promise to the PK? There is no question many men enter solely for the betterment of their marriage and are not of this narrow mindset—at least not going in. What is troubling is how many will walk out accepting the PK's myopic vision. Many of the men who innocently become involved in the PK are married to women who were not raised in such oppressive homes, and they are therefore unlikely to accept their partner's domination. They will likely resist such attempts at control. Here is where the danger lies. These men may be more inclined to relate to their families in a dictatorial fashion. In the worst circumstances, this could lead to spousal abuse.

At the same time these men are learning sexist attitudes from their affiliations, women are indoctrinated by religious leaders and fundamentalist literature in which the Bible and her religious convictions arc repeatedly used against her. Many Biblical passages from the New and Old Testaments are used to support this patriarchal view:

> To avoid confusion and establish order, someone needs to be the head and God has ordained that this should be the man (I Corinthians 11:3). . . . Christ is subject to God, man is subject to Christ, and woman is subject to man. . . .

> As the church is subject to Christ, so let wives also be subject in everything to their husbands. (Ephesians 5:24)

> As in all the churches of the saints, the women should keep silence in the churches. For they are not permitted to speak, but should subordinate, as even the law says. If there is anything they desire to know, let them ask their husbands at home. For it is shameful for a woman to speak in church. (I Corinthians 14:33-35)

> Let a woman learn in silence, with all submissiveness. I permit no woman to teach or to have authority over men: she is to keep silent. . . . [w]oman will be saved through bearing children, if she continues in faith and love and holiness, with modesty. (I Timothy 2:11-12, 2:15)[256]

Conservative males also manipulate women into buying their patriarchal worldview by glorifying submissiveness. Woman's role is referred to as "one of the greatest privileges in the world . . ." softening the blow by creating an illusion of specialness:

> with Christ she will be able to live a self-denied life. . . . He will grace her life with humility, modesty, and with that inner 'ornament of a meek and quiet spirit, which is in the sight of God of great price' (I Peter 3:3,4).

> She [woman] was a direct gift from the hand of God, made from man and for man. (I Corinthians 11:9).

> Although the woman is considered the 'weaker vessel' (I Peter 3:7), this does not make her inferior.

> In the Garden of Eden, God said, 'It is not good that the man should be alone,' and He made a help mate for him—a companion, someone to satisfy needs (Genesis 2:18).[257]

Again, her religious convictions are taken advantage of, and the Bible is used against her to cement these views. Of course, "someone to satisfy needs" (as quoted above) is primarily what patriarchy is about. Patriarchal men are in search of the woman who can offer companionship and unquestioning obedience. They want a woman to serve as nanny, housekeeper, and cook. All the while, these men are building their own potential in the workforce or business world. What will be a wife's compensation? Food, clothing, and a roof over her head—so long as she never leaves this confined life. As these men well know, once she accepts this lifestyle, she becomes trapped as she is prevented from doing anything that could eventually lead to independence.

Another reason women are seduced into female submission, according to Alice P. Mathews, of the Conservative Baptist Seminary of the East, is that many Christian women hear promises of gratification.[258] Mathews's point is illustrated by conservative author, J.M. Miles of *The Femine Principal: A Woman's Discovery of the Key to Total Fulfillment.* He claims:

> What does the woman gain by submission to her own husband? Only the infinite security of yielding to the duly constituted chain of authority in the universe; only the deep joy of living with a real man who grows stronger everyday; only the fulfillment of fully participating in a genuine love relationship; only the completing of what is partial in her human nature; only the opening of her yielded being to the influence of God's Spirit, who comes where humble and yielded spirits are seeking Him.[259]

Conservative church leaders and patriarchs are well versed in the female psyche. Portraying the oppressive role fundamentalist women are subjected to as a high and noble cause is commonplace. L. Christenson, author of *The Christian Family*, similarly claims:

> To be submissive means to yield humble and intelligent obedience to an ordained power or authority [the husband]. . . . God did not give this law of wives being submissive to their husbands because he had a grudge against women; on the contrary, he established this order for the protection of women and the harmony of the home. He means for a woman to be sheltered from many of the rough encounters of life. Scripture knows nothing of a 50-50 'democratic marriage.' The wife is 100% a wife, the husband is 100% a husband. . . . A wife's primary responsibility is to give of herself, her time, and her energy to her husband, children, and home." (Christenson, 1970, pp. 32-33, 40).[260]

Clearly, conservative Christian leaders know the emotional triggers to appeal to women. To many, it is inconceivable any woman would be unable to see through these sugarcoated messages, especially when they are sprinkled throughout calling for her to give, give, give. But, many women who fall into this trap have been raised in homes and churches indoctrinating these beliefs from the time they were young. Raised in authoritarian homes, these women have mistakenly come to perceive such control as love. Moreover, women raised in such controlling and often abusive environments grow up with a potent need for male love and approval, and they unknowingly seek to fulfill it through their spouse. He becomes the "loving" father they never had, despite the fact they have chosen partners as controlling as their fathers.

Marital harmony and hierarchy

A common argument for patriarchy by conservative Christians is that a woman's submission acts as a protective shield against marital dissatisfaction and divorce, in comparison to non-hierarchical marriages. Convincing women their submissiveness is the road to everlasting happiness is one of the ways women come to accept male headship. In reality, though, the only dissatisfaction this shields against is a man's. Obviously, a man who has someone at his every beck and call, will likely never be discontent, or so it would seem. Yet, once such a relationship has been established, the woman's dissatisfaction is likely to cause major unhappiness, as she feels bound to a life she cannot escape. Women in patriarchal homes generally do not work outside the home. Even when they do, they are often without the financial means to leave because their partners control the type of employment and hours they can work. These women are not afforded opportunities to further their education and attain job skills, mainly because it could eventually lead to financial independence.

Regardless, the argument that patriarchal families are less likely to destruct is without support. According to an undocumented report discovered by Mathews of the Conservative Baptist Seminary, "a small but well-known evangelical denomination recently announced that in the course of a year, it lost one clergy couple per week to divorce."[261] Mathews explains what happens, more often than not, is a wife's self-surrender leads to alienation rather than fulfillment. The traditional hierarchical marriage leads to marital pressure, dissatisfaction, and even divorce.[262] It is not difficult to imagine how many other reports and studies with similar findings have been quietly filed away.

A recent study by Mathews revealed the true level of unhappiness and dissatisfaction evangelical women feel. The study interviewed all married and previously-married women who staffed an evangelical Christian organization. The study asked women, among other things, to list the five most advantageous reasons to marry. Companionship was listed by seventy-five percent of the women.[263] Yet, when these same women were asked their personal experiences, companionship was often lacking. Less than twenty percent found their need for companionship to be met.[264] One woman revealed:

> Companionship—this has been possibly the biggest disappointment for me personally as I chose to marry someone with very different interests than mine. . . . Hence the companionship relationship in my marriage has been disappointing, frustrating, hurtful, at times abusive—emotionally, mentally, not physically.[265]

As would be expected, the disadvantages of male headship women mentioned were:

> Loss of potential for growth, and development of talents.

> All-consuming responsibility for others (spouse and children).

> Loss of one's own vision for ministry.

> Loss of independence, freedom to 'do my own thing.'

> Time is no longer my own.

> Loss of freedom to make my own decisions.[266]

Another question asked the women to rate their own marital experience, in which they indicated:

> All I do is work and do childcare. Have to fight depression, fight to be innovative and pursue anything creative.

> I struggle to find time to do what I want to do, and I feel guilty and selfish for wanting time to myself.

> Sometimes I feel 'controlled' or restricted in independence and freedom, which sometimes makes me depressed. . . . My identity is rather confused—as a single I felt whole, but as a married I feel like half a person, and it's hard to know my identity.[267]

Furthermore, according to more than half of the women surveyed, those with strong commitments to their church and religious convictions felt, rather than helping their adjustment, the church had actually hindered them.[268]

More telling of the reality of dissatisfaction, was a study published by Barna Research Group, Ltd., a California, Christian-based marketing research company. A Barna article titled "Christians Are More Likely to Experience Divorce Than Are Non-Christians," reported that Baptists, born-again Christians, and nondenominational Christians are more likely to divorce than non-born-agains, mainline Protestants, atheists, agnostics, and several other religious groups. The study, below, which was published in December 1999, involved interviews with 3,854 adults in forty-eight states, asking whether they were currently or had previously been divorced. According to the research group, the large sample size indicates a high level of accuracy and makes the difference in divorce rates "statistically significant."[269]

Divorce Rates for Persons Who are Currently or have Previously been Divorced, by Religious Belief or Affiliation

Nondenominational Protestants	34%
Jews	30%
Baptists	29%
Born-again Christians	27%
Mainline Protestants	25%
Mormons	25%
Non-born-again Christians	24%
Catholics	21%
Lutherans	21%
Atheists/Agnostics	21%[270]

Marital dissatisfaction and divorce is only one problem related to the hierarchical marriage. A study was completed in 1989 by Carolyn Holderread Heggen, one of the coauthors of *Women, Abuse, and the Bible: How Scripture Can Be Used to Heal or Hurt*. She found women who believed in subordination to men scored lower on self-esteem measures than women who believed in gender equality.[271] The negative effects of male domination on women's emotional health, revealed through the evangelical women's responses, is undeniable and disheartening.

John Swomley, Professor emeritus of Social Ethics at St. Paul School of Theology, has written extensively on women's issues, the Christian Right, and Catholicism. He points out that defining and institutionalizing women's role as mother and caregiver, through "religious, economic, and political systems and enforced by legislation and custom," is merely a covert form of violence against women.[272] The effects of emotional abuse related to the hierarchical marriage, while invisible to the naked eye, leads women into depression, at best, to trauma, suicide, and worse. This was evidenced when Andrea Yates drowned her five children.

Battered into submission

Every fifteen seconds a woman is beaten in the United States—and one-third of all women murdered in the nation are victims of boyfriends, husbands, and former partners. More alarming, domestic violence is the leading cause of death for women around the world between the ages of fourteen and forty-four.[273] Violence against women, however, is not a new phenomenon. The battery of women very likely goes back as far in history as patriarchy.

To be certain, a historical review of domestic violence was made in 1979, by sociologists R. Emerson Dobash and Russell Dobash. They concluded, according to sociologists Richard J. Gelles and Ann Levine, "that violence against wives is an extension of patriarchy; ancient customs and laws designed to give men domination and control over women."[274] Patriarchy is the common family structure among fundamentalists today, and universal male domination is one of the key goals of the religious right. Historical examples of the relationship between patriarchy and domestic violence can be seen by glimpsing into early Roman society. There, a wife was considered her husband's property having "no more rights than a child or slave." A wife merely suspected of adultery could be punished by death.[275]

In early Christian society, women did not fair much better. Gelles and Levine explain:

> The Bible was interpreted as teaching that woman was created from Adam's rib, as an afterthought, to serve man's [sic] needs; that she was weak by nature and easily lured into temptation; and that as punishment for Eve's transgression, she must live a life of subjugation.[276]

A husband, in those days, had the authority to enforce his wife's servitude through beating. Even the United States, the birthplace of democracy in modern times, did not pass laws until the late 1800s to protect married women from "excessive" physical force.[277] Statistics reveal today, the problem of spousal abuse continues. An alarming number of men still believe violence is an acceptable means to gaining a woman's compliance.[278]

One of the characteristics common to batterers is "the traditional belief in male superiority and the stereotyped masculine gender role within the family."[279] But, where do these beliefs come from? According to James and Phyllis Alsdurf in *Battered into Submission: The Tragedy of Wife Abuse in the Christian Home*, "the probability of wife abuse increases with the rigidity of a church's teachings, especially teachings pertaining to gender roles and hierarchy."[280]

As Heggen, an elder of the Albuquerque Mennonite Church found, certain types of religious beliefs relate to spousal abuse. Among Christians, four of those beliefs are that: 1) women should be subordinate to men, 2) women are inferior to men, 3) it is a Christian virtue for women to suffer, and 4) as Christians, women must forgive their abuser.[281]

Worse, fundamentalist pastors often condone domestic violence, or at the very least, are unsupportive of battered women and unhelpful in protecting them from further abuse. This is evidenced by one battered woman who was told by her pastor:

> No matter what he is doing to you, he is still your spiritual head. Respect those behaviors that you can respect and pray for those that you can't respect. But remember, no matter what, you owe it to him and to God to live in submission to your husband. You'll never be happy until you submit to him.[282]

Battered women have several common characteristics. These include: strong support for family unity, traditional values pertaining to the home, and acceptance of the female gender-role stereotypes assigned by the church.[283] Unfortunately, religious beliefs and values are one of the main reasons women remain in abusive relationships.[284] Those with strong religious backgrounds who accept male headship are often "the least likely to believe that violence against them is wrong,"[285] as was found in a study by Leonore Walker in 1979.

Wives and girlfriends are not the only victims of battery resulting from beliefs in male domination. For highly religious women, whether the assault is by a male partner or just an acquaintance, the result is often the same. Shirley Gillett, founder of Women Won't Forget, had been sexually assaulted by another member of her church. Following the attack, she felt worthless, because she had not upheld her duty to control the offender's sexual urges. She had learned in Sunday school, it was the woman's responsibility to control. The assault was then compounded by feelings of helplessness because Gillett knew "women's words were worth nothing." So, she did not report it. As a result, Gillett grew severely depressed and eventually stopped attending church.[286]

Gillett's fears regarding the reaction she would have received may not have been far off base. One woman who had been physically and sexually abused by her father was told by her pastor, "Only a bitter, self-pitying woman would even remember these things after all those [twenty] years."[287] Similarly, as Christine E. Gudorf wrote in the *Christian Century*, "Victims of domestic battery are especially likely to hear [from Christians] that this cross of theirs should not be shirked, that their duty is to remain with the abusive spouse."[288] Therefore, helping battered fundamentalist women is difficult. According to a 1987 report by Vicky Whipple in the *Journal of Marital and Family Therapy*, they are encouraged to seek help from the church, often rely on faith, are encouraged to forgive, are male dominated, and oppose divorce.[289] Thus, they are unlikely to see how wrong the abuse really is.

As Heggen points out, the only way to prevent domestic violence is to eliminate the belief God's plan is for a patriarchal society.[290] This may be easier said than done. In spite of all the evidence, many religious leaders fail to see or at least acknowledge the connection between patriarchy and domestic violence. Many continue to push for the further subjugation of women. Instead of recognizing the role male headship plays, an evangelical minister once insisted to a sociologist, "Wife beating is on the rise because men are no longer leaders in their homes. I tell the women they must go back home and be more submissive."[291]

No way out—the woman trap

Unbeknownst to many are two ways in which the Christian Right pursues the reinstitution and maintenance of the patriarchal family. This is through local, state, and federal proposals to either eliminate or reform welfare and other government assistance programs and through proposals to make divorce more difficult, if not impossible, to obtain. To onlookers, these proposals are often seen as ways to put a stop to abuse of the welfare system and to make married couples work harder to resolve conflict—just as the Christian Right intends. However, for many women in abusive relationships their only hope for getting out of a potentially lethal situation is with the help of welfare.

Many battered women come from fundamentalist homes where they've not been allowed to work, or at least not earn enough to financially support themselves, so few would ever be able to leave without assistance. Keeping battered women tied to their abusers through difficult to obtain divorces and lengthy waiting periods is unacceptable. It increases the odds they will remain with or return to an abusive partner. In most cases, such proposals would allow for divorce under certain circumstances, such as physical abuse or alcoholism. Still, it is often difficult and sometimes impossible to prove battery because battered women frequently hide the abuse from family and friends and do not report it. Therefore, no records or witnesses may exist to support a woman's claim. It then becomes his word against hers in a court of law, leaving it to a judge to determine a battered woman's fate.

Yet, how much political support do these divorce and welfare reform packages really have, and who is proposing and supporting them? A September 1996 article appearing in *Policy Review*, a publication of the Heritage Foundation, sheds light on this question. The foundation, founded by Paul Weyrich, of the New Right, and Joseph Coors ,"is best known for its production of tomes that compile recommendations for reducing or abolishing government policies, regulations, and agencies,"[292] says Political Research Associates. These are sent out to "7,000 congressional and administrative officials, staff journalists, and major donors."[293] *Policy Review* asked several right-wing and Christian Right "family experts" how the government can "make sure that the overwhelming majority of American children grow up with a mother and father."

Attorney General John Ashcroft, who was a senator at the time, offered the following doublespeak: "Government must encourage families to come together and stay together through cultural, not governmental, pressures." Government encouragement, concealed as "cultural" pressure, is nonetheless "governmental pressure." Ashcroft further insists, "The most important role for government is to remove the perverse incentives of the welfare state."[294]

Another expert was James Dobson who believes, "The primary responsibility for the provision of authority in the home has been assigned to men."[295] His Focus on the Family has exhibited strong political interest in restructuring welfare. Dobson offers four "imperatives for government." He sets forth that marriage should be defined as "a lifelong commitment between a man and woman," no-fault divorce laws should be reformed, tax policy should be tilted in favor of marriage, and welfare must be reformed "to end current incentives for conceiving children outside of marriage."[296]

The notion single women are getting pregnant to live a glamorous life on welfare is outrageous. But Dobson makes it sound as if welfare recipients are not only given enough to support their families, but they are offered a large supply of rainy-day cash, enough to go out and splurge. The only splurging most welfare families are doing is purchasing the bare essentials to keep their family clothed and in good health. The only thing a woman gets from welfare by having another child is a slight increase in a far smaller-than-necessary amount of assistance. This comes mainly in non-cash form such as food stamps, a Medicaid card, a shelter allowance often paid directly to the landlord, daycare assistance paid directly to the provider, and minimal cash barely covering utilities and other needs.

There are no "incentives" in the welfare system for women to conceive out of wedlock, as welfare opponents would have us believe. The only incentive welfare offers is mere survival. Yet, by creating such a gross misperception in the eyes of Americans who are footing the bill for these women's survival, the Christian Right creates a vast network of support for its version of welfare reform.

Another proponent of divorce law reform is former Governor John Engler of Michigan. Engler reveals, in *Policy Review,* that Michigan state legislator Jessie Dalman has been leading the way nationally. Dalman has sponsored twelve bills that would require either mutual consent to divorce or proof of desertion, infidelity, physical or emotional abuse, or other serious problems. In other words, he seeks to abolish Michigan's thirty-year-old no-fault divorce law. Engler praises, "The growing impact of groups like Focus on the Family and Promise Keepers—all these signs give me encouragement." There is no question of Engler's involvement in Christian Right politics. His name is repeatedly linked to the most prominent religious right names in literature and the media. Engler is one of the three founders of the Mackinac Center for Public Policy, the Michigan-based right-wing think tank advocating school vouchers, school privatization, and free market-based policies.

To an even further extreme is Paul Weyrich, president of the Free Congress Foundation, who recommends the suggestions of William S. Lind and William H. Marshner, authors of *Cultural Conservative: Toward a New National Agenda.* In Weyrich's words, we should "Permit employers to offer a 'family wage,' that is, a higher wage to heads of families."[297] And who is the head of the family? If you guessed man, you have already begun to see through the "family wage." As described by Dr. Carl J. Cuneo of McMaster University, Ontario, Canada, the family wage is the practice "in which men control the sources of household income on which women and children are totally dependent."[298] Under the "family wage," men were commonly paid much higher wages because of the assumption men had families to support and that women were either supported by a husband or would eventually be supported by a spouse. The family wage was outlawed in 1966 by the Department of Labor's interpretation of the Equal Pay Act of 1964. The interpretation was adopted by the Equal Employment Opportunity Commission as well, in interpreting Title VII of the Civil Rights Act. But, Weyrich and his comrades have called for new laws to reverse the nondiscriminatory nature of current laws.

How else do Lind, Marshner, and Weyrich propose to keep women at home? "Make the child-care credit universal, so parents who care for their own children receive the same benefits as those who send their kids to daycare."[299] Although it may be difficult to argue against encouraging parents (women, as usually tends to be the case) to stay home with their preschoolers, this contradicts conservatives' position on welfare. Moms on welfare who stay at home are accused by conservatives of taking advantage of the system. The underlying motive in making the child-care credit universal is evident. If families can be paid to care for their own children, they can easily have a half dozen or more. This serves first and foremost, fundamentalists who believe in procreation. Furthermore, it reinforces woman as caregiver and at the same time creates a society in which families can build their own daycare businesses. But, unlike daycare homes, which must be licensed in most states and are limited to only a handful of children, these families can have many children, with no restrictions.

Another proponent of patriarchy, David Blankenhorn, president of the Institute for American Values tells *Policy Review* he favors elimination of the "antimarriage bias" of the Earned Income Tax Credit.[300] Of course, there is no bias in this credit, which is based on the size of the family and its income. Blankenhorn calls for many other tax changes favoring married couples as well. He advocates the discriminatory practice of giving priority to married couples in public housing. He also recommends the government appoint and hire people to tell Americans how they should live by insisting in the evils of "unwed childbearing."

Here is how he would handle teen pregnancy. Expectant girls and teen mothers would be prevented from attending regular public schools; thereby, unlikely to ever earn a high school diploma, a common requirement for many jobs. Moreover, with the further reforms to the welfare program recommended by Christian conservatives, these girls would be without financial assistance as well. Blankenhorn would have teen fathers only miss sports and extracurricular activities.[301] Boys would not only have the opportunity to earn their high school diploma, but by finishing high school, they could go on to earn a college degree and a decent living.

D. James Kennedy, president of Coral Ridge Ministries Media is considered by secularists as one of the more dangerous among the religious right. This is because most of his viewers accept his distortion of facts because of his ability to project an image of being reasonable—in spite of his extreme views. He claims today we are "subsidizing illegitimate children" in the same manner as the government once "subsidized pigs."[302] His views on welfare and divorce are nearly identical to those of Blankenhorn, Lind, and Marshner.[303] These proposed changes to our laws offer a disturbing picture of what fundamentalists have in store for American society. While the immediate danger is to women in fundamentalist homes, there's growing concern of what divorce legislation and welfare reform could ultimately do to advance the patriarchal agenda.

Already, in West Virginia, a $100 monthly bonus has been offered to married couples on welfare. To middle and upper class Americans, this hardly seems substantial enough to cause concern. Still, Sue Jilian, with the West Virginia Coalition Against Domestic Violence, explains the predicament this places women in who are battered. "When financial stress and domestic violence coexist in the same relationship," says Jilian "an additional $100 per month can easily be used as leverage by batterers to keep women living in poverty committed to the marriage."[304]

It is difficult enough for most women to leave an abusive relationship. However, in a poor home to a family on welfare, $100 can mean the difference between keeping a home comfortably warm, making an automobile payment on a used vehicle, paying for a child to participate in school sports, and many other things most of us take for granted. The loss of this small financial bonus is substantial to a poor woman who wants to offer the best life she can to her child. Therefore, this $100 bonus to married welfare recipients could be enough to keep a battered woman from leaving a painful and dangerous situation.

The likelihood of this scenario is not insignificant. According to a 1999 report by Taylor Institute, five major research studies found an alarming trend. Twenty to thirty percent of welfare recipients had been experiencing domestic violence at the time the studies were conducted.[305] This was actually an improvement over 1996 studies that found between fifty and seventy-one percent of recipients were at the time experiencing domestic violence.[306] Thus, rewarding married couples through government assistance, which ultimately takes away from funds that could be distributed evenly to all welfare recipients, serves only to keep women in abusive situations.

The Heritage Foundation and its members, however, are not concerned with reinstating patriarchy only in America. They want to preserve patriarchal societies around the globe. Patrick F. Fagan, in "The Heritage Foundation Backgrounder Executive Summary" expounds:

> how various U.N. agencies are attempting to force countries to implement a radical interpretation of treaties on women's and children's rights. . . . A close examination of the reports issued by U.N. committees monitoring implementation of the Convention on the Rights of the Child (CRC) and the Convention to Eliminate All Forms of Discrimination Against Women (CEDAW) shows that these committees are pushing an agenda that counters traditional moral and social norms regarding family, marriage, motherhood, and religion.[307]

Misinterpreting the treaties, Fagan continues to complain that these and similar policies advise nations to make societal changes that "decrease emphasis on marriage, the nuclear family, parental authority, and religious beliefs." He is disturbed mothers are encouraged to seek fulfilling lives outside the home and that these policies remove "social and legal restraints" on teen sexuality. He fails to see the purpose of the policies, which is to protect against oppressive measures violating individual rights. Fagan goes on to claim U.N. committees ignore that children of "married parents who worship" have "far superior outcomes" pertaining to health, intellectual development, crime reduction, teen pregnancy, welfare dependency, educational attainment, and income levels.[308] It is an interesting claim he not only fails to substantiate, but is contradicted by much current research, especially pertaining to fundamentalist religious beliefs.

According to the National Center for Policy Analysis, while teens cite religion, values, and morals as important factors in their decision to abstain from sex, religious teens who have sex are less likely to use contraceptives.[309] Moreover, a study conducted by the Federal Bureau of Prisons found Catholics, which represent twenty to twenty-five percent of the U.S. population, make up thirty-nine percent of the prison population. Less than one percent of the prison population consists of atheists, who make up between thirteen and sixteen percent of the U.S. population.[310]

It is easy to conceive Third World countries controlled by the church, where women and children have no rights, would oppose such protective measures as outlined in these treaties. For the United States to oppose such policies is reprehensible. Although the Clinton administration had supported these U.N. policy statements, the United States, under George W. Bush has refused to ratify the CRC, CEDAW, and the Convention on the Rights of Women (CRW). Today, 191 states have ratified the CRC—it is lacking only Somalia and the U.S.[311]

Eros Unplugged

It shall be unlawful for any person to knowingly distribute, possess with intent to distribute, or offer or agree to distribute any obscene material or any device designed or marketed as useful primarily for the stimulation of human genital organs for any thing of pecuniary value. Material not otherwise obscene may be obscene under this section if the distribution of the material, the offer to do so, or the possession with the intent to do so is a commercial exploitation of erotica solely for the sake of prurient appeal.

-Alabama Code Section 13A-12-200.2 (1998)

For most Americans, the notion of a law prohibiting the sale of vibrators and other sex paraphernalia, especially in exclusively adult stores or through home party plans, is preposterous. These were exactly the sentiments of Sherri Williams, owner and operator of the Alabama-based Pleasures boutiques, and B.J. Bailey, who sells sexual devices through home parties. In an affidavit, Williams stated the $20,000 worth of adult toys and paraphernalia she sells in a period of six months would be enough to cause her business to fold if the vibrator law were enforced. Bailey, who sells Saucy Lady products, has estimated tens of thousands of Alabama women have attended her parties and would, therefore, be equally affected by enforcement of the law. As would be anticipated, the case was immediately taken on by the American Civil Liberties Union on behalf of six women, including Williams and Bailey. The ACLU's stance was that the law is an invasion of privacy and, therefore, unconstitutional.

The Alabama code had become law in 1998, making it illegal for Alabamans to sell, distribute, manufacture, possess with the intent, or even just agree to distribute vibrators or any other device used for genital stimulation. The penalty under this section could result in a $10,000 fine and a year in jail. A second or subsequent violation becomes a class C felony, carrying a penalty of up to $50,000 in fines.[312] The production of these obscene items immediately holds a Class C felony charge upon the first violation.

What is most unsettling is the law, written by state Senator Tom Butler, mustered enough support to pass both Alabama's House and Senate unanimously, despite being in violation of five amendments to the U.S. Constitution, the First, Fourth, Fifth, Ninth, and Fourteenth.[313] But anything goes in a state known for its ultraconservatism where fundamentalist Biblical law has become the cornerstone for its government. Near the turn of the twenty-first century, conservative Christian politicians had gained enough seats in Alabama to substantially violate the Constitution, especially the Separation Clause of the First Amendment.

In 1999, U.S. District Judge Lynwood Smith ruled in favor of the ACLU "describing the law as 'overly broad' and saying people would be 'denied therapy, for, among other things, sexual dysfunction.'"[314] But that would not be the end of it for Alabamans. The case was appealed, and in October 2000, the 11th Circuit Court of Appeals made a unanimous decision to uphold the Alabama vibrator law. The state's attorney general contended, "a ban on the sale of sexual devices and related orgasm-stimulating paraphernalia is rationally related to a legitimate legislative interest in discouraging prurient interests in autonomous sex."[315]

Supporters of the law included Reverend Dan Ireland, executive director for the Alabama Citizens Action Program (ACAP). He considers devices for the sake of pleasure "a nuisance and they certainly are conducive to promiscuity and loose morals."[316] Senator Butler and the ACAP are also highly involved with churches and the Christian Coalition on other political matters[317] that would, in effect, do away with religious freedom for all but Christian conservatives.

For two years, women in Alabama were forced to rely on out-of-state mail order companies for purchasing sexual devices like vibrators sight unseen. The obvious intent of the law was to suppress a woman's sexual pleasure. Indeed, although such intent was not written into the state code, Alabama went so far as to say there is "no fundamental right to *purchase* [emphasis added] a product to use in pursuit of having an orgasm."[318] For these women, the law did not simply limit the ways in which they can pleasure themselves or be pleasured by their partner. It limited whether they can reach orgasm at all. The Alabama law and this statement in particular, implied women have no right to even purchase vibrators by mail or to have sexual pleasure.

As an aside, Attorney General John Ashcraft holds similar views and has "equated masturbation with pruriency,"[319] points out Maxine Parshall, president of the Detroit-area National Organization for Women. This a big issue for fundamentalists relating to "the sin of Onan and spilling your seed."[320]

Fortunately, in October 2002, U.S. District Judge Lynwood Smith Jr. ruled, again, in favor of the ACLU. He wrote it was a violation of "the fundamental right of privacy, long recognized by the Supreme Court as inherent among our constitutional protections, [which] incorporates a right to sexual privacy."

Female sexuality is not affected only by laws imposed by the religious right. There is a high rate of sexual dysfunction among women. According to a 1999 study by the University of Chicago, it was found nearly half of all women have sexual dysfunction. Many are unable to climax or only able to climax with the use of a vibrator.[321] According to Masters and Johnson, one of the several possible "historical antecedents" to sexual dysfunction is religious orthodoxy. In many conservative religious homes, sexuality for the sake of pleasure is scorned. What Masters and Johnson found was "many of their sexually dysfunctional patients had negative views of sexuality as a consequence."[322]

In one case, a female patient "had been taught as she was growing up not to look at herself naked in the mirror and that intercourse was reserved for marriage and then only to be endured for purposes of having children."[323] Women raised in fundamentalist homes, therefore, not only may never find enjoyment in the act of sex, but also may find it uncomfortable and even painful. Yet, it is an obligation they must fulfill to procreate and satisfy their husband's sexual desires.

To exemplify the perverseness placed on female sexuality, Ann Landers replied to a man in one of her columns in 1994 "that he should not marry a woman whose hymen was not totally intact or he would always consider that he had settled for 'damaged goods.'" Landers went on to recommend potential spouses be medically examined to determine their virginity.[324] Shirley Gillett, contributing author to *Women, Abuse, and the Bible: How Scripture Can Be Used to Heal or Hurt*, says that many evangelical books warn men against considering marriage to a woman unless she's a virgin. Therefore, even women who have been raped or sexually abused as a child are considered 'damaged goods.'[325] Women who've engaged in teen sex or premarital sex as an adult are demonized by fundamentalists. This plants images in women's minds that sex is a filthy act from which they failed to abstain. It can affect both their emotional and sexual health, as they eventually come avoid sex altogether.

There are a couple of female sexual disorders that can develop from the fundamentalist upbringing. These include hypoactive sexual desire disorder, in which sexual fantasies and urges seem absent, or sexual aversion disorder, in which genital contact with another is completely avoided. Little is known about people with low sex drives. But, "Religious orthodoxy" or "trying to have sex with a partner of the nonpreferred sex"[326] has been seen clinically as a common cause of these dysfunctions.

A woman may also know little about her body and never have learned what arouses her, leading to female orgasmic disorder. With this, a woman is unable to reach orgasm even after normal stimulation and sexual excitement. In these women, there may also be a lack of sexual knowledge and familiarity with their genital anatomy.[327] These disorders can clearly be seen as outgrowths of fundamentalists' opposition, in fact refusal for their children to participate in sexuality education programs. That is not to mention the evilness often projected about the naked female body and sex altogether.

Your body . . . is not *your* body

The fertility rates of fundamentalists and evangelicals, according to Christopher G. Ellison and Patricia Goodson, in the *Journal for the Scientific Study of Religion*, are considerably higher than those of mainline Protestants. They are less likely to use contraception the first time they have intercourse,[328] regardless of marital status, because of their lack of knowledge regarding sex and reproduction and, just as often, because of their opposition to birth control.[329] Furthermore, to many fundamentalists, any sexual conduct not for the purpose of procreation is "perverted." So fundamentalists not only reject artificial contraceptives, but often, natural family planning as well.[330]

Such views create problems with fundamentalist women's emotional, physical, and sexual health, overpopulation, and poverty. But these views also can affect mainstream women as fundamentalists attempt to impose their beliefs on society. Contraceptive opponent Janet E. Smith, associate Professor of Philosophy at University of Dallas, postulates that using contraceptives creates a "barnyard morality." Millions of people, she complains, are having sex out of wedlock. "Our culture is so obsessed with sex and hostile to babies," she insists. According to Smith, birth control pills should not be allowed on the market, and natural family planning is the only appropriate form of birth control. This is because "contraception violates fertility and caters to the animal propensity for self-indulgence."[331]

Smith's characterization of sex for pleasure as animalistic is amusing, if not a complete contradiction. Animals, unlike humans, do not act on sexual impulses purely for pleasure, as do humans. Females of most species are unwilling partners when not fertile. And males less interested, if interested at all, in females when they are not in season. Therefore, while mammal behavior (or "barnyard morality") is not necessarily bad, which group tends toward "animalistic" behavior? Such exaggerations and comparisons by Christian fundamentalists could almost be seen as comical were it not for the Christian Right's power to meet such irrational objectives.

In 1998, Republican Representative Chris Smith of New Jersey, an anti-abortion extremist, proposed to legally define a variety of birth control measures, including the IUD and oral contraceptives, as abortifacients.[332] This would prohibit insurance coverage of contraceptives through Federal Employees Health Benefit (FEHB) plans, since the FEHB plans ban abortion services. As the National Organization for Women points out, "Though the amendment failed, the Smith initiative is part of a larger effort to undermine acceptability of contraceptives and to eventually restrict—or perhaps even ban—their use."[333]

The greatest issue of the moment pertaining to reproductive freedom, however, is abortion and the Christian Right's desire to overturn *Roe v. Wade*. Almost immediately following the January 22, 1973, Supreme Court *Roe v. Wade* decision, the "right to life" movement began. Leading the crusade was the Roman Catholic Church, which in 1975 devised a full-scale right-to-life educational and political campaign. It was called the Pastoral Plan for Pro-Life Activities. [334] The National Conference of Catholic Bishops' (NCCB) detailed, 4,000-word strategy set forth:

> In fulfillment of our pastoral responsibilities, the members of the National Conference of Catholic Bishops have repeatedly affirmed that human life is a precious gift from God; that each person who receives this gift has responsibilities toward God, toward self, and toward others; and that society, through its laws and social institutions, must protect and sustain human life at every stage of its existence. Recognition of the dignity of the human person, made in the image of God, lies at the very heart of our individual and social duty to respect human life.[335]

The plan was clear. Not only must Catholics live in accordance with Catholic views on abortion, but so must everyone else. As the plan revealed, the NCCB would seek "to activate the pastoral resources of the

Church in three major efforts." One would be "a public policy effort directed toward the legislative, judicial, and administrative areas so as to ensure effective legal protection for the right to life." The plan describes many objectives and ways to achieve these goals by involving Catholics, from national Catholic organizations all the way down to laypersons.

Furthermore, the plan imparts:

> Dialogue is most important–and has already proven highly fruitful–among churches and religious groups. Efforts should continue at ecumenical consultation and dialogue with Judaism and other Christian bodies, and also with those who have no specific ecclesial allegiance. Dialogue among scholars in the field of ethics is a most important part of this interfaith effort.[336]

The Pastoral Plan describes how different committees, from the diocese to the parish, work toward meeting its objectives. They will make "a continuing public information effort to persuade all elected officials and potential candidates that abortion must be legally restricted." This will be done by electing "members of their own group or active sympathizers to specific posts in all local party organizations." And they'll encourage "the development of 'grassroots' political action organizations,"[337] for starters.

Regardless of pro-life action, abortions continued to increase, motivating some fundamentalists to mobilize their forces. Women in need of abortion were soon faced with crossing angry picket lines that sometimes grew violent. Many clinics were firebombed; others received threats, attempted bombings, and were vandalized. According to Flo Conway and Jim Siegelman of *Holy Terror: The Fundamentalist War on America's Freedoms in Religion, Politics and Our Private Lives*, "The pro-life movement pioneered the fundamentalist right's use of personal intimidation and gruesome scare tactics."[338] Promotional literature was distributed by mail and within the anti-abortion circle, often with photos of aborted fetuses, gorily detailing the abortion procedure.[339]

The Catholic Church, through its campaign, knew just what it was doing. And with the assistance of other conservative Christian denominations and sects, it had become a massive movement. By the end of the 1970s, a drive to overturn *Roe v. Wade* was well under way. A Human Life Amendment to the Constitution was proposed. If passed, it would have deemed life to begin at conception, granting the fetus full legal status.[340] Thus began fundamentalists' first efforts in terrorizing Congress through a "March for Life." Tens of thousands of antiabortion protestors marched on the capital with "banners, posters, black crosses, coffins and toy babies on sticks."[341] They were unsuccessful at overturning the 1973 Supreme Court decision. But this was only the beginning of what would become an ongoing and undying attempt at overturning *Roe v. Wade*.

During the 1980 election, Christian fundamentalist preachers, along with special interest groups took on a new strategy. In addition to brochures and mailings, pro-lifers began using every form of media to spread its message. This included publishing articles and airing television commercials.[342] Reverend Jerry Falwell made the issue a priority in his Moral Majority platform. This led the Republican Party to give way to Falwell and the fundamentalists' pro-life cause, as the party adopted the platform and endorsed "pro-life judges and passage of the Human Life Amendment." Ronald Reagan became the first serious presidential candidate to favor the fundamentalists' extreme anti-abortion position.[343] Reagan, an actor, used his rhetorical skills to convince anti-abortionists he was their guy, and it worked like a charm to get their votes.

The following years saw continued attempts to overturn *Roe v. Wade* and to place restrictions on abortion. In 1989, in *Webster v. Reproductive Health Services*, the Supreme Court heard arguments on a Missouri law declaring life begins at conception. It placed burdensome restrictions on abortion such as "forbidding the use of public funds for the purpose of counseling a woman to have an abortion not necessary to save her life." It also forbid "the use of public facilities for abortions not necessary to save a woman's life."[344] Thirty-three pro-choice briefs were filed on behalf of "a broad range of groups, representing every major sect of American society" opposing the Missouri law. A narrow range of groups, consisting of Catholic fundamentalist and antiabortion organizations, filed forty-five briefs favoring the Missouri restrictions.[345] The conservative Court upheld the Missouri law, which opened the door to similar restrictions in other states.

While still unable to overturn *Roe v. Wade*, the movement has undoubtedly seen significant gains. The evangelical Randall Terry, founder of Operation Rescue, an extreme antiabortion coalition, reveals social unrest in large numbers can cause politicians to give in to such groups in an effort to calm the nation.[346] In 1993, Operation Rescue formed the Institute of Mobilized Prophetic Activated Christian Training (IMPACT). Antiabortionists from around the country took part in the drills. They learned how to harass and expose anyone involved in abortion clinics and even those associated with the pro-choice movement.[347] At one IMPACT training session, Terry proclaimed, "Intolerance is a beautiful thing. We're going to make [abortionists'] lives a living hell."[348] Terry has been heavily influenced by Reconstructionism, one of the more extreme forms of Christian fundamentalism.

Another antiabortion group, Rescue America, began distributing "wanted posters" for doctors who perform abortions. This, however, was only the beginning of what would grow into a violent and deadly form of pro-life activism.[349] On March 10, 1993, a Rescue America participant, Michael Griffin, shot Dr. David Gunn, outside the doctor's abortion clinic. Radical groups such as Operation Rescue and Rescue America lost followers as a result of the violence. Nonetheless, the organizations reached out for new recruits. According to William Martin, "At a July [1993] rally, [Terry] urged a group of Denver Christians to become 'intolerant zealots [of] baby killers, sodomites, condom-pushers and that pluralism nonsense.'"[350] Another Operation Rescue member, Reverend Keith Tucci had also declared, regarding the RU 486 (Mifeprex) abortion drug, "When they invent new ways to kill children, we will invent new ways to save them."[351]

In July 1994, former Presbyterian minister Paul Hill murdered Dr. John Bayard Britton and his driver, Jim Barrett outside a Pensacola abortion clinic. In November 1994, the saga continued as Operation Rescue attempted to justify the use of violence. Another activist added, "It isn't always wrong to kill." It was claimed, "Violence doesn't necessarily beget violence. Sometimes it solves violence." A month later, two female clinic workers, Lee Ann Nichols and Shanon Lowney, in Brookline, Massachusetts were shot to death by John Salvi, a Catholic anti-abortionist.[352]

The contradictory views of pro-lifers who are willing to murder are not surprising, since the dogmatic views held by fundamentalists are not allowed to be questioned. As Conway and Siegelman found through personal interviews with fundamentalists, the positions they hold on various issues are often contradictory and hypocritical. Those who claimed to be for life on the abortion issue most often favored the death penalty and America's nuclear weapons. They were generally unsympathetic to the needs of the poor and were against government health care for poor mothers or hot school lunches for needy children.[353]

Now, with the new millennium, the antiabortion crusade is, in many ways, as strong as ever. Fundamentalists have managed to have more restrictions placed on abortion. These include waiting periods, parental permission, and elimination of public funding. However, nothing short of a complete halt to abortion will satisfy the campaign, even when the lives of women are at stake.

The Catholic public information campaign, along with its Protestant fundamentalist anti-abortion allies, has gone so far as to misrepresent the reasons women often seek abortion. This has become evident in the so-called "partial-birth" debate—a term created by anti-abortionists to mislead the public about late-term abortions performed only to save the life and health of the mother.

Anti-abortionists misrepresent abortion as the birth control method of choice for most women who seek abortion. In actuality, failed contraceptives are the cause of nearly half of abortions. From 1979 to 1982 alone, there were 1.61 million pregnancies resulting from contraceptive failure.[354] All the studies found contraceptives to be the preferred method of birth control, and women choose abortion "as a last resort." Unwanted pregnancies occur frequently among women who have inadequate family planning materials or services.[355] Yet, anti-abortionists fail to acknowledge these common reasons women turn to abortion. They instead paint a picture that abortion is the birth control method of choice among most women seeking the procedure.

Such misrepresentations, along with the Catholic anti-abortion movement's considerable financial means for waging its media campaign, have led to public confusion and growing support of the antiabortion endeavor. According to a June 2000 *Los Angeles Times* poll, support for *Roe v. Wade* dropped from fifty-six percent in favor of choice in 1991 to only forty-three percent in 2000.[356] Regardless of the Church's stance, the abortion rate among Catholics is thirty percent higher than that of Protestants.[357]

More troubling, George W. Bush's selection of John Ashcroft as U.S. Attorney General was a significant blow to the safety of women's reproductive freedom. While serving as attorney general of Missouri, Ashcroft sought to overturn *Roe v. Wade* through U.S. Supreme Court cases. He also cosponsored a resolution, as U.S. senator, for a Constitutional amendment "to ban abortion even in cases of rape and incest."[358] During Bush's administration, it is expected sixty-three federal bench vacancies, as well as Supreme Court vacancies, will occur. The danger Ashcroft poses by being a part in selecting candidates for these nominations is imminent.[359] To think otherwise would be a gross miscalculation on the part of the choice movement.

Of course, while antiabortionists' ultimate goal is very clear—to overturn *Roe v. Wade*—most of the anti-abortion cases that go to court stem from state laws. These are far easier to pass. Antiabortionists know that even if challenged, the amount of time that would lapse between implementing a law and opponents gaining a judgment against the law would be significant. Enough so as to impede at least a substantial number of girls and women's access to abortion. This makes passing laws in violation of the Supreme Court's *Roe v. Wade* decision a tempting option for the religious right. There seems no shortage of politicians willing to violate the law of the land. This is especially so at state and local levels. In the last legislative session of 2000 in Michigan alone, twenty-three bills were introduced to restrict abortion and reproductive rights.[360]

The anti-abortion campaign, as John Swomley, Professor emeritus of Social Ethics at St. Paul School of Theology points out, stems from the doctrine of the Roman Catholic Church "that every sexual act must be open to procreation."[361] This is also the view held by fundamentalist Protestants who have been most publicly visible in the drive against choice—just as I suspect the Catholic campaign intended. Regardless of the Catholic stance, as Swomley explains, the Vatican created the anti-abortion campaign in opposition to Biblical scripture. Not only is there no Biblical basis to support the anti-abortion sentiment, there are many passages in the Bible that support abortion.[362] In one such passage, Numbers 31:17, God orders: "Now therefore kill every male among the little ones." This hardly supports fundamentalists' pro-life stance.

It is Swomley's belief that the right to life movement not only wants women to be subordinate to men, but to their fetuses as well. In 1988, the Republican Party platform declared "that the unborn child has a fundamental right to life which cannot be infringed." Platform committee member Marjorie Bell Chambers "argued that in the conflict between saving the fetus or the life of the woman, the phrase, 'cannot be infringed' meant 'that men and fetuses have a right to life at all times, but women lose that right when they become pregnant.'"[363] Chambers moved to amend the platform to eliminate the last four words. However, those on the committee defeated Chamber's amendment that would have protected the life of the mother. This was by a fifty-five to thirty-three vote, with eleven abstentions.[364]

Despite the Christian Right's efforts to overturn *Roe v. Wade*, a number of Christian denominations and other religious groups have taken a pro-choice stance, holding abortion is a personal choice. These denominations agree it is a decision individuals should make according to their own religious and personal beliefs.[365] The organization Catholics for a Free Choice believes similarly. It is fighting against Catholic fundamentalist attempts to impose their religiously based views on others.

On December 12, 2000, CBS's *60 Minutes* featured a report by Morley Safer on Catholic-controlled hospitals in America. According to the report, four out of ten of America's largest health care systems are owned by or are under the control of the Roman Catholic Church. In almost half of the hospitals that have merged with or made alliances with the Catholic Church, services have been cut. Catholics for a Free Choice opposes Catholic doctrine being instituted in medical practices. According to the organization's president, Frances Kissling, when hospitals merge with Catholic institutions, many services are eliminated. Family planning, contraceptives, including condoms, sterilization, fertility treatment, and abortion are not available in these facilities. Moreover, they cannot even be discussed. Kissling pointed out, "Medical decisions about reproductive health care in Catholic hospitals or non-Catholic hospitals that merge with Catholic hospitals are made by religious authorities, not doctors."[366]

Catholic control of hospitals is not the only issue affecting women's reproductive health. Controversy over the procedure known as "partial-birth abortion" has drawn many unsuspecting proponents of choice into the Christian Right's bandwagon regarding the procedure. The medical term most closely resembling the description of the "partial-birth abortion" is properly termed "intact dilation and extraction." This method is sometimes used because prior to thirty-six weeks, the cervix is resistant to dilation. This resistance causes much physical pain during the two to four days it takes to dilate at this stage. Inductions done before this time also pose risk of uterine rupture. Therefore, continuous nursing supervision is required if drug induced labor is carried out rather than performing intact dilation and extraction.[367]

In the campaign against late-term abortions, pro-life activists have created the illusion women are deciding at the eleventh-hour that they suddenly do not want to have a baby and, with no concern for their pre-born, decide to abort. By creating this misperception and graphically depicting the procedure to appeal to the emotions of the public, even many pro-choice advocates argue the procedure must stop.

The reasons for the use of late-term abortion are not for women who have a last minute change of heart. The procedure is used for the sake of the woman's health and, in some cases, when there is "severe fetal abnormality," says obstetrician Dr. Allan Rosenfield, who is also the dean of New York's Columbia School of Public Health. Many complications can arise late in pregnancy threatening a woman's life. Tragically, it is also sometimes discovered a fetus would be unable to survive birth. In these instances, continuing the pregnancy could pose other serious health risks to the mother or result in the inability to conceive again.[368]

Furthermore, the reality is only 1.4 percent of all abortions are performed twenty-one weeks into pregnancy or beyond.[369] The estimated number of abortions performed beyond twenty-six weeks is fewer than five-hundredths of a percent.[370] Considering the number of babies born with severe defects and the number of health complications that women face during pregnancy or delivery, this number is exceptionally small. Still, anti-abortionists would have us believe pregnancy and childbirth are completely without risk. It matters not that the World Health Organization reports "585,000 women die each year during childbirth and pregnancy." And "for every maternal death," it is reported "as many as thirty women sustain often times crippling and lifelong health problems related to pregnancy."[371]

Maureen Mary Britell of Sandwich, Massachusetts learned from a sonogram her fetus was not developing a brain. Medical experts confirmed the baby would not survive, so the couple, with the support of their priest, chose to terminate the pregnancy by inducing labor. Unfortunately, complications arose during the delivery, which required cutting the umbilical cord to abort the fetus to prevent health risks to Britell.[372]

In another case, Coreen Costello of Agoura, California desperately wanted her daughter. But she discovered the fetus had lethal neuromuscular disease and would be unable to survive. Even after it was discovered dangerous levels of amniotic fluid had built up, the Christian couple struggled with the decision to terminate the pregnancy for more than two weeks. Finally, it became absolutely necessary for Costello to abort for the sake of her health.[373]

Regardless of the health risks it would pose to expecting mothers, anti-abortionists propose legislation to ban the use of the procedure under all conditions and in spite of the recommendations of major medical associations. The American College of Obstetricians and Gynecologists argues, "The physician, in consultation with the patient, must choose the most appropriate method based upon the patient's individual circumstances."[374] The American Nurses Association agrees: "It is inappropriate for the law to mandate a clinical course of action for a woman who is already faced with an intensely personal and difficult decision."[375] Nonetheless, anti-abortionists place the life of the unborn, non-breathing fetus ahead of the life of the mother.

The antiabortion movement poses another health risk to women as well. According to Flora Davis, in *Moving the Mountain: The Women's Movement in America since 1960*, abortion was legal in the country until around 1900.[376] By that time, male physicians desiring to increase business by taking on child birthing, had gained the support of churches and the clergy in condemning the practice.[377] Previously, women saw midwives and others for their reproductive health. Churches had originally not opposed abortion, until the business-cause of the male physicians took hold.[378] Regardless of the illegalization of abortion, by the 1960s, more than a million abortions were performed annually in the United States "by moonlighting clerks, salesmen, and barbers, and, less often, by doctors willing to risk imprisonment."[379]

Bernard Nathanson, M.D., a recently converted anti-abortion activist describes in his 1996 autobiography, *The Hand of God*, the horrors women faced before *Roe v. Wade*:

> At least two-thirds of the clinic females ambulanced to our emergency room in the middle of the night, bleeding profusely and in severe pain, were the victims of botched illegal abortions, not spontaneous miscarriages. . . . Those of us practicing gynecology no longer see the results of illegal induced abortion: the raging fevers, the torn and obstructed intestines; the shredded uterus requiring immediate hysterectomy; the raging infections leaving many women sterile, exhausted, in chronic pain. . . . Illegal abortion was in 1967 the number one killer of pregnant women.[380]

"Every year," according to Davis, "more than 350,000 women who had an illegal abortion suffered complications serious enough to be hospitalized; 500 to 1,000 of them died."[381] Today, approximately 70,000 women die from unsafe abortions each year, 69,000 of them from less developed countries. A significantly larger number of women suffer complications from the estimated 20 million unsafe abortions undergone annually around the world.[382]

Should *Roe v. Wade* be reversed, the situation in the United States would be no different today than it was decades ago or than current conditions in less-developed countries across the globe. Since the legalization of abortion, a survey administered by Reproductive Health Services in St. Louis has been given to patients at their three-week medical check-up after abortion. It found every woman would have sought an illegal and unsafe way to end her pregnancy if legalized abortion were not available or else they would have considered suicide.[383]

Perhaps the most disturbing part of this whole right-to-life effort is that fundamentalists and the religious right refuse to take part in the prevention of pregnancy. This could easily be done by advocating for appropriate sex education and contraceptive use or by improving the economic conditions for low-income women to support a baby.[384] Yet, they have gone to great lengths to prevent appropriate and adequate sex and family planning education. And they have worked to make birth control difficult, if not impossible, to obtain. This has been especially so with the most effective contraceptives, and not only for youth, but for many adults, especially the poor.

While fundamentalists insist on abstinence-only or celibacy as an answer to pregnancy prevention, it has proven an unrealistic method of birth control for a majority of the population. As a result, girls and women become pregnant. Abortion then becomes the only suitable solution for the many who are unable, at the time, to take on the responsibility of having a baby and who are emotionally unable to give up a baby for adoption. In turn, the fundamentalists who prevented these women from obtaining and, therefore using contraceptives, accuse these women of using abortion as their method of choice for birth control. Then, in contrast, when unmarried women choose not to have an abortion, they're accused of having many children to take advantage of the welfare system. In reality, having more children was the last thing they wanted. Either way, pregnant women are punished.

Immense suffering takes place for women around the world. This is a result of lack of knowledge pertaining to and access to contraceptives and in many parts of the world, where safe abortion is inaccessible. Regardless, on May 28, 1992, the *New York Times* reported that Vatican diplomats were preparing for the upcoming Earth Summit in Rio de Janeiro. The diplomats were campaigning to ensure any decisions on the population issue would not be "in conflict with Roman Catholic teaching on birth control," points out Swomley.[385] The Vatican has standing as a member nation of the United Nations and has been criticized by Catholics for a Free Choice for holding this special status.[386] But in the end, it had its way. It succeeded in gaining enough right-wing support, as Swomley reveals:

> to block the United States from paying its debt to the United Nations by attaching an amendment to ban the use of federal funds by any private or government organization that supports abortion overseas or counsels women on where to get an abortion.[387]

Most alarming, almost immediately upon taking office in 2001, President George W. Bush placed a ban on U.S. aid to overseas organizations that, according to the ACLU, "use their own money to counsel women and girls on their reproductive choices."[388] Such decisions do not affect just women. In the May 1991 issue of the *American Journal of Psychiatry*, Dr. Paul K. B. Dagg found that women who are denied abortions are not the only ones to suffer serious psychological and social problems. Their children, who otherwise would have been aborted, suffer immensely, as well.[389] These children lack a secure childhood, require more psychiatric care, and have an increased rate of juvenile delinquency, among other problems.

Furthermore, 14 million American children go to bed hungry every night. And in the United States, the infant mortality rate ranks twentieth among industrialized nations.[390] In 1984, according to *The New York Times*, the United States had more than 50,000 children available for adoption.[391] Many have multiple handicaps, requiring lifetime medical care. So how will our nation care for more unwanted children should *Roe v. Wade* be overturned? It is clear that concern for the unborn is not the issue at hand. The anti-abortion campaign is, largely, just one more way for patriarchs to keep women under their control.

The dangers fundamentalism poses to women are many. Women raised in Christian fundamentalist homes suffer emotionally, sexually, and physically as adults. This is because of the beliefs with which they have been indoctrinated and, ultimately, from their acceptance of male domination in the marriage. As a result, their marriages suffer also. Women in the mainstream, as well as fundamentalist women, suffer from legislation affecting their reproductive rights and sexual gratification. They often lack education and access to information pertaining to reproduction and contraception. They are impaired by stereotyping affecting educational attainment, job opportunities, and equity in wages. Women's health is compromised by religiously-based medical decisions not conducive to maintaining life. They are also affected by stereotypes leading to rape as well as divorce legislation and unfair welfare initiatives. Finally, they are hindered by a wide range of acts meant to keep women barefoot, pregnant, and in their "proper" role.

CHAPTER 5

THE SOCIAL IMPLICATIONS
OF ARMAGEDDON

by Kimberly Blaker

We are engaged in a social, political, and cultural war. There's a lot of talk in America about pluralism. But the bottom line is somebody's values will prevail.[392]

Gary Bauer, former head of Family Research Council

The war Gary Bauer warns of is not against our age-old communist enemies or "America's New War" as CNN dubbed our actions against Osama Bin Laden and other Islamic terrorists. Bauer specifically speaks of a civil war, in which Americans fight each other for the right to dictate morality and social standards for everyone in the United States. Most will react to this with detachment. "I didn't enlist. I wasn't drafted. This is not my war. I'm not the one they're attacking." Americans see things happen and how they are affected, but do not necessarily see these as acts of war.

Yet, looking around at the world, the war becomes easier to see. Instinctively, the truth of Bauer's statement can be accepted. Yes, there is a war. Yes, eventually, someone will probably win. In and of itself, his statement is not so confrontational. His colleague, however, Coach Bill McCartney, head of the Promise Keepers sheds a bit more light on the fundamentalist role in this fight:

> What you are about to hear is God's word to the men of this nation. We are going to war as of tonight. We have divine power—that is our weapon. We will not compromise. Wherever truth is at risk, in the schools or legislature, we are going to contend for it. We will win.[393]

Bauer warns of being surrounded by a war touching every corner of Americans' lives. McCartney informs that his army is leading the fight,

114

and God is its weapon. Therefore, looking at the effects of fundamentalism on society is a matter of identifying the battleground, understanding the weapons, and assessing the casualties. Battlegrounds are not something with which most Americans are familiar. It has been more than half a century since a national government attacked any part of the United States. It has been far longer since America has experienced an ongoing war on its home turf. So, it comes as a surprise to many to learn that the battleground of the war is right in their own backyards, as demonstrated by the aims of fundamentalism.

Several fundamentalist battles and weapons pose serious danger to society. Fundamentalists are the main supporters in what they refer to as pro-life issues. They oppose abortion and often all forms of birth control—not just for adherents, but for all of society. This ultimately leads to high rates of poverty and increased expense to the public. More problematic is the domino effect that ensues. Poverty causes a vast array of social problems from low educational attainment and unemployment to drug abuse, alcoholism, and even crime.

Another battle is the fundamentalist desire to rid society of those it perceives as its enemies or, if nothing else, to reduce the status of those enemies. Based on fundamentalist prejudices, such enemies include women, gays and lesbians, other races, and adherents of other religions or no religion.

Crime and violence is a key battle of fundamentalists. However, their inability to see other than in black and white terms leads to proposing and frequently implementing laws that are ineffective in practice. More often, those practices actually promote crime and violence. Although religious conservatives claim their stringent moral code reduces the rates of murder, rape, and other crimes, this is generally not so. It may actually lead them to criminal behavior.

One of the weapons used by Christian fundamentalists with devastating effects is cult-like recruitment practices. This characteristic places those with certain vulnerabilities at risk for getting involved and often trapped into emotionally damaging and sometimes deadly movements.

When speaking of the fundamentalist war, it is generally understood to be one in which democratic principles are used by both sides to propose and oppose local, state, and federal laws. Some fundamentalists are physically preparing for a lethal war they perceive as imminent. Heavily-armed militias are scattered throughout the country and are training armies for war-like battles that could take place in Americans' own backyards. All of this necessitates a review of the moral development or lack thereof, of those claiming to have the market on this attribute. The fundamentalist claim fails to hold up to sociological theory.

The fundamentals of poverty

Christian fundamentalist beliefs and practices pertaining to sexual abstinence and procreation lead to poverty. This affects not only those within the fundamentalist religious culture, but society at-large. This is demonstrated as fundamentalists advocate policies or prevent measures that would protect against untimely or unwanted pregnancy and childbirth. Such policies promoted by fundamentalists include minimizing or eradicating sex education programs, withholding birth control options, and measures to restrict abortion.

Although not all Catholics fit the fundamentalist criteria, there is a large Catholic fundamentalist population. The reality of the fundamentalist desire to populate and force the whole human race to continue multiplying is demonstrated best by the Vatican. It "has been one of the most adamant opponents of contraceptive birth control and worldwide family planning for decades,"[394] says John M. Swomley, Professor emeritus of Social Ethics at St. Paul School of Theology.

To exemplify this, the *Pittsburgh Tribune Review* reported on April 4, 1998, that in the 1980s, Pope John Paul II counseled Kenyans in Nairobi. They had the fastest-growing population in Africa and "probably in the world," at the time, yet were told to "be fruitful and multiply."[395] Such practices and policies promoting population growth ultimately lead to poverty and welfare dependency, where welfare is still even available, for both fundamentalists and a large segment of society. In turn, these practices indirectly cause crime, health problems, mental illness, drug addiction, alcoholism, unemployment, and other serious social problems.

The relationship between the promotion of population growth and poverty can easily be illustrated. "The United States' child poverty rate is substantially higher—often two to three times higher—than that of most other major Western industrialized nations,"[396] says the National Center for Children in Poverty. The U.S. poverty rate ranged between 22.4 and 25 percent from 1986 to 1997. The Netherlands is one of the least religious regions and with the most liberal of policies pertaining to sex education, drugs, and other social issues. Yet, its poverty rate ranged between only 5.2 and 8.1 percent during the period of 1987 to 1994.[397]

High poverty rates are associated with a number of factors. These include populations that are more rural, offer fewer educational opportunities, or suffer governmental mismanagement through practicing or enacting laws that have an indirect effect on poverty. The conditions breeding poverty, as listed above and discussed in more detail below, are not cut and dry. According to much data, many of the states with the highest poverty rates also have the highest fundamentalist populations.[398] Though this does not mean in and of itself fundamentalism causes poverty, it does show it fails to alleviate it. Furthermore, if the connection is reversed, it shows poor people are more likely to become fundamentalists, as has been suggested by social scientists.

Several characteristics of fundamentalism increase the odds or maintain the cycle of poverty. To understand this fully, one must look at the causes and nature of poverty. A wide variety of factors can lead to poverty, while at the same time stem from it as well. Low education levels, drinking, gambling, drug addiction, high unemployment rates, medical and emotional problems, and racial and sexual discrimination are causes and symptoms of poverty.

Typically, poverty is passed from one generation to the next. It begins with a "poor family with young children," which "results in substandard living conditions."[399] This generally leads to lack of interest in school.[400] From there the cycle may be cut short by teen pregnancy, resulting in single parenting. This continues the cycle of poverty.[401] Alternatively, the cycle may progress as youth try to escape substandard living conditions and drop out of school. This leads to the circumstances that will forever trap him or her into poverty.[402] Those who have young children as well, are even more financially strapped. This ultimately "lock[s] them into poverty for the rest of their lives." As the cycle is completed, the children from this poverty-stricken family continue down a similar path.[403]

How this relates to fundamentalism can be observed in many ways. First, there is a definite negative correlation between fundamentalist beliefs and educational attainment. In 2000, only 18.7 percent of those who said they believe the Bible is the literal word of God had any education beyond high school. Yet, 30.8 percent of all respondents had gone on to junior college or better. Even more telling, 22.6 percent of the Biblical literalists never finished high school, compared to only 14.8 percent of the general population.[404] It should be noted, however, this is not necessarily the case for fundamentalists that are politically active, as they are often highly educated.

Discrimination is another factor of poverty that is also related to fundamentalism. Discrimination results in limited employment opportunities and equity in pay for women, other races, and gays and lesbians. The relationship between fundamentalism and discrimination will be discussed in depth later in this chapter.

Certainly not all emotional and mental health problems can be attributed to fundamentalism. Still, it does lead to a wide variety of mental health problems as has been revealed so far and will be further examined.

Most notable, however, is the fundamentalist attitude promoting childbearing, regardless of the economic condition of the teenager, woman, or couple. This results in scores of children brought into a world of poverty, to continue the ongoing cycle.

Teenage pregnancy rates are an indicator of social conditions. As a nation, the U.S. dominates the economic world of the most developed countries. Nevertheless, ABC News has reported the U.S. teen pregnancy rate nearly matches Russia's and is higher than all of Eastern Europe. Teen pregnancy is four times as likely to occur in the United States as it is in Japan or France.[405] Although the U.S. teenage pregnancy rate has steadily dropped over the past decade, even the rate of decline does not match that of Western Europe. "We've made some progress," says Susheela Singh, lead author of a year 2000 study on teen pregnancy that was performed by the Guttmacher Institute. "[B]ut we haven't caught up [to the other developed countries],"[406] she points out.

A strong correlation between high rates of teen pregnancy and greater prevalence of fundamentalism is evident from the available data.[407] More than half of the states falling into the top bracket of fundamentalist activity are also in the top third for teen pregnancy rates. While this alone does not demonstrate a causal link, it is clear that fundamentalist activity does little, if anything, to prevent teens from having sex or becoming pregnant. If it does have any effect, it is more likely to increase, rather than reduce teen pregnancy.

Beyond the attempts by fundamentalists to keep women barefoot and pregnant, as covered in the previous chapter, countless tactics are used by pro-lifers to prevent women from obtaining abortions. As of 1992, approximately 1,500 to 3,000 Crisis Pregnancy Centers (CPC) were operating across the country. These facilities counsel between 700,000 and one million women annually.[408] Many CPCs, especially those affiliated with the Pearson Institute, are set up to intentionally give women the false pretense they are contacting or visiting a medical clinic that offers abortions. Once the women are inside, many of these CPCs use shock tactics and other misinformation to scare teen girls and women out of undergoing abortion. Such tactics include dispensing false information pertaining to abortion related death rates, as well as showing visitors gory visual imagery of shredded fetuses. In such clinics, women are filled with guilt for contemplating abortion, even when a single mother already has several children and no income.[409]

Of course, not all CPCs use such devious tactics. Yet, even those that are up front do admit the problems experienced by women in their clinics. Many, if not most of the women entering, are poor and unsure how they will manage another mouth to feed.[410] The responsibilities posed by another child when the mother-to-be is an adolescent or already physically taxed is yet another concern not adequately addressed. Clinic workers confess they are often able to convince a teen girl or a poor woman to continue a pregnancy. They do this by offering donations such as a microwave or assistance in meal planning to reduce some of the time expended in parenting.[411] While such propositions may be well intentioned and seemingly helpful, in the scheme of things, such donations and assistance are a minute fraction of the total costs, time, and energy required to raise a child.

Therefore, a poor woman or young girl makes the decision not to abort. After the baby arrives, it is likely to be discovered the mother is not up to the task when coming face-to-face with the full brunt of the financial, physical, and emotional stress of parenting. Ultimately, this poses a variety of problems, most notably locking the family into a cycle of poverty.

Fundamental differences: the cultivation of prejudice

Perhaps one of the most obvious characteristics of Christian fundamentalism, yet the most vehemently denied by its adherents, is the fundamentalist relationship to prejudice and discrimination, and ultimately hate crimes, whether based on race, religion, gender, or sexual orientation. While fundamentalism is not the only factor contributing to prejudices, there is a strong relationship between the two. Conservative Christian biases have been observed in a preponderance of events throughout American history. As noted in the previous chapter, only within the last hundred years did women gain the right to vote, as well as many other rights long afforded to men. Also evident is that the misogyny of the Christian Right has far from dissipated.

Bigotry toward those of other religious beliefs has been repeatedly demonstrated. In fact, Protestants and Catholics have each been at the giving and receiving end of discriminatory practices toward each other. Jews, Muslims, and atheists have also been victims of Christian fundamentalist prejudices.

While slavery itself did not originate from Christian fundamentalism, it did ultimately come to be favored by conservative Christians, as they eventually led the fight for its preservation. Even following the conservative South's loss in the Civil War, fundamentalists diligently strove to maintain segregation.

Psychologists and psychiatrists now consider homosexuality an inborn trait and normal for a small percent of the population rather than a disorder. Regardless, Christian fundamentalists view homosexuality as a sin. They are responsible for preventing policies offering equity to gays and lesbians and for torturous hate crimes against homosexuals, who they perceive as wicked and immoral inhabitants of society.

Although slavery may have originated without religious motive, when the North American practice became challenged, the Bible and conservative Christian doctrine were used to uphold it. Conservative Christianity became one of the strong motivators for keeping it intact. Although the evangelical South had once condemned slavery, the movement eventually took the proslavery stance,[412] "with the belief that the Bible sanctioned it."[413] Conservative followers of the Christian faith were not the only ones to endorse the practice, however. As Brinkley notes, the southern Protestant clergy was the most effective in the 1820s and 1830s in defending it. The majority of southern Christian ministers argued that because of the inferiority of blacks, it was the duty of whites to maintain slavery for the sake of the African-Americans' "physical and spiritual needs. . . ."[414]

But beyond simple concern for the welfare of blacks, as George Brown Tindall, Kenan Professor of History at University of North Carolina reflects, the following were the Biblical sentiments of the 1800s:

> Had not the patriarchs of the Old Testament held bondsmen? Had not Noah, upon awakening from a drunken stupor, cursed Canaan, son of Ham, from whom the Negroes were descended? Had not Saint Paul advised servants to obey their masters and told a fugitive servant to return to his master? And had not Jesus remained silent on the subject, at least so far as the Gospels reported his words?[415]

Regardless of the Biblical basis for slavery, the more liberal northern Protestant clergy disagreed with the institution. And in the 1840s, the northern clergy's opposition to slavery led to a split in Methodist and Baptist churches, dividing the branches into the north and the south.[416] Over the years, tensions grew between the North and South over various issues. White southerners were opposed to the North's abandonment of "traditional American values." Eventually they became dangerously militant in their proslavery stance, one of the factors contributing to the Civil War in 1861.

When the defeated South reluctantly surrendered in 1865, all slaves were finally freed. But many in the south were outraged over the end of slavery, and in 1867, believing whites were God's chosen people, the Ku Klux Klan was formed. Its purpose was no secret: to intimidate blacks or those who defended them and to keep blacks "in their place." From the period of 1889 to 1918, the hatred of the Klan was revealed as it "captured and hung 3,224 men, women, and children, mostly black."[417]

"Christian fundamentalism was a cornerstone of institutional racism," explains Forrest G. Wood, Professor of History, at California State University, Bakersfield and author of *Black Scare: the Racist Response to Emancipation and Reconstruction*. Before the 1900s, most Christians held a fundamental view of the infallibility of the Bible and its literal interpretation; and the story of Noah's Curse was used to justify slavery.[418] The twentieth century, however, marked the fight for segregation—and fundamentalists' fight to maintain the status quo.

In *Brown v. Board of Education* (1954), the United States Supreme Court made the landmark decision to end segregation. This led Reverend G.T. Gillespie to speak before the Mississippi Synod of the Presbyterian Church. There, he reaffirmed his belief in Noah's Curse.[419] Although Presbyterians are typically mainstream, there have been rifts in the movement. This has been observed in many denominations. Differences in views on Biblical inerrancy and literalism have led to splits, as eventually happened with Presbyterians in 1973.[420]

Gillespie, one Presbyterian who strayed from the more liberal views of the movement, had been inspired by Jefferson Davis. Davis had spoken nearly a century beforehand to the Mississippi Democratic State Convention in defense of the slave trade and chattel slavery. He had alluded "to the 'importance of the race of Ham' as a fulfillment of its destiny to be 'servant of servants.'" Gillespie's reaffirmation was distributed by the white supremacist Citizens' Council of Greenwood, under the title, "A Christian View on Segregation."[421]

Today the Biblical basis for holding racist views has become less acceptable and therefore, less visible. But there is, undoubtedly, a relationship between modern-day racism and fundamentalism. Perhaps the best evidence comes from the continuation of the Ku Klux Klan as well as other extreme Christian based sects such as the Aryan Nation, also known as the Church of Jesus Christ Christian, and the Christian Identity movement.

Less recognized for racism, but still of issue is the Reconstructionist movement. Although Chalcedon Institute, the organization founded by the late R.J. Rushdoony, denies its interest in reinstituting black slavery, the movement does favor slavery as a means of paying off debts. The Ontario Consultants on Religious Tolerance has noted Reconstructionists' desire to reestablish slavery. The organization has received e-mail from unhappy Reconstructionists who deny such a desire.[422] Nonetheless, the organization has also received many letters from Reconstructionists in support of slavery who point out it would be good for North America.[423] There is an overlapping of many fundamentalist sects and movements. Therefore, the likelihood that a large number of Reconstructionists' desire to enslave other races is a high probability, regardless of the claims or views of the Chalcedon Institute.

This is demonstrated by many white supremacists and their organizations. They have begun linking their websites to Reconstructionist pages and taking up the Reconstructionist philosophy. One such example is at the website of God's Order Affirmed in Love. This site claims, "Christianity has historically been a religion of the white race regardless of how hard whites have tried to convert the world."[424] God's Order insists, "In addition to being grounded upon a Biblical foundation, Reconstruction must be built upon preserving our families which includes the greater racial family (nation) that we were born into."[425] There has also been much support by the Christian Identity and Aryan Nations movements for Reconstructionism.

Although in most instances racism is not openly a part of the fundamentalist repertoire, there is a definite correlation even among other fundamentalist groups. Such prejudices are evident as was witnessed in the 1970s. Approximately one hundred religious schools lost their tax-exempt status when they avoided integration.[426] While most of this has changed, even by 1988, most Christian schools had disproportionately white populations.[427] The reason for such, as Nancy Ammerman suggests, is that, "there is often an implicit, if not explicit, assumption that many black students are simply unwilling or unable to live by their [conservative Christian] standards."[428] And as Susan Rose, of the Fundamentalist Project points out, there is still commitment by many fundamentalists today, if not to segregation, at least to separation.[429]

In June 2002, the Civil Rights Project at Harvard University released data confirming the continuation of this trend. It found that today, private religious schools have the highest levels of segregation over both private secular schools and public schools, with Catholic the most segregated of religious schools.[430]

Best known for its separatist racist policies is the conservative Bob Jones University (BJU), which lost its tax-exempt status in 1982 for its policy of banning interracial dating and marriage. BJU's attorney argued before the Supreme Court insisting that as an exclusively religious organization, it qualifies for tax-exempt status regardless of its racist policy, because the policy is based on religious belief. Evangelicals joined forces in speaking out on behalf of BJU. Nonetheless, BJU lost the case and continued running without tax-exemption. The school maintained its belief that "God intends the races to be separate."[431] The ban on interracial dating finally was lifted in 2000 following a wave of media attention to BJU's practice.[432] While today, many BJU faculty and students deny the policy was racist, the meaning behind the policy is undeniable when looking at its founder.

Bob Jones, Sr., who was a fundamentalist preacher "was a Ku Klux Klan mouthpiece who preached against Catholics and foreigners . . ."[433] Jones, Sr. once clamored, "I would rather see a saloon on every corner than a Catholic in the White House. I would rather see a nigger as president."[434]

More recently, Bob Jones III rationalized in reference to the Curse of Ham:

> (A) Negro is best when he serves at the table. When he does that, he's doing what he knows how to do best. And the Negroes who have ascended to positions in government, in education, this sort of thing, I think you'll find, by and large, have a strong strain of white blood in them. Now, I'm not a racist and this school is not a racist institution. I can't stress that enough. But what I say is purely what I have been taught, and what I have been able to study is the teaching of the Scripture.[435]

James A. Landrith, Jr. of The Multiracial Activist, applied to BJU in 1998. He received a letter from BJU informing him of the university's ban on interracial dating. Since Landrith is interracially married, only he or his wife could be students at BJU, but not both of them.[436] Later, BJU's community relations coordinator, Jonathon Paite, wrote to Landrith:

> God has separated people for His own purpose. He has erected barriers between the nations, not only land and sea barriers, but also ethnic, cultural, and language barriers. God has made people different one from another and intends those differences to remain. Bob Jones University is opposed to intermarriage of the races because it breaks down the barriers God has established. It

mixes that which God separated and intends to keep separate. Every effort in world history to bring the world together has demonstrated man's self-reliance and his unwillingness to remain as God ordains. The attempts at one-worldism have been to devise a system without God and have fostered the promotion of a unity designed to give the world strength so that God is not needed and can be overthrown.[437]

Interestingly, BJU, from which Attorney General John Ashcroft received an honorary doctorate and delivered his acceptance speech in May 1999, is a favorite among Christian conservatives. Moreover, many conservative politicians have campaigned at BJU. This includes Republican Senator Strom Thurmond and former Republican Vice President Dan Quayle, who appeared with President George W. Bush. Many politicians have also graduated from or hold honorary degrees from the university.[438]

The issue of racial discrimination by fundamentalists is far from limited to academic institutions. According to a year-2000 survey, those who take the Bible literally and view it as the actual word of God, are three times as likely to favor laws against interracial marriage as those who do not take the Bible literally. They are twice as likely to not vote for a black candidate for president, even if their own political party nominated the candidate.[439]

More telling, in February 2001, ten African-American employees filed suit against the Christian Coalition; the charges were of discrimination. It was alleged that the blacks were barred from using the front door and must eat in segregated facilities at the Coalition's Washington, D.C. headquarters, simply because they are black.[440] The Coalition also played a role in the 2000 Florida election debacle. It sent lawyers to help avert the correction of the myriad of problems in getting an accurate vote count. This included the major issue of African-Americans who had been prevented from voting at all.[441]

The group least tolerated both vocally and visibly today, however, is homosexuals. In the past, fundamentalists received a great deal of support from the more mainstream population. It has been nearly thirty years since the American Psychiatric Association removed homosexuality from its register of mental disorders. Still, the culture at large has only recently begun to accept this behavior, which was traditionally considered deviant. Most mainstream society today accepts and promotes tolerance and equality for gays and lesbians. But, those who continue to speak venomously regarding homosexuality generally do so from a selective literal and inerrant interpretation of the Bible. They use Christian doctrine to support their contempt.

To fundamentalists, the possibility of gay marriage is extremely threatening to the envisioned American family. This is regardless of the fact the American Academy of Pediatrics' recently reported that children raised by gays and lesbians are no more likely to be maladjusted than their heterosexually parented peers.[442] Even so, gays and lesbians are the target of much criticism and attempts at conversion or correction. It matters not whether the homosexuals are actually attempting to create a family.

Gays and lesbians often suffer from family rejection and verbal abuse. Similar to the discrimination once endured by African-Americans (that is to a disturbingly large degree still experienced today), homosexuals suffer from housing and job discrimination, to threats, and, occasionally, actual violence.[443] Unfortunately, gays have more difficulty protecting themselves from discriminatory practices today because in many states there are few laws to protect them.

Legislation has been proposed to protect the rights of homosexuals, and there have been some successes. Still, most bills see strong opposition from fundamentalists, many within the political system, and the bills are therefore, unable to muster enough support. As an example, Attorney General John Ashcroft, while serving in the Senate, opposed a bill aimed at stopping employment discrimination of gays and lesbians. He insisted homosexuality is a choice that can be changed and that such a bill would send the wrong message to the youth in America.[444] The legislation failed to pass the conservative-controlled Senate by a single vote.[445]

Del Stover, editor of *Urban Advocate*, the newsletter of the National School Boards Association, describes the tragedy of the fundamentalist view on homosexuals. Gay and lesbian students feel alienated in a society that treats homosexuality as a plague. Parents of one child threatened: "If I thought you were gay, I'd smother you with a pillow."[446] Anyone growing up in fear of being disowned, ostracized, or killed for something they cannot change about themselves is likely to grow up with emotional problems.

Suicide is an all too common response to the emotional impact of fundamentalist attitudes toward homosexuality. It is estimated that thirty percent of teen suicides are by gay, lesbian, bisexual, or transsexual youth.[447] Yet, only an estimated four to ten percent of the population is homosexual. Although the American Academy of Pediatrics, the National Education Association, and the Child Welfare League of America are unanimous on the need for more services helping gay youth, Stover indicates that such relief for a gay teenager is not likely to happen. The battles imposed on school districts by religious conservatives in regards to intervention for gay students and opposition to sex education in general, make this a no-win situation.[448] Unfortunately, members of this at-risk population rarely receive intervention. This is because some religious conservatives protest so fiercely against anything possibly giving an appearance of accepting homosexuality, which they "decry . . . an abomination. . . ."[449]

When gays and lesbians force themselves to conform by marrying traditionally, their families can suffer greatly from the eventual revelations of their true orientation. Stanton L. Jones wrote in an article appearing in *Christianity Today* about a gay friend, Peter, who married a woman. Peter tried, unsuccessfully, to repress his urges for fifteen years. During his marriage, he had affairs with other men. When his wife eventually learned of the affairs, their marriage and lives were destroyed.[450] Although Peter was finally able to have a healthy relationship with a man, his ex-wife remained distraught from the destruction of their marriage.[451] Had Peter not been placed in a position of needing to repress his feelings, he would never have married a woman. This would have prevented the painful and traumatic experience.

Tragically, Matthew Shepard learned very well the pain homophobia can cause. Shephard's fate resulted from a society inundated by conservative Christian opposition to and outright contempt for gays. It came on October 12, 1998, because one of his assailants had been embarrassed when Shepard allegedly made a pass at him in a bar. In retaliation the assailant decided to steal Shepard's money. But it went far beyond robbery when Aaron McKinney and Russell Henderson brutally beat Shepherd and then abandoned him on the side of the road, tied to a fencepost.[452] McKinney and Henderson are now serving two consecutive life sentences each, with no possibility of parole, for Shepard's murder. The assailants were spared the death penalty at the behest of the slain student's father.[453]

Although highly visible, Shepard's case is not as rare as one might hope. In 1999, the FBI's Uniform Crime Reporting Program recorded 1,487 offenses motivated by sexual orientation against 1,558 individuals. Three of those resulted in death for the victim; another 180 were aggravated assault cases, which was the original charge against Shepard's assailants. Amazingly enough, gays, lesbians, and bisexuals are about as likely to be targeted for hate crimes as racial minorities, even though their "difference" is much less visible.[454]

The other side of the efforts to repress homosexuality is most dramatically illustrated by the case of Jeffrey Dahmer. The insistence that homosexuality is a disorder and a sin has taken a visible toll on society. Convicted serial murderer Dahmer suffered from severe self-hatred because of his own homosexuality. He was convinced by his fundamentalist upbringing that he was at heart a sinner and that his family would never accept him if they knew of this. Dahmer's rage was catastrophically turned against seventeen men and boys. He murdered and then performed sex acts on them before mutilating their bodies. Psychiatrist George Palermo testified in Dahmer's trial. He said to the *Milwaukee Sentinel*, "I believe Jeffrey Dahmer killed his victims because he hated homosexuality."[455]

In 1996, Henry Adams, Lester Wright Jr., and Bethany Lohr, all of the University of Georgia, conducted an experiment. It lent credence to the long-held hypothesis that homophobia, usually meaning a hatred of homosexuals, rather than simply fear, may be a reaction to unacknowledged "homosexual inclinations." In this experiment, heterosexual men viewed videotapes of homosexual, lesbian, and heterosexual acts while hooked up to a penile plethysmograph.[456]

The men were given a questionnaire before the experiment to determine their attitudes toward homosexuality. Those men who were categorized as homophobic before the experiment showed sexual arousal while viewing the homosexual videos. Those who had not been categorized as homophobic did not. Nevertheless, when they completed a closing questionnaire, the homophobic group denied their sexual arousal during the homosexual video. This would indicate that homophobics are repressing or at least unwilling to acknowledge homosexual feelings.[457] It may also suggest some turn to fundamentalism as a way of coping with and repressing their own homosexuality.

Fortunately, attitudes are changing—although slowly. In 1984, seventy-four percent of Americans responded that sexual relations between adults of the same sex were "always wrong." But by 2000, only fifty-nine percent chose this answer.[458] Still, how long and painful the change will be is unknown. Just less than two-thirds of the population still holds such a view. Rosie O'Donnell, who graced the cover of *People Magazine* in March 2002, was hailed for her bravery in coming out of the closet to the nation on ABC's *Primetime Thursday*. Her long-standing reputation as an adoptive mother and all-around friendly gal, makes it difficult for fundamentalists to convince people there is something evil or harmful about her desire to be a parent.

Many companies, including Apple Computer, Disney, and AOL Time Warner now offer health plans including benefits for same-sex partners of employees. But such companies have not managed these policies without censure. Disney faced a boycott from the Southern Baptist Convention when it added domestic partnership benefits to its health plan in 1995 and for a laundry list of other reasons. Most had to do with positive portrayals of gays and lesbians.[459] Although Disney stood its ground, it is likely that many smaller companies have been swayed from doing so because of the potential costs of fundamentalist actions.

In some states, despite fundamentalists' strong opposition, there is also a real possibility laws allowing gay marriage could pass. Unfortunately, as a pre-emptive strike, thirty states have passed laws defining marriage as a union between "one man and one woman." This is an evasion of the Full Faith and Credit clause of the U.S. Constitution.[460]

The religious right is fighting tooth and nail to prevent people from socially accepting homosexuality. So, there are bound to be more Matthew Shepards and a need for more Rosie O'Donnells. It can only be hoped it comes more easily and more quickly, than came acceptance of African-Americans or women as full citizens of this country. This is especially so, since even those battles are not yet decisively won.

The fundamentalist agenda and characteristics, however, do not support changes in public opinion. It is not surprising, then, fundamentalism fosters prejudice of many kinds. In more recent years, specific approaches to religiosity have been great indicators of prejudice. Religious rigidity, and even more so, authoritarianism, have the highest relation to prejudice.[461] The relationship between prejudice and fundamentalism echoes through all kinds of studies. Researchers James Forest and Linda Wylie of the University of Manitoba found a high correlation between fundamentalism and authoritarianism. It was also found that fundamentalism was a strong predictor of racism, homophobia, ethnocentrism, and punitiveness.[462]

A survey by Lee Kirkpatrick at the College of William and Mary found prejudice toward homosexuals, women, blacks, and communists was higher among Christian fundamentalists than orthodox Christians.[463] And a 1993 review of studies on the relationship between religion and prejudice by three sociologists[464] found that nineteen out of twenty-three studies published from 1960 and before showed that people who were more religious were also more inclined toward prejudice. Only one of the studies indicated religion alleviates prejudice, with three finding no relationship either way.[465]

Bruce Hunsberger, a Professor of Psychology at Wilfred Laurier University in Ontario, Canada, agrees that a large amount of research reveals religion is related to prejudice.[466] In his work with B. Altemayer,

Hunsberger defined fundamentalism for purposes of studying the relationship between the two as:

> the belief that there is one set of religious teachings that clearly contains the fundamental, basic, intrinsic, essential, inerrant truth about humanity and deity; that this essential truth is fundamentally opposed by forces of evil which must be vigorously fought; that this truth must be followed today according to the fundamental, unchangeable practices of the past; and that those who believe and follow these fundamental teachings have a special relationship with deity.[467]

Although this definition is more specific than the one presented in the introduction of this book, it does bring home the authoritarian nature of fundamentalist doctrine and shows how easily it fosters prejudice. As Hunsberger puts it, "both religious fundamentalism and authoritarianism encourage obedience to authority, conventionalism, self-righteousness, and feelings of superiority."[468] He points out that although the studies he reviewed have been consistent in relating religious fundamentalism to higher rates of prejudice, there is a need for more empirical studies. What seems to be lacking in most of the studies to date are various measures of religiosity.[469]

It is also important to note that the correlation between religious fundamentalism and prejudice does not necessarily mean fundamentalism is the cause of prejudice. Further study is needed to determine a causal relationship, although the possibility of such cannot easily be dismissed.[470] Hunsberger concludes that religion in and of itself may not cause prejudice. Instead it may be "the way in which religious beliefs are held," as in fundamentalism and right-wing authoritarianism, that creates the association.[471]

It is common in religious institutions where prejudice is taught as unacceptable that some religious individuals will indicate they are not prejudiced on surveys or questionnaires. [472] "Since they see themselves as religious persons," Hunsberger explained, "they will 'toe the party line.'" Yet, in cases where the church does not openly oppose specific prejudice, or even when covert measures are used, those same people, "will admit to their discriminatory attitudes, since such prejudice is not inconsistent with the teachings of their religious community."[473]

A popular contemporary study of the New Testament makes this tendency toward prejudice seem out of step with Christian doctrine. However, the tendency for fundamentalists to see the world in terms of indisputable absolutes does make prejudicial attitudes easier to adopt and keep. Furthermore, prejudice serves the role of simplifying the world, by making decisions easier and cutting down the amount of information needed to get through daily life. When struggling to adapt an explicit ancient moral code to modern society, any means of reducing complexity can be a welcome relief.

A number of scholars believe there are certain aspects of religion typically found in fundamentalists that possibly lead to prejudice and discrimination. These include belief in absolute truths,[474] teachings of out-groups' inferiority,[475] "stimulating nationalism,"[476] "encouraging authoritarianism, ethnocentrism, and in-group out-group stereotyping,"[477] the fostering of dogmatism and opinionation,[478] and "emphasizing the importance of submission to authority."[479]

Although even mainstream religions may incorporate some of these elements to a mild degree, fundamentalist faith is very dependent on most, if not all of the above characteristics. This makes its adherents far more susceptible to prejudicial ideas. Mark Nathan Cohen, Distinguished Teaching Professor at the State University of New York at Plattsburgh, explained, "Intolerance grows out of the need to find scapegoats." Because no system is perfect, yet culture requires an undying faith in its rules, people within the system seek out reasons for failures of the system. Blame must be placed somewhere outside the system to elevate or at least maintain faith in the culture. One of the most basic needs religion addresses is the need for explanation and understanding; blame is often an integral part of this.[480]

Fundamentalists target women, homosexuals, Jews, atheists, African Americans, and a host of other groups when confronted with imperfections within our culture. "Scapegoats," Cohen explained, "are safety valves for the cultural system against the pressure of disappointment." Leaders are especially likely to point blame at outsiders to avoid discontent among members. This also can "justify their own initiatives."[481]

Therefore, as America becomes more global and inclusive, conservative elements tend to be more insular and exclusive. Religion has always played a major role in defining groups. Cohen explained that intolerance and racism do not result from the visible and biological differences of a group, nor "cultural inadequacy." Rather, such feelings stem from misunderstanding and misinterpreting other groups when these populations live together.[482] Cohen says:

> We fail to recognize that most problems can be approached in more than one way. People on all sides are unable to recognize

what is arbitrary and conventional in their own behaviors and beliefs. Cultures not only blind their members to alternatives but also actively foster chauvinism and intolerance as a way of reinforcing group identity.[483]

Intolerance grows as leaders discourage any efforts for groups to intermingle[484] and come to terms with each other's differences, which ultimately stems from the leader self-interests. This is revealed in the practice at Bob Jones University and the Christian Coalition's Headquarters.

Legitimizing extremism

When extremist viewpoints are given validity by society at-large, it becomes difficult to determine what is taking things "too far." This may have the affect of making people think their beliefs can justify any number of antisocial actions, such as those stemming from prejudices. It may also make some people more susceptible to forming or recruitment into a more extreme sect or cult. To appreciate this likelihood and the effects, a basic understanding of the differences between churches, sects, and cults, and how religious groups change, is necessary.

Denominations, or churches, are to what mainstream Christians belong. Denominations are generally accepting of other religious beliefs and comfortable with society.[485] They generally favor an intellectual approach to religious teachings, while avoiding emotionalism in their services. Churches are attended more by the middle and upper classes, and members tend to participate from the sidelines by acting mainly as an audience.[486]

In contrast, sects are often to what Christian fundamentalists belong. Sects are deviant religious groups holding traditional beliefs. They claim to be the only true believers,[487] or true Christians, and satisfy the masses, or those who are low in the stratification system.[488] Sects stress "emotionalism and individual mystical experiences." Members actively participate in the religious experience, which offers them "a strong sense of community and solidarity."[489]

It must be pointed, however, that there is overlap, just as with many other issues pertaining to fundamentalism. So, whether fundamentalists are part of a sect or denomination is not always cut and dry. Many fundamentalists are also Southern Baptists, which is considered a conservative denomination rather than a sect. But the reason for this situation can be more readily understood by looking at the church-sect theory.

In an increasingly secular world, it is difficult to understand how and why there is, at the same time, a rapid growth in sects. The church-sect theory, derived from Ernst Troeltsch and developed by H. Richard Niebuhr, helps to explain this phenomenon.[490] As has been historically the case, sects and churches change over time. In his book *The Social Sources of Denominations* (1929), Niebhur said the growth of religious organizations leads to increased memberships in the middle and upper classes. Over time, these classes influence the organization to take a more worldly approach in which material success is no longer considered a punishable offense to God. In turn, the religious needs of the lower classes are no longer met. As discontent grows, the masses break off from the less-spiritual church to form a sect to satisfy their needs, as did the former organization, originally. The cycle then repeats itself.[491]

Similar discontent was observed in recent years in the Southern Baptist Convention, resulting in a major division. In this instance, a sect was not formed because the massive ultra-conservative membership of the SBC was able to maintain control over the denomination, forcing out the more liberal of its membership. Therefore, the needs of its conservative and fundamentalist adherents were able to be maintained by the denomination.

While sects are simply new organizations attempting to revive old religion, cults, on the other hand, are movements that either are altogether new or are different from traditional religious organizations. After many cycles of the church-sect process, a religious tradition loses its ability to satisfy a large segment of the population. Thus, secularization also gives rise to cults. The term "cults" has come to have negative connotations because of the tensions "between these movements and their social environment."[492]

All religions, including Christianity, begin as cults,[493] most of which are benign. In contrast to sects, cults emphasize converting individuals rather than attempting to change society.[494] Nevertheless, cults tend to assault the value of individuality and place heavy emphasis on group conformity from dress and lifestyle to thoughts and even sex patterns. Therefore, some can become very damaging to their members.[495]

Cult researchers Flo Conway and Jim Siegelman did a study in 1980 on cult rituals and their long-term effects. Out of forty-eight cult groups studied, more than thirty "had emerged out of fundamentalist or other branches of conservative Christianity." The long-term effects of these cult-like sects ranged from depression, suicide, and fear, to amnesia and hallucinations, to name just a few.[496] Furthermore, Conway and Siegelman found "these thirty Christian sects combined ranked higher than the most destructive cults . . . studied in terms of the trauma they inflicted upon their members."[497]

Typically, even among "more legalistic churches," members of Christian-based cult-like sects are taught that the Bible has all of the answers to life's questions. "Specific verses are invoked to address the most complex issues of human existence. The verses are then quoted whenever members are faced with uncertainty in their lives," explains Doni P. Whitsett, in "A Self Psychological Approach to the Cult Phenomenon," in *Clinical Social Work Journal*. "Thus, individual thinking and talking is replaced by 'group-think' and 'group-talk.'"[498]

According to Whitsett, it has been estimated that between:

> two to three million Americans have been involved in approximately 3,000 cults (West and Singer, 1980). The figure becomes astronomical when family members and friends who have been affected are considered. Additionally, numerous other people seen in clinical practice exhibit symptomatology and emotional states associated with cults.[499]

Regardless, little attention has been given to this widespread problem by the mental health field.[500]

There are several common characteristics of cults, points out sociologist Donald C. Swift. They generally have charismatic leaders, questionable recruitment practices, "fanatical loyalty and obedience," and surrender of assets and income to the leaders.[501]

Johan D. Van der Vyver, former Professor of Human Rights Law at the University of the Witwatersrand in Johannesburg, South Africa offers further explanation. Many cults and self-professed evangelists use religion as a ploy, he says. They "exploit the miseries of persons in need, through illness or poverty, in order to secure their subservience."[502] The television pleas of icons such as Billy Graham show fundamentalism bears relationship to cults in some of these characteristics as well. These televangelists exploit their viewers, whom the televangelists are most certainly aware, cannot afford the donations they are called on and easily persuaded to make.

The line between sects and cults certainly becomes blurred when looking at the International Churches of Christ formerly known as Church of Christ/Boston Movement or Church of Christ/Crossroads Movement. Some call it a fundamentalist church; those with personal experience call it a cult. While the Church of Christ's beliefs are not out of the ordinary for a fundamentalist group, its method of operation is very aggressive. New recruits are assigned a "discipler," an older member who mentors them[503] and makes sure that new recruits go to Bible studies, barbecues, and other events. New members are strongly discouraged from keeping ties with family members and friends who are not in the church. When operating on college campuses, members are often expected to live in the church co-op or with other church members. The entire organization is extremely insular, with the exception of their recruitment. Former members tell of sneaking out in the middle of the night, leaving all their personal possessions behind, to escape.[504]

Cult experts have found people in transitional phases or experiencing a life crisis are more susceptible to recruitment.[505] Therefore, college students are an appealing target. Another example of fundamentalist cult-like practices and their effects are described by Whitsett, in the case of a twenty-one year old referenced as "C." C grew up in a fundamentalist church that taught Biblical literalism and that all answers, regardless of the question, could be found in the Bible. As a result, "C. never learned to think for herself." C's mother always responded to C's questions in the same manner, resulting in the failed emotional connection needed for healthy development.[506] Moreover, the church group's "strong prohibitions against any sexual activity, against masturbation, against homosexuality . . . against anger" resulted in obsessive thoughts for C. This led her to perceive of herself as being "of the devil." Treatment for C., including psychotropic drugs, was ineffective in eliminating her obsessions and suicidal thoughts. Eventually, she became hospitalized.[507]

C's story is not unusual. Whitsett discovered "that a disproportionate number of young adults aged (19-21) within this church community had made serious suicide attempts and some had succeeded." In one case, the church was sued when parents learned that the church had discouraged their son, who was depressed, from seeking professional help. According to C., suicide was considered a "viable alternative" to those in the church who were unable to "live according to God's teachings. . . ."[508]

Other fundamentalist groups also use cult-like methods in recruiting or at least in maintaining their memberships. Kris, whose name has been changed to respect her anonymity, shared stories from one evangelical Lutheran church that her family had attended regularly in a small town in Michigan. Over time Kris observed what she increasingly found to be outlandish beliefs, and eventually, her family quit attending the services. Several months later they received a guilt-inducing letter that was riddled with threats of eternal punishment.

The letter admonished: "He [the rich man] was always too busy to hear God's Word. . . . How sad that his laxness in and towards 'the one thing needful' cost him an eternity of pain and suffering in hell." The missive continued:

> TODAY, while you still have time, the Lord calls you to sincere repentance—to do a U-turn, an about face, and to turn from your sin of worshiping created things and to come back to your Savior, His Word and Sacrament which alone can save your soul. . . . It's pretty foolish, pretty sad when anyone <u>for any reason</u> neglects their soul salvation. . . . but turn from your evil ways to Him who alone can forgive sins; . . . Otherwise, like the poor "rich(?)" man you too shall perish.

The letter, dated 1997, closes by threatening that if the couple does not "have a change of heart concerning this sin," their names will be brought before the church's Voter's assembly. The Board of Elders will then recommend that the couple "be put out of the communicant membership for living in the unrepentant sin of idolatry." It is signed, "Sent out of Christian love."

Fortunately, this couple was not brainwashed enough during their attendance to heed the churches call. In fact, because the church failed in its attempts to brainwash, it was the final straw in the couple deciding not to return. Nonetheless, it can only be assumed that some members would take such a letter wholeheartedly, hastening a return to the church for further inducement.

The effect fundamentalism has on legitimizing extremism undoubtedly helps cults and other radical movements in their efforts, by obscuring the line where religion becomes fanaticism. The emphasis fundamentalist sects place on the "End Times" may also ease the path of doomsday cults. The thirty-nine Heaven's Gate members who committed mass suicide in March of 1997 are a good example. So is the Branch Davidians, whose fifty-one day standoff with the U.S. Bureau of Alcohol, Tobacco and Firearms dominated the headlines of mid-1993.

The First Amendment's guarantee of religious freedom cannot and should not be curtailed simply because something is considered "extreme." Nevertheless, as with all rights, this right must go hand-in-hand with responsibility for actions affecting others.

Crime: morality and reality

Most Americans, Christian or otherwise, see fundamentalist philosophy as extreme. Still, it is difficult for many to perceive it as truly dangerous or criminal. This is especially so in light of the fact that the Christian Right attempts to endorse its beliefs and practices through proposed laws that it claims are necessary to reduce crime and violence in an anti-religious, immoral society. Christian fundamentalists commonly propose laws to reduce teen violence, drug use, child and spousal abuse, property crime, murder, and more. But contrary to Christian Right claims, the fundamentalist proposals often do nothing to alleviate such problems and may even aggravate criminal behavior. Yet, it is not simply their methods of dealing with social problems that make fundamentalists dangerous. Many fundamentalists are perpetrators of a wide variety of crimes and violent acts.

To begin, if fundamentalist activities were consistent with their goals, it would be expected that violent crime would be lower in areas with higher fundamentalist concentrations. But generally speaking, the opposite is the case. When reviewing available data, six of the states with the highest violent crime rates also fall into the highest bracket for fundamentalist believers. At the same time, seven of the states with the lowest fundamentalist church membership rest in the bottom third for crime rate.[509] Overall, violent crime is far more influenced by urbanization than by religion; New York, California, and Illinois contain the three largest cities in the nation, and all have relatively high crime rates. They occupy tenth, eleventh, and seventh places respectively, so urbanization is not a complete predictor of violent crime.

Although the U.S. "is the most religious of all industrialized nations" it has a murder rate five times that of Sweden, six times that of Britain, and seven times the murder rate of France. Japan, perhaps the most urbanized country of all, has the lowest violent crime rate of almost any country— and few Christians. In Louisiana, the churchgoing rate is the highest in the country, yet it has a murder rate greater than twice the national average.[510]

Even if there were a stronger correlation between religion and high crime rates, these figures would not necessarily mean fundamentalists cause crime. It is just as possible a high crime rate or a tendency toward criminal behavior makes people more likely to adopt fundamentalist beliefs. It is also possible that ineffective and even counterproductive laws, as typically proposed by the Christian Right, in areas with heavy concentrations of fundamentalists, contribute to the violent crime rate. What these patterns do show, however, is that if fundamentalist activity has any effect on the prevalence of violent crime, it is more likely to increase rather than reduce it.

One of the problems of fundamentalism in relation to crime is, as criminologists D. Stanley Eitzen and Doug A. Timmer in *Criminology: Crime and Criminal Justice* point out:

> contemporary conservatives like those conservatives before them who 'have successfully posed as the guardians of domestic tranquility for decades' typically promote social and economic policies 'that bear a large part of the responsibility for the level of crime and violence we suffer today.'[511]

This can easily be understood by looking at the effect legalized abortion has had on violent crime. John J. Donohue III, Professor of Law and Academic Associate Dean for Research at Stanford University, and Steven D. Levitt, economics professor at the University of Chicago, explained this. They found in their analysis of crime trends in various geographical areas that about half of the dramatic drop-off in crime rate during the 1990s can be logically attributed to the legalization of abortion in the 1970s.[512] The idea that fewer unwanted children and fewer unwilling mothers reduce the crime rate is not counterintuitive to most Americans. Yet, it is close to heresy to fundamentalist Christians. If their findings are correct, the success of fundamentalist efforts at reducing the availability of abortion could change the violent crime map a great deal in the future.

Fundamentalist attempts to make undesirable elements such as pornography, a scapegoat for violent crime, may be another reason fundamentalism has failed in making the world a safer place. Beyond just ignoring solid data to the contrary, groups opposing pornography may occasionally fabricate evidence in their favor. This was apparently the case with a supposed Michigan State Police study. This study, allegedly conducted in the 1980s, has been cited repeatedly by pornography opponents. Gael Parr, the acquisitions librarian for the J.V. Barry Library in Australia requested a copy of the report for its records.

Detective Sergeant David Minzey informed Parr, "the truth is that no such study was ever conducted." Then Minzey attempted to replicate the study using the department's extensive database on more than 75,000 sex offenses reported from 1955 to the present. But he was unable to support the original claim. No more than a weak correlation between pornography and sexual assault was found. This could have simply meant the perpetrators of sexual crimes have a stronger tendency to view pornography. Other factors, such as use of alcohol, showed a much stronger correlation to sex crimes.[513]

What have also been found to have a strong correlation to these crimes are beliefs and practices typical of fundamentalists. According to Dennis Coon in *Introduction to Psychology: Exploration and Application*, sex role socialization likely plays a role in the perpetuation of rape. Many people believe women should not display sexual interest, and men are taught to take the lead in sexual intimacy. Therefore, "even when the woman says no," rape is often the result.[514] Misogyny, hatred of women, is another cause of rape. Many rapists have been found to "harbor deep-seated resentment or outright hatred of women." Sexual intercourse, it is widely believed, is not typically the main goal of the rapist. Rather, it is a desire to humiliate, degrade, subordinate, and even injure a woman.[515]

Fundamentalists continue to oppose equality between the sexes and to reinforce sex roles. This makes rape for any reason more likely. In fact, the church's interpretation of the crucifixion and resurrection of Jesus Christ can play into rapists' hands. According to Christine E. Gudorf, Professor of Theology at Xavier University in Cincinnati, Christians often tell sexual violence victims "that it is good to suffer" and through such that they will "earn God's special favor."[516] Victims of sexual violence are often told by Christians the violation occurred out of God's will, they will soon forget the incident, and to just go on with life, or worse, to forgive an unrepentant offender.[517]

Holding such views may perpetuate rape as the perpetrators realize there will be no repercussion for their actions. They may even use these views to justify their violent acts. More telling, it has been reported that nearly thirty percent of all nuns have experienced "sexual trauma" from within the church, according to Catholic researchers. Southern Baptists have also found "14.1 percent of their clergy have sexually abused members."[518]

Other criminal behavior that has a strong relationship to fundamentalism has been discussed in other chapters. There is a high relationship between spousal abuse and fundamentalist views on a woman's role. It has also been found that child abuse is more typical in fundamentalist homes where parents adhere to a "spare the rod, spoil the child" mentality, as discussed in chapter 3. Studies have found incest rates to be higher among fundamentalist fathers. As has been seen for years, in a report by Reverend Tom Economus, it is estimated between 6.1 percent and 16.3 percent of priests are pedophiles.[519]

Exhibitionism, a prevalent form of sexual deviancy, also appears to be related to fundamentalism. Common characteristics of exhibitionists are that they are male, married, and "most come from strict and repressive backgrounds."[520] Such backgrounds are commonly found in fundamentalist households.

There also seems to be a possible link between fundamentalism, or the fundamentalist religious upbringing, and mass murder or serial killing. This trend was found by Paul O'Brien during 1980 and 1981. He conducted a study spurred after his friend, a schoolteacher, murdered the man's own family. According to O'Brien, the teacher became very religious and started carrying a Bible. Less than a year later, the teacher murdered his own wife and three children. On a tape that he made before his death in the Arizona gas chambers, the inmate remarked, "My wife and children are now in heaven. I'm happy to join them now."[521]

In an attempt to understand his friend's shocking action, O'Brien clipped every article pertaining to mass murder or serial killing appearing in the *Flint Journal* for an eighteen-month period. Out of twelve mass murderers and serial killers, O'Brien found the common link among eleven was either a very religious upbringing or belief in demons and devils. "Most carried a Christian Bible with them at all times,"[522] says O'Brien.

Some of the stories O'Brien studied included Sampson Kanderayi, a Christian known as the Ax Killer. He murdered more than thirty people "to appease evil spirits." Another man by the name of Douglas went on a search to find a woman home alone. When one was found, he stabbed her to death. Douglas, reportedly, was a frequent Bible reader and believed he had received a message from God to do the killing.[523]

The teenager David Kellers murdered his parents with a shotgun, according to the *Flint Journal*. Says O'Brien, "David's whole life revolved around church and religion."[524] Patricia Dueweke dropped her three children off a hotel balcony. She had extensive religious training and had gone to a Catholic convent to be a nun.[525] Curtis Martin took his three children to a factory and put them in a steel melting pot. He turned it on and walked out reading the Bible aloud as his children "turned into charred ash."[526]

It should be noted that there has been much controversy surrounding criminal profiling, and it has not been found overly effective in catching criminals. Nonetheless, the religious commonality found in so many mass and serial killings cannot be denied. An abusive and repressive upbringing may not be a direct or sole cause for violent behavior, since many abused children do not grow up to commit murder. Still, such an upbringing does appear to play at least some role.

According to the article, "What Makes Serial Killers Tick?"

Some parents believed that by being harsh disciplinarians, it would "toughen" the child. Instead, it often creates a lack of love between parent and child that can have disastrous results. If the child doesn't bond with its primary caretakers, there is no foundation for trusting others later in life. This can lead to isolation, where intense violent fantasies become the primary source of gratification.[527]

This parenting style is common in fundamentalist homes where parents are often authoritarian and punitive in nature. They see their child's immature or unruly behavior as inherently evil and in need of being broken.

A 1995 study by David Lester, a world-renowned authority on murder, as well as a 1992 study by M.H. Medoff and I. Lee Skov, "found that fundamentalism has not been successful in reducing murder." Moreover, these criminologists concluded that fundamentalism may be a cause of murder, because of the oppressiveness of fundamentalists' strict moral code. They believe that fundamentalists "may be unable to conform . . . and suffer emotionally and spiritually with adverse consequences."[528] It has also been concluded, write Michael Franklin and Marian Hetherly, that "'evil imagination'—which includes diverse forms of hostility, hatred, and violence—is a response to the anxiety and fear associated with powerlessness, and absolute dependence on faith."[529]

Also telling of religion's failure to prevent crime is an increasingly familiar pattern. This is recorded in the Annual Statistical Table on Global Mission, compiled by research Professor of Missiometrics David B. Barrett at Regent University. Ecclesiastical-related crime, or crime in religious institutions, has grown from $300,000 annually a century ago to $3 billion by 1990. It is estimated the year 2024 will bring $65 billion in ecclesiastical crime.[530]

Whether or not such crimes are committed mostly by fundamentalist ministers, it contradicts fundamentalist beliefs and their insistence that religion is a deterrent to crime. One example is of Robert R. Courtney, a deacon in an Assemblies of God church where his father had formerly ministered. Courtney was accused of diluting over a hundred doses of chemotherapy drugs to help pay off his $600,000 federal income tax bill and his $330,000 pledge to the church in which he was raised.[531] Courtney's father, now retired from the ministry, had been working as Courtney's bookkeeper during the time of this fraud. He describes Courtney as, "an ideal son in every sense of the word." Courtney was jailed without bond, charged with at least twenty counts of felony drug tampering.[532]

In 1991 an illuminating study was reported. According to a Roper survey, born-again Christians deteriorated in their behavior following conversion. Respondents had gone from only four percent driving while intoxicated before conversion to twelve percent doing so afterward. Illegal drugs were used by only five percent beforehand, but after being born-again, the number rose to nine percent. And illicit sex increased from two percent before conversion to five percent following.[533]

For the reasons just discussed, the Christian Right's pursuit to post the Ten Commandments in courtrooms and public schools to alleviate crime and create a more moral society meets serious objections. Martin E. Marty of the Fundamentalism Project and the Fairfax M. Cone Distinguished Service Professor of the History of Modern Christianity at the University of Chicago makes a more needed suggestion. He says, instead, maybe the Commandments should to be hung in church sanctuaries.[534]

Militancy to terrorism: morality goes to war

Contrary to what much of mainstream society may believe, fundamentalism is not receding. In some sects it is becoming increasingly militant, according to Karen Armstrong who teaches for the Study of Judaism at Leo Baeck College. She is one of the foremost commentators on religious affairs in the United States and Great Britain.[535]

Most fundamentalists do not want violence. Still, there is a problem with the fundamentalist relationship to it. This is because, according to Charles B. Strozier, the more extreme tend to take on the responsibility of punishing sinners.[536] And while fundamentalists seem to have a "half-wish" for destruction, they are generally quick to back off once they have expressed the desire.[537]

But beyond the types of violent crimes already discussed, some fundamentalists are known for their terrorist acts and violence. Reverend Lester and others are looking forward to "nuclear war to hasten the return of Jesus." He has confided, "I'm kinda looking forward to all this stuff [nuclear destruction], to the whole thing because once the rapture takes place the church is glorified."[538] While only a small fraction of fundamentalists is so extreme, the number holding such attitudes is undoubtedly significant. When fundamentalists turn to militancy, and even violence, they risk the support of many adherents or potential supporters of the movement. Still, there are those who are willing "to suspend the ethical norms of the religious tradition for the sake of the religious tradition."[539]

Fundamentalists can be overtaken by ideology and politics. This makes it difficult, if not impossible, to draw obvious lines between different forms of fundamentalism. Separatists, or those who practice separation from society, can easily become political activists[540] or even gun-toting militants.

While not strictly a Christian fundamentalist practice, the militia movements developing in every state around the country have a strong relationship to Christian fundamentalism. It is estimated that 400 militia-type groups are in the U.S., most of which are Christian based. Christian Identity followers are at the forefront of the militia movement, numbering in the area of 40,000.[541] However, there are many other Christian militia groups, as well as Christian movements with connections to militias.

Behind the militia movement is the view, like that held by Christian Identity followers, that there is a conspiracy regarding a New World Order and it is the intent of the United Nations to take over the world. This theory is not owned by Identity proponents alone. Pat Robertson sold 500,000 copies of his book *The New World Order* in 1991. It introduced "mainstream evangelical and Pentecostal Christians" to these extreme ideas.[542] There is also the fundamentalist "idea that certain Americans have a greater claim on the country's traditions and rights than others." This is attractive during times "of uncertainty, when people fear that 'our' society is under attack."[543]

Following the collapse of the Soviet Union, militias and the Christian Right expanded, Kenneth Stern wrote in *A Force Upon the Plain: The American Militia Movement and the Politics of Hate*. He explained:

> Our old, comfortable 'evil empire' upon which we could project our worst fears, no longer exists. For those who believe in Christian supremacy and those who believe in white supremacy, the enemy has become internal: the United States government. This shared new enemy has helped create ideological images which empowers both the Religious Right and the far right.[544]

The Christian militia movement justifies its warmongering the same way fundamentalists justify all of their beliefs, by referring to the Bible. *The Field Manual of the Free Militia* attempts to prove the inerrancy of the Bible. It is then used to support the militia's claim that Christians have not only been authorized by Jesus to arm themselves, but that arming themselves is a Christian's duty.[545]

In his article, "What Does the Bible Say About Gun Control?" Christian Reconstructionist and Executive Director of Gun Owners of

America, Larry Pratt, made this clear. He argued: "Both the Old and New Testaments teach individual self-defense, even if it means taking the assailant's life in certain circumstances."[546] Interestingly, Pratt was formerly an aide to Pat Buchanan. But Pratt's views on gun control go beyond simply a need or desire for self-defense. He declared:

> In Matthew: 15 (and in Mark" 7), Christ accused the religious leaders of the day of also opposing the execution of those deserving of death—rebellious teenagers. They had replaced the commandments of God with their own traditions. God has never been interested in controlling the means of violence. He has always made it a point to punish and, where possible, restore (as with restitution and excommunication) the wrongdoer. Control of individuals is to be left to self-government. Punishment of individuals by the civil government is to be carried out when self-government breaks down.[547]

Apparently, what Pratt promotes is the self-government that Christian Reconstructionists desire. With this, incorrigible children are punished by death at the hands of the "self-government" who determine, at will, what constitutes "rebelliousness."

Moreover, Pratt complains: "Man's wisdom today has been to declare gun-free school zones, which are invaded by gun-toting teenage terrorists whom we refuse to execute. We seem to have learned little from Christ's rebuke of the Pharisees."[548] Does Pratt propose then that school zones should not be declared gun-free? More telling of the lack of concern extreme fundamentalists have for the welfare of children, Pratt concludes: "Surely in protecting against accidents we cannot end up making ourselves more vulnerable to criminal attack, which is what a trigger lock does if it is in use on the firearm intended for self-protection."[549]

The magnitude of the problem of Christian militancy is visible in many ways. United Patriot Radio (UPR) is an illegal (unlicensed) station run by militiaman and Christian Identity follower Steve Anderson, out of Tennessee. It broadcasts militia-related news and advocates "resistance to further encroachment by the Federal government on the lives of America's citizenry." UPR is "on the air more than twelve hours at a time." During Anderson's personal program, "The Militia Hour," he "advocates a Christian-only philosophy of what America should be." At the same time, he denounces those of minority religions and preaches that those who do not wish to convert to his brand of Christianity should leave the country.[550]

Troublingly, some Christian fundamentalist summer camps for children seem fronted to look like weeklong recreational outings. Yet, upon close examination, they have a strong military-style bent. One such camp is Camp Peniel in Marble Falls, Texas. Like many summer camps, it offers a wide variety of fun activities from volleyball and softball, to arts and crafts. There is no doubt children attending the camp have a blast. But, it chillingly has the semblance of a youth military training ground, though it may not be the camp founders' and directors' intent.

At the camp, boys become "braves," typically meaning "warriors," in its Tehas Indian Tribe; girls take on the label of property by becoming "Kings' Daughters."[551] Referring to the children, Camp Peniel asserts, "Jesus took the disciples away from their homes."[552] Contrary to what most parents would hope from a summer camp, Camp Peniel claims that from the experience, along with bonds of trust that develop, so does "dependence," rather than independence.[553]

Military jargon abounds, as the day's agenda begins with a "reveille." This is defined in the dictionary as a bugle call to signal the first military formation of the day. Twice daily, children go to a "canteen" for refreshments. In addition, they enjoy a suppertime "retreat"[554] following their afternoon of vigorous activity. Camp activities include skeet shooting, archery, survival, and riflery.[555] There are other "Scary activities, like rappelling down a cliff, tubing behind a speed boat, dropping from a swing into a cold river, [that is] tried—and mastered."[556] There is also rock climbing, canoeing, and white-water rafting.[557] The site's picture gallery sports snapshots of Christian campers following what was apparently a mudding adventure, with their bodies, hair, and faces plastered and painted in mud,[558] resembling camouflage.

The intent of the military focus could be innocent enough. But the strong emphasis on such and the glorification of it likely creates a comfort zone and appeal for the military lifestyle. This, combined with other characteristics of fundamentalism, may ultimately induce fundamentalists into militia-style Christian groups.

One of the biggest problems related to militant Christian fundamentalists is that many believe they are above the law. The Supreme Court has upheld a ban on demonstrations within fifteen feet of abortion clinics. However, according to a 1997 report in *Christianity Today*, President of Operation Rescue Flip Benham insisted, "It has no effect, because the Supreme Court is not supreme."[559] Operation Rescue is known for its ties to militia groups, and the lines between anti-choice organizations and militia movements have become increasingly blurred.[560]

Reverend Matthew Trewhella, leader of Missionaries to the Preborn spoke at the Wisconsin convention of the U.S. Taxpayers Party in 1994.[561] He urged, "churches can form militia days and teach their men to fight." Classes were also held in Trewhella's own church on "the use of firearms."[562] On the video of his speech released by Planned Parenthood Federation of America, he was captured recommending that parents buy "each of your children an SKS rifle and 500 rounds of ammunition."[563]

The Aryan Nations, or the Church of Jesus Christ Christian, is a white racist militia movement with heavily-armed compounds in Utah and Pennsylvania. It "has been linked to at least several dozen murders since 1980."[564] And Christian Identity leader David Lane was "convicted of racketeering, conspiracy and violating the civil rights of a slain Jewish talk-show host," writes Don Lattin. Lane explained "his racist 'end times' prophecies" from a jailhouse.[565] "I am the symbol that is going to stop the Judeo-American murder of the white race," bragged Lane. "Killing is always justified for the preservation of your kind."[566]

Examples of the potential for violence can be found in the 1993 Branch Davidian standoff with authorities. David Koresh and more than seventy followers finally accepted their fate of going out in "a blazing inferno." At the Waco, Texas compound, Koresh stockpiled arms and weapons, while teaching his Adventist theology.[567] Moreover, Oklahoma City bombers, Timothy McVeigh and Terry Nichols had inspiration from a Texas militia movement. It had ties to extremist Christian groups, including the Christian Identity sect.[568]

One way fundamentalists find it so easy to use violence is with the view, "We cannot value ourselves and degrade and ultimately kill the other unless we call God onto our side in the struggle."[569] H. Newton Maloney, Senior Professor of Psychology at Fuller Theological Seminary, explains similarly. Many fundamentalists believe literally in the devil and demonize others, and by doing so, violence is more likely to occur.[570] To the fundamentalist, explained Strozier, "Those who refuse Jesus are not only dumb, but also different, dangerous, and possibly contagious . . . Such thinking can lend itself to potentially dangerous stereotyping." Because the fundamentalist sees the nonbeliever as only "tentatively human," nonbelievers are viewed as dispensable.[571]

Interestingly, nonbelievers to fundamentalists are not only atheists and adherents of other religious beliefs. They are also liberal and mainstream Christians who do not accept the dogma of Christian fundamentalism. For fundamentalists who were not born into such views, there may be a tendency to pity and sympathize with the nonbeliever. He or she may be a reflection of the fundamentalist before salvation. Even this, however, can have a reverse effect. The reformist can often turn on the unreformed, who symbolizes the abandoned enemy of the self.[572]

Many in the Christian militia movements are Reconstructionists, the movement founded by Texas economist Gary North and Rousas John Rushdoony. Reconstructionists' envision a totalitarian society based on literal interpretation of the Bible. Their goals include the reintroduction of slavery, elimination of birth control, and a non-intervenable capitalist society.[573] Karen Armstrong admits it is highly unlikely for such a movement to gain enough popularity in the United States; however, she says it is not wholly impossible in an emergency state such as an economic or environmental catastrophe. "Christianity, after all, was able to adapt to capitalism, which was alien to many of the teachings of Jesus," Armstrong reminds. "It could also be used to back a fascist ideology that, in drastically changed circumstances, might be necessary to maintain public order."[574]

Reverend Norman E. Olson, a Baptist and the commander of the Northern Michigan Regional Militia has expressed a desire to form a national militia for purposes of creating an alliance between all of them.[575] This desire should not be dismissed. According to the United Nations, during the brief period of 1989 to 1992, seventy-nine of the world's eighty-two armed conflicts were within, rather than between countries. These were a result of religious zealots, "destroying the opportunity of millions worldwide to receive family planning, birth control, and legal abortion services."[576] It is difficult to fathom and even improbable for such to take place on American soil. But it is by no means an impossibility.

You are here: theories on social development

In discussing a segment of the population claiming to have the market on morality, it seems inevitable that the development of moral and social behavior come to be understood. Lawrence Kohlberg, a Harvard University professor until his death in 1987, was the author of a landmark work on moral development. He isolated six discrete stages of individual moral maturity, which he divided into three main groups. The pre-conventional level is observed mostly in early childhood; the conventional level is what most of society subscribes to; and the post-conventional is a level most adults never achieve.

The first two stages, under the pre-conventional level, are known as "Punishment orientation" and "Pleasure-seeking orientation." They are commonly recognized on the school playground. This is behavior reinforced by authority figures, which threatens reprisal for misbehavior or promises rewards for good behavior.[577]

The next two stages, under the conventional level are referred to as "Good girl/ boy orientation" and "Authority orientation." These are based on the desire to please others, gain approval, and to uphold the law and higher authority.[578] Interestingly enough, religious morality holds to these most rudimentary stages of morality. This is because it is based on absolute pronouncements from God, the promise of heaven, and the threat of hell.

The third level, post-conventional, includes the "Social-contract orientation" and the "Morality of individual principles" stages. Under this level of morality, decisions are controlled internally going beyond self-interest and laws. Laws, although a necessity, are believed at this stage to be based on rational thought and "mutual agreement." The welfare of the community is of concern at this higher level. And moral decisions are based on "justice, dignity, and equality."[579] This final and highest level of morality is in direct conflict with Christian fundamentalism. For fundamentalists, everything is viewed in black and white terms, as subject to the authority of God or a society's laws. And these laws, they believe, should be based on conservative Christian doctrines.

In the early 1900s, Emile Durkheim laid a foundation for modern sociological theory. This can be viewed as the moral development of society, in contrast to individual moral development. In his essays in "The Division of Labor and Society" and "On Morality and Society," he described two stages of sociological development. They are characterized by their form of solidarity, in other words, a union of community interests and responsibilities.

The first is a period of "mechanical solidarity" and the second, a period of individualism. The "mechanical" society's connection is based on features that people share. It is rooted in common ritual and routine. Religion is a strong basis of mechanical solidarity, as it reinforces the common code and societal expectations.[580] As time goes on, however, societal structures become more complex and require people to play different roles. Organic solidarity develops out of the need for division of labor and fosters a growing sense of individualism. It relies mainly on the interdependence between people to reinforce social connections. As with organs in a body, each person may do something very different from another. But without the others, an individual could not survive. Reality television shows are a nightly reminder of just how far people have come from a time when survival was something they had to do on their own.

The transition from mechanical to organic solidarity is not easy. Writing at the dawn of the twentieth century, Durkheim discussed the moral crisis that had arrived with industrialization in terms people still find very familiar a century later. He named this crisis of moral confusion anomy. It originates from a Greek term literally meaning lawlessness. He warned, however, "the remedy for the evil is not to seek to resuscitate traditions and practices. These no longer respond to present conditions of society, so they can only live an artificial, false existence."[581] Instead, a new morality is needed to cope with the new demands of society.[582]

David Riesman similarly described societal evolution as occurring in stages. His work, more recent than Durkheim's, goes on to discuss a third stage. There are definite similarities between Riesman's first two stages and Durkheim's mechanical and organic solidarity. But Riesman had a different emphasis. He defined stages of development in terms of where people find moral direction.

In the initial "tradition-directed" stage, the society has high growth potential due to a high birth rate outpacing a high death rate. Tradition-directed societies are based on ideological uniformity. They are "ruled by fear of shame."[583] The tradition-directed society gradually reduces the death rate through scientific advancements. Without moving to an "inner-directed" transitional growth model, it will face severe population pressures.[584] Unless the birth rate is reduced to match the declining death rate, excessive population will be addressed by mass deaths, such as through famine, warfare, or ritual sacrifice.[585]

Riesman described the next two stages also in terms of population growth. Inner-directed societies are in a transitional growth stage, where a falling death rate is followed by a falling birth rate. The inner-directed society is marked by nuclear parenting and centralized schooling as well as being ruled by inner morality. This is possible because of parenting practices conducive to such moral development that can be used in a complex society.[586] As a society becomes more other-directed, it sees growth begin to decline. Constant movement of groups leads to individual adaptability. Peer pressure and media control the other-directed society.[587]

The society of the Biblical era, which fundamentalists are trying hard to resurrect, falls squarely into the tradition-directed category. The Old Testament requests, "Be fruitful and multiply,"[588] "Servants be obedient to them that are your masters," and "Wives be in subjection to your own husbands." Fundamentalism's disdain for diversity fits well with the tradition-directed society's need for like beliefs. Here, shame is the measure used to gain conformity.

As hinted by its name, tradition-directed society functions according to an explicit and relatively inflexible moral code. This is seen in the Biblical code fundamentalists would like to force all of society to follow. As with Durkheim's mechanical solidarity, this rigid code works when there are only a few situations possible. People must generally carry the same role in society when they are at home, at work, at church, or at play, for the code to function.

Inner-directed society begins to emerge when people's roles become more situational. It looks for moral guidance from an internal "moral gyroscope." This guides a person through a variety of situations with a more flexible set of general rules. In today's world, people can be fired from their jobs for saying things that are normal in a less formal situation, such as with family or friends. They might also end up divorced if they treat their spouses exactly as they treat their employees. Therefore, a flexible moral code is needed for social survival.

So, what does fundamentalism mean for Durkheim's and Reisman's descriptions of social development and Kohlberg's moral development? Perhaps the best way to illustrate the clash between where we are and where fundamentalists want to take us is to examine the Ten Commandments. The 1980 Supreme Court decision *Stone v. Graham* settled the debate over this relic by ruling that the display in courthouses and public schools was unconstitutional.[589] In the wake of the 1999 Columbine High School shooting there was, again, a strong movement to post the Commandments in public buildings across the nation, especially public schools.

Leading the charge was Judge Roy Moore of Alabama. He was challenged in 1995, over his own posting of the Ten Commandments in the courtroom.[590] His battle picked up speed when conservative Americans suggested that posting the Commandments in schools might have averted tragedies such as the shooting in Littleton, Colorado. This proposal, says the ACLU, "represents the worst possible thinking."[591] In spite of this flawed logic, sales of Ten Commandments merchandise increased dramatically. For one business, the Lighthouse Christian Bookstore in Pikeville, Kentucky, sales for these items increased by more than 400 percent between 1998 and 1999.[592]

Because fundamentalists take the Bible literally, they firmly believe these commandments are both necessary and sufficient to regulate society. For a pre-industrial tribal society, fundamentalists may be right. But there are many risks to imposing outdated rules on modern America. First of all, the first five commandments have little relevance to creating a moral society. The first four deal with establishing a new, monotheistic religion, that is, a doctrine that accepts there is only one God. "Thou shalt have no other gods before me" and "Thou shalt not make any graven image" establish there is no room for other deities.

Rule three makes sacred any words that refer to the Judeo-Christian God in the command, "Thou shalt not take the name of the Lord thy God in vain." The fourth sets up the Sabbath. And the fifth commandment requires adherents "Honor thy father and thy mother: that thy days may be long upon the land which the Lord thy God giveth thee."[593] This commandment may have some value. But without a companion piece for parents to treat their children in a manner deserving of a child's respect, it is inefficient and even dangerous.

Commandment six, "Thou shalt not kill,"[594] is one upon which everyone can agree. A secular American law, however, has remained intact without the need for the religious order of it. This "common-sense" mandate originated at a time when people actually did need to be told killing was wrong. By the twenty-first century, contemporary society recognizes that killing other humans is generally wrong. It is also developing definitions of when it is necessary to break this rule such as in war or self-defense. Broad theological prohibitions only hamper the development of suitable exceptions, while offering anti-abortionists justification for their cause.

Ironically, the death penalty, most favored by fundamentalists, is employed to punish people for breaking the same commandment. Fundamentalists lead the fight against euthanasia, because this injunction prohibits the causing of death. Yet, today our lives span entire centuries without any specific prohibition against prolonging suffering. The American life expectancy has more than doubled in the last century;[595] as our lives change, so do our needs. Therefore, the generalized language of this commandment fails to even accomplish the initial task of defining proscribed behavior. This leads to increased confusion, rather than resolution and accord.

According to the seventh commandment, "Thou shalt not commit adultery."[596] Marriage is one of the three cultural universals;[597] that is, every known culture defines marriage in one way or another, though definitions of marriage vary widely over time and location. The Old Testament defines marriage and adultery for a new religion, and our current law regarding marriage mirrors this definition in many basic respects, including the definition of adultery.

The exception is that the Old Testament laws pertaining to adultery did not pertain to men, but rather women, except for men who had affairs with married women. Today, thirty-seven states and the District of Columbia recognize adultery as at least a misdemeanor. Several states still consider it a felony. It is also grounds for divorce in all states allowing fault-based divorce.[598] When considering what social rules should govern marriage, recognizing changes in life span and lifestyles is necessary.

While people marry much later and divorce more often than a century ago, the average amount of time-spent married has changed very little.

Many alarmist publications from fundamentalist organizations misuse facts. They claim the average American marriage lasts only six or seven years, neglecting to mention this includes only marriages ending in divorce. On average, Americans spend twenty-six years married during their lifetime, and only sixteen percent have been married two or more times.[599] Marriages ending in the death of a spouse last on average forty-three years today, compared with only twenty-eight years at the dawn of the twentieth century.[600] Given that the circumstances surrounding marriage have changed so dramatically, our standards must be revised. Today, adultery has lost its dominant position as a threat to the institution of marriage and domestic harmony. It is replaced by spousal and child abuse.[601] Therefore, a more appropriate commandment would be "Thou shalt not beat thy child or wife."

"Thou shalt not steal"[602] is the succinct eighth commandment. This is firmly on "common sense" ground. From petty theft to grand larceny, stealing is the subject of a huge proportion of criminal law. Today, the Golden Rule can easily cover theft. Therefore, this commandment, while not actually counterproductive, serves no explicit purpose in defining morality and law. Our society universally recognizes the desirability and practicality of ownership.

Commandment nine is, essentially, an injunction against lying: "Thou shalt not bear false witness against thy neighbor."[603] However, as sweeping and broad as most of the commandments are, the restriction "against thy neighbor" sets this one apart. There are a number of interpretations of the "neighbor" clause. Critics of Biblical ethics interpret it most literally to mean it is perfectly all right to lie about any number of things, including total strangers. But it is only a violation to be disloyal and untrue about those of your community or tribe.

David R. Weissbard of the Unitarian Universalist Church shed a bit more light on the subject. He pointed out that at the time of writing this commandment, it meshed very well with Hammurabi's Code of Laws and was specifically about respecting the brand-new judicial process.[604] He said, "While [behavior in legal judgments] was apparently critically important at the time, people's behavior in a court is hardly among the greatest moral issues of our time." Hammurabi may deserve credit for his invention of a justice system. But today's trial law is significantly more advanced and includes penalties for perjury and other abuses of the system.

The final component of the commands is perhaps the most telling when considering the era of this rule set: "Thou shalt not covet thy neighbour's house, thou shalt not covet thy neighbour's wife, nor his manservant, nor his maidservant, nor his ox, nor his ass, nor any thing that is thy neighbour's."[605] Like bearing false witness, restricting covetousness could be a useful injunction in our current society, if it did not as a piece include the definition of what is owned. Our laws against owning people are seventy years younger than the U.S. Constitution. They were the breaking point in our only Civil War. There may be value in denouncing covetousness in today's competitive social arena. Yet, the reference to a wife or servants as the property of another person is completely inappropriate for our contemporary moral code. It can serve as a justification to those who would undermine the civil liberties of vulnerable groups.

Three thousand years ago, this top-ten list of moral pronouncements functioned as a foundation of a new faith. It established revolutionary social agreements taken for granted today. As American society has developed, older moral predicaments have been resolved only to see them replaced by brand-new complications. As a documentation of our moral and legal heritage, the commandments may have value. Still, as a comprehensive guiding principle, they fall far short of addressing our needs.

Given the extreme stress placed on society by the clash between fundamentalist and mainstream ideals, it is clear our nation is not anytime soon going to give in to the pressure and adopt Biblical law as our main code of ethics. In spite of this, religious conservatives continue to exert influence on nearly every facet of our lives. This results in often undesirable and, occasionally, disastrous, consequences.

To apply a single explicit moral code, our social environment would have to dramatically simplify in ways none of us are prepared to cope with. It is simply not possible to remove the effects of progress that are changing the world without also removing progress itself. The fundamentalist vision of returning to a high-growth potential, traditionalist, mechanically solid society is, therefore, an unfeasible dream. To do so, Americans would have to give up medical advances that increase lifespan, as well as much industry and technology that depends on highly specialized roles.

It is not possible to accomplish fundamentalists' goals without setting back the technological clock at least a few hundred years. Yet, fundamentalists are actively working against social progress. In so doing, they increase the difficulty of developing a new moral code to regulate an other-directed society. They even ask that the inner-directed morality Americans have depended on for more than a century be dismissed. At the same time, by showing admiration for fundamentalist faithfulness to the

Scripture, mainstream Christianity is in a position to unwittingly foster this moral dilemma. Most churches and adherents inwardly reject many of the "fundamentals" that most conservative movements are based on. But they are usually hesitant to explicitly denounce all but the most obviously harmful social policies.

The effects of fundamentalism ripple through the entire population as poverty, crime, and general unhappiness permeate society. Unwanted children raised by their birth parents often face serious abuse and neglect and are ultimately responsible for high crime rates. Those waiting for adoption have few chances of securing a loving home. Even children resulting from unplanned pregnancies who are not mistreated or neglected by their birth parents often live in poverty. This in itself has negative consequences on the child's physical and emotional health and intellectual development. Thus, it leads to a bleak outlook for escaping poverty later in life.

Those most targeted by the religious right, such as gays and lesbians, find their basic rights violated and even legislated out of existence. This is because of the inherent evil placed on homosexuality by fundamentalism. African-Americans and other races continue to face many less noticeable discriminatory practices that persist. And both groups suffer from hate crimes.

Others, especially as they enter adulthood, are at risk for recruitment into emotionally-damaging, even traumatic, sects or cults. All Americans are at increased risk for victimization from a wide variety of crimes that result from ineffective and counterproductive laws. Fundamentalists' repressive beliefs may also have a role in mental illness. This plays out in the form of mass murder, serial killing, and other violent crimes. Finally, there is the strong potential for acts of terrorism and armed conflict resulting from fundamentalists' glorification of war and the growth of their military complexes and weapons arsenals.

Many lessons have been learned in the turbulent history of the world and even America. It is hoped they are sufficient to prevent the fundamentalist agenda from gaining further strength in its attempt to do away with America's diversity—and to reverse what damage has already been done.

CHAPTER 6

THE PATH TO THEOCRACY
THE PURGATION
OF THE FIRST AMENDMENT

by John M. Suarez, M.D.

The "wall of separation between church and state" is a metaphor based on bad history, a metaphor that has proved useless as a guide to judging. It should be frankly and explicitly abandoned.[606]

Justice William H. Rehnquist (1985)

> Congress shall make no law respecting an establishment of religion, or prohibiting the free exercise thereof; or abridging the freedom of speech or of the press, or of the right of the people peaceably to assemble, and to petition the government for a redress of grievances.[607]

The first sixteen words of the First Amendment, ordinary and commonplace, address the relationship between government and religion. This would be a seemingly hopeless task for even hundreds, nay, thousands, of words. Yet, the last two centuries have revealed the sociopolitical experiment, embodied in those bitterly hammered out and ultimately well-chosen words, has been nothing short of unique and revolutionary. Nonetheless, so few words cannot anticipate or cope with the inevitable complex situations that will arise. And so, different interpretations have blossomed and will continue to do so indefinitely.

True "separationists," those favoring separation of church and state, in contrast to "accommodationists," find themselves frequently fighting uphill. Separationists rely on the recorded deliberations and decisions of the Founding Fathers and subsequent clarifications from the United States Supreme Court, when available. Such efforts are necessary to convince the rest of Americans as to the essence of the concept and the wisdom of keeping government and religion separate.

Most wars, conquests, and bloodsheds throughout human history have featured a strong religious element. This has not relented into the present. The twentieth century saw religion-fueled carnage in Northern Ireland, the Middle East, the Balkans, and many regions in Asia and Africa. Religiously-fueled and maintained wars are incredibly savage. But besides this, the most common element of such wars has been the inability to resolve the conflict and allow the populations involved to exist in reasonable harmony and mutual acceptance. This is so, despite ongoing efforts from seasoned negotiators.

The opening of the twenty-first century has been just as foreboding. The unimaginable, well-orchestrated events of September 11, 2001, have plunged the world into an apparent confrontation. It is between Islam, a religious tradition that has evolved very differently from Christianity, and what is often referred to as the "Modern World." Here too, the efforts of religious scholars and well-meaning peace promoters have thus far been impotent in dampening the fires of religious passion and misunderstanding.

It is against such a background that the wisdom and power of the First Amendment can best be appreciated. This basic concept of the Founding Fathers has occasionally been clarified and amplified by the courts. But it has single-handedly kept our society over the past 200 years from plunging into the bottomless pit of religious war. This has been far from easy, not surprisingly. Our society serves as home to the world's largest number of religions, large and small, well recognized and hardly known.

Some sociologists have even credited the First Amendment with the fact the United States is a more religious country than any of its western counterparts. In many countries, there exist various levels of government subsidization of religion. The combined enlightenment of the Free Exercise and Establishment Clauses, they contend, has been a better stimulus to religious activity than tax revenues. Given all of the above, it is a remarkable success story by any political standard. So, why is there discontent, and what is causing the attempts to revise or totally dismantle the First Amendment?

The dissatisfaction stems directly from the success of the First Amendment. It has served as a catalyst for the creation of a society with true religious freedom and harmony in the context of religious pluralism. At the same time, the rights of those who profess the absence of religious belief have not been overlooked. But, there are those in our midst unwilling to coexist and tolerate such differences. Their ideology demands their belief system be paramount and exclusive of others. They would like their particular brand of religion to permeate all aspects of private and public life. They are overtly threatened by the availability and circulation of alternatives. Most importantly, the First Amendment, they are painfully aware, constitutes the most powerful remedy against the establishment of a theocracy.

Thus, we see many efforts, like those of Republican Representative Ernest Istook of Oklahoma. He unsuccessfully attempted to legislate the Religious Freedom Amendment several years ago. It was a constitutional amendment with the intent of neutralizing the First Amendment as it has evolved over the past 200 years.[608] What is most worrisome is that Istook elicited so much support from fellow legislators. Efforts to topple or weaken the First Amendment are not limited to one-punch attempts to "vote" it out. They also come in subtler, gradual steps. Examples of such are judicial decisions by courts with a majority of jurists who have a very different perspective on what the Founding Fathers had in mind. These steps can eventually erode the First Amendment's protective elements.

Another section of the First Amendment has also come into play in the ongoing juggling between religious freedom and maintaining a secular government. The First Amendment also provides for "freedom of speech." It is listed second to highlight its importance, right behind freedom of conscience. As was readily discovered, scenarios can be constructed in which one freedom is pitted against the other, with the primary goal of eroding the wall of separation between church and state. For example, a public school teacher might attempt to promote his faith directly in the classroom or include materials from it into his assignments. If, and typically only if, a student or family makes an issue of it and the school administration sets limits on such behavior, will the matter come to light. In such an event, ample support may come from fundamentalist organizations. So, it is not uncommon for the teacher, under such circumstances, to claim his or her freedom of speech has been violated. This has become a powerful tool to undermine the religion/government segment of the First Amendment and the practice likely to become more extensive.

Antecedents to religious liberty

Not all residents in pre-Revolutionary America favored the Democratic model that ultimately emerged. The predecessors of today's fundamentalist Christians opposed the contemporary notion of religious freedom and were very troubled by the blossoming pluralism around the

Colonies. The diverse aspect of our present society will continue to fuel such discontent given the historical judicial interpretations of the First Amendment. As Boston has pointed out, Pilgrims and Puritans who came to these shores to escape religious persecution seemed perfectly content to establish their own brand of theocracy, creating "religious freedom" only for themselves.[609]

Roger Williams is the best-known dissenter of his time. Despite his absolutistic religious views, he took issue with any government's role in promoting and enforcing orthodoxy. The colony he settled in Providence, Rhode Island, was the only region coming close to the practice of religious freedom as we conceive it today. Yet, his contribution to the eventual Constitution and Bill of Rights has been underplayed historically. His writings clearly reflect his understanding and promotion of diversification, or the separation of church and state, as well as the inherent value of pluralism.[610]

As Christian historian Robert R. Handy has pointed out, state support of religion correlated little to the extent of religiosity among the population.[611] Outside of Rhode Island, the situation varied among the colonies including taxes to support specific religious ideologies; the persecution of Catholics, Quakers and other minorities; and, of course, the execution of witches in Massachusetts.[612]

Although theocratic rigidity probably softened gradually, significant winds of change were not felt until the contributions of Virginia's two most famous sons. Thomas Jefferson and James Madison served as catalysts and spokesmen for progressive trends. Madison struggled with the concept of religious liberty eventually abandoning the popular notion of "toleration" in favor of the more radical notion of the right to "the full and free exercise of religion."[613] He was influenced by European philosophers, particularly John Locke, a proponent of political secularism and the keeping of religion and government separate.[614]

Madison was most articulate in arguing on behalf of what ultimately became the Establishment Clause. Jefferson's writings were crucial to the notion of religious freedom. He rightly insisted his bill was designed to protect all religious persuasions, including "the infidel of any denomination," that is, non-believers.[615] Therefore, the Founding Fathers proceeded to create a framework for the revolutionary concept of democracy, a secular state, and the coexistence of government and religion. It derived from a combination of personal experiences and the writings of Enlightenment philosophers.

Most people are unaware the Bill of Rights was originally controversial. Even Madison had doubts. Not because he opposed civil liberties, but out of concerns that listing specific rights might lead to the interpretation that only those rights were guaranteed by the Constitution. Eventually, luckily for us, the need for clarity and emphasis overcame this concern. The Bill of Rights was developed as a necessary complement to the Constitution.[616]

The detailed evolution of the First Amendment, which Madison drafted, is fascinating, but beyond the scope of this writing. But consideration of the framers changing of wording and whether or not to include certain amendments throughout the process is essential to developing insight as to their intent. Most scholars have come to the consensus, as Boston puts it, that "the First Amendment is a command to government to keep its hands off religion—neither aiding nor hindering it—to the fullest extent possible."[617]

Years later, in 1802, Jefferson characterized the First Amendment as building a "wall of separation between church and state"[618] when he wrote to the Danbury Baptists:

> I contemplate with sovereign reverence that act of the whole American people which declared that their legislature should 'make no law regarding an establishment of religion, or prohibiting the free exercise thereof,' thus building a wall of separation between Church and State.[619]

Anti-separationists, including United States Supreme Court Chief Justice William H. Rehnquist, have criticized Jefferson's metaphor as "based on bad history" and a poor guide to "judging," concluding that "it should be frankly and explicitly abandoned."[620]

This brings us to a key argument of Christian fundamentalists, namely, that the United States was founded as a Christian nation. As Boston points out, this assertion confuses the fact that our government was created as a political unit and the broader historical perspective of the conquest and settlement of North America by Europeans.[621] There were minority attempts during the Constitutional Convention favoring recognition of Christianity in shaping our laws, but these ideas were rejected.[622] This led to the Constitution's emergence as a purely secular document. It is, therefore, no accident the entire document is devoid of religious references.

This was made clear in 1797, when the Treaty of Tripoli was approved by the Senate, under John Adams. It unequivocally stated, "the Government of the United States is not, in any sense founded on the Christian religion."[623] Of course, none of those revelations are surprising to those who appreciate the wisdom of the First Amendment and the sociopolitical benefits it has reaped over the past two centuries.

Yet, Christian fundamentalists continue to contend, in ever more frequent and louder claims, this is a Christian nation. The United States has lost touch with its Christian origins, they argue. This has come about because of a pluralism that is out of control, misguided legislation, and "incorrect" decisions by "liberal" judges. This is such a key issue to anyone seeking a theocratic direction, that it will not be abandoned regardless of historical evidence to the contrary. The myth of the United States being a Christian nation allows for the promotion and insertion of religion into all aspects of public and governmental endeavors. This is justified on the grounds all contemporary social ills are the result of the removal of God and religion from the public square. When bounds of sensitivity and the Establishment Clause are crossed and people react, the situation is misrepresented as "another" example of Christian persecution by faithless or misguided individuals, usually accompanied by a fair share of distortion and hype. The broader version, found particularly among younger persons, involves claims that religion in the abstract is under assault. Unless they have been properly prepared, however, they are usually hard pressed when asked by whom or for what purpose is the assault.

The law of the land

As Trustee of Americans United for Separation of Church and State, I address general audiences on the topics of the First Amendment and separation of church and state. I often begin by quoting the first sixteen words of the First Amendment and asking what they mean. Most of the answers focus on specific issues and reflect some general understanding of the concept. These responses allow me, as the speaker, to size up the audience's level of sophistication, so I can adjust my presentation accordingly. Eventually, I offer them the punch line: "they mean whatever the United States Supreme Court says they mean." This leads to the most pertinent issue, the composition of the Supreme Court.

Early in its judicial history, the First Amendment was dissected into two components. These are commonly referred to as the Free Exercise Clause and the Establishment Clause.[624] Free Exercise focused on making sure the government, through all of its manifestations, did not interfere with the practice of religion. At the same time, it protected all traditions, particularly minority ones. Establishment, understandably far more controversial, dealt with the limitations imposed on government in terms of involving itself in religious activity. Conservatives repeatedly comment that the Establishment Clause was intended only to limit government from espousing or establishing a particular religion. Secularists and freethinkers, those who reject religious authority and dogma, on the other hand, interpret the Establishment Clause as providing "freedom from religion." Religious freedom, at least outwardly, is not a major concern for most in our society. It is therefore, not surprising most of the judicial cases, particularly those making their way through appeal process, deal with the Establishment Clause.[625]

Some years ago, the radical religious right tried to document its claim of epidemic assaults on religion and persecution of religious Americans. But it was hard pressed to come up with significant numbers of cases and ended up parading old and distorted ones. In school settings, situations sometimes lead to repression of appropriate religious expression inadvertently or through poor judgment. Most individual situations as these are typically resolved and corrected quickly and informally, thus not leading to litigation and judicial opinions.

The two Clauses of the First Amendment are best conceptualized as two distinct edges of the same sword. In fact, many judicial pundits consider the Establishment Clause as the most potent protector of the Free Exercise Clause. This is because of its limitations on the government in terms of promoting or establishing a major religion, thus maintaining all religions on a level plane.

It is impossible, under the limitations of this chapter, to cite every judicial decision over the past two centuries that has helped to mold our contemporary interaction between church (religion) and state (government). In mid-nineteenth century, Horace Mann, a Unitarian, was instrumental, both as a member of the Massachusetts Board of Education and as a legislator, in opposing sectarianism in public schools. This ultimately promoted a concept of public education as religiously neutral.[626]

The conflicts between the overwhelming majority of Protestants and Catholics throughout the nineteenth century were mostly resolved outside of the courts. This revealed a very different approach to church and state conflict resolution as compared to today. The Catholics lost most of the battles. This led to the creation of Catholic parochial schools as a way to resolve differences as to the type of prayers and Bible readings practiced in the schools. Nevertheless, it is interesting that the earliest judicial challenges to religious exercises in public schools, in Ohio and Illinois, were brought by Catholics. This is in contrast to the complainants in contemporary cases.[627]

What are today viewed as the key cases in the evolution of the First Amendment blossomed in the second half of the twentieth century. The 1947 *Everson v. Board of Education* case allowed the use of public bus services by parochial school students.[628] Justice Hugo Black's writing raised the bar in terms of public money and religion, as he argued:

> The First Amendment of the Constitution means at least this: Neither a state nor the federal government can set up a church. Neither can pass laws which aid one religion, aid all religions, or prefer one religion over another. . . . No tax in any amount, large or small, can be levied to support any religious activities or institutions, whatever they may be called, or whatever form they may adopt to teach or practice religion.[629]

In the 1948 *McCollum v. Board of Education* (8-1) decision, Black again concluded clergy and others should not be allowed on school grounds for religious educational purposes.[630] However, in the 1952 *Zorach v. Clauson* opinion, the Supreme Court allowed public school students to be released to attend religious classes away from public school premises.[631] Then ten years later, two monumental decisions returned the Court to a clearer separationist stance. In *Engel v. Vitale* (6-1) the Court rendered unconstitutional school-sponsored prayer.[632] Similarly, a year later, public school Bible reading in the *Abington Township School District v. Schempp* (8-1) experienced the same fate.[633] Contrary to claims by fundamentalists today, the practices of school-sponsored prayer and Bible reading were not widespread throughout the country anyway. In the Engel case, Black added that the Establishment Clause's "first and most immediate purpose rested on the belief a union of government and religion tends to destroy government, and degrade religion."

In 1971, the Court in *Lemon v. Kurtzman* rendered laws unconstitutional in Pennsylvania and Rhode Island that allowed for public funds to be used to cover parochial school teachers' salaries while dealing with "secular" subjects. Even more importantly, in that decision, the Court created a three-part test to gauge First Amendment violations. A government practice or law was considered to violate church-state separation if (1) it does not have a secular purpose, (2) it has the primary effect of advancing or inhibiting religion, and/or (3) it fosters excessive entanglement between government and religion. The Lemon Test has been invoked frequently in subsequent decisions, to protect church and state separation leading to a crescendo of calls by religious right proponents for its discontinuation.[634]

The past two decades have seen both solid judicial victories for the "wall of separation" and definite erosions. In 1980 *Stone v. Graham* (7-2), a Kentucky law requiring public schools to post copies of the Ten Commandments in every classroom was declared unconstitutional.[635] Then in 1985 *Wallace v. Jaffree* (6-3) struck down an Alabama law requiring public schools to set aside a moment of silence for meditation.[636] In 1992, *Lee v. Weisman* (5-4) disallowed public schools from sponsoring invocations at graduation ceremonies.[637] In that case, Justice Anthony Kennedy, writing for the majority, said, "The First Amendment's Religion clauses mean that religious beliefs and religious expressions are too precious to be either proscribed or prescribed by the state." And, in the 2000 *Santa Fe Independent School District v. Doe* (6-3) decision, school-sponsored prayers at athletic events were disallowed.[638]

Looking at the flip side, the 1990 *Board of Education v. Mergens* (8-1) case was less than reassuring. The Court upheld the Federal Equal Access Act of 1984 requiring public secondary schools to allow religious clubs to meet on campus if other non-curriculum clubs are also allowed.[639] This opened the door to the 2001 *Good News Club v. Milford Central School* (7-2), which allowed evangelists access to public schools after school hours.[640]

The judicial history of evolution deserves individual attention. It models the nature of the conflict between the First Amendment and fundamental Christianity. Darwin's *On the Origin of Species by Means of Natural Selection* was published in 1859. But conservative Christians had the upper hand in blocking the teaching of the scientific theory of evolution for more than a century. In the unanimous 1968 *Epperson v. Arkansas* decision, the Court struck down an Arkansas law prohibiting the teaching of evolution in public universities and secondary schools.[641] Almost twenty years later, in the 1987 decision *Edwards v. Aguillard* (7-2), the Court invalidated a Louisiana law that required public schools to offer "balanced treatment" between evolution and creationism.[642] These developments, however, have not slowed down the creationists and their allies one bit. Evolution remains a taboo subject in many areas of the country, and creationism is smuggled regularly into public school science classrooms. This is almost exclusively an American phenomenon. Other industrialized countries around the world have resolved the scientific issue unequivocally.

The judicial evolution of the Free Exercise Clause has been slow, in contrast to its much flashier sibling. There was a development in 1990, which took some people by surprise and which is now beginning to come into focus. Prior to 1990, the Supreme Court seemed committed to a liberal interpretation of the Free Exercise Clause. In cases involving a conflict between law and religious activity, the state was expected to bend and yield, within reason, through the notion of the "least restrictive" alternative. Then along came *Employment Division v. Smith* (6-3), a case involving the use of peyote, an illegal drug, in a Native American religious ceremony.[643] In a radical turn around, Justice Antonin Scalia, writing for the majority, advanced the notion the government need not have a "compelling reason" before applying existing laws, which incidentally happen to interfere with religious practice.

The decision triggered complaints and concerns in many quarters. Protectors of religious freedom feared the conceptual change in the decision raised doubts as to the potential for minority religions to survive. The loss of protection for one faith endangers all faiths, including the status of non-believers. Majority religions are not immediately affected since their long-standing practices have been accommodated to existing laws or more likely, the reverse, that is, existing laws have been shaped to coexist with established religious practices. There have been attempts to legislate a return to the "good old days." The Religious Freedom Restoration Act (RFRA), which was rejected by the Supreme Court is but one example. So far, the efforts have not been successful. The RFRA attempted legislation to reestablish the notions of "compelling reason" and "least restrictive" alternative as guides to religious practices in conflict with general law.

In summary, the last decade has seen a major shift in how the United States Supreme Court is disposed to interpret both the Free Exercise and Establishment Clauses of the First Amendment. There have been outright reversals from a longstanding, predictable trend that was indisputably separationist such as the 2001 Good News Club decision trumping the 1948 McCollum decision. More subtly, the Justices' votes within each decision have become closer. The days are no longer when our anxiety was low and we could inherently trust the Supreme Court to decide properly. That is, to preserve the Founding Fathers' basis for the First Amendment and a robust wall of separation between Church and State. The composition of the Supreme Court has become the issue. At the turn of the twenty-first century, it was unbalanced, with the future looking ominous. The administration, under George W. Bush, made no secret its intention to nominate judges, to both the Supreme Court and the federal bench, who adhere to its views of the world and the First Amendment, in particular. Implementation of drastic policies by the Bush Administration, affecting the economy, the environment, international relations, and more, will have long-term effects. Regardless of political orientation, these will all pale in comparison to the impact its judicial appointments will have for decades to come. We are only able to glance at a fleeting moment in a complex, unfolding process.

Visions of violations

As a long-time social activist, I find myself dealing with several "hot" issues at once. There is no question the number of challenges to the First Amendment has skyrocketed over the past decade. It has become even worse after the horrible events of September 11, 2001. Our "firemen" are having to fight many blazes and infernos simultaneously, both nationally and regionally. These result in the thinning of resources to a dangerous level. Given this reality, to a greater degree than ever, we have to make priority lists and difficult choices.

In this context, I have found definite value in classifying church and state issues into two conceptual categories. I label these the "symbolic" and the "substantive." These are clearly not pure categories. As will be illustrated, each situation contains elements of both. Nevertheless, the categorization helps us make choices and understand strategies operating below the surface.

By "symbolic," I mean issues that manifestly insert religion into the public square, and in the process, defy the generally agreed limits of separation. They impact the climate, moving us away from the notion of a secular society. Examples include "In God We Trust" in the currency, the posting of the Ten Commandments in public schools and courthouses, and government sponsored prayers in public contexts. "Substantive" issues, on the other hand, including school vouchers, Charitable Choice, and curricular censoring, focus on altering the very fiber of our society.

Symbolic issues attract immediate attention. A majority of the population has some awareness the pot is percolating. In contrast, substantive matters lie below the public radar. Until recently, the man in the street had no inkling about the inherent complications in using public funds for parochial school vouchers. Even more dramatically, although Charitable Choice was enacted back in 1996, to this date, very few hands go up when I ask audiences if they have heard of it.

The radical religious right's strategy is simple. They flaunt the symbolic challenges, perfectly happy to draw maximum attention to them. They have no illusion of winning all, or even most, of them. What they accomplish is distraction from the substantive matters. Those are the real battles they must win to achieve the necessary socio-political power to advance us toward a theocracy. This creates a real dilemma for the protectors of the First Amendment. Both types of issues should be opposed whenever they surface. But the resources are not there to fight on all fronts. At the very least, separationists must pay close attention to public awareness or the lack thereof. Thus, substantive issues must not be resolved without full public scrutiny.

Symbolic challenges to the concept of separation of church and state were on the sharp rise well before the events of September 11, 2001, which opened the floodgates. The Good News Club case was a major victory for fundamentalists and their allies. This was the first time overt religious activity coupled with proselytization, or recruiting, had entered the school setting. The Child Evangelism Fellowship, for example, is committed to recruiting children, ideally starting in kindergarten. The child, they believe, can open the door to the possibility of evangelizing the whole family. They have even developed materials for preliterate children.[644]

On another front, in 2000, the Reverend Donald Wildmon, who runs the American Family Association, began pushing for the passage of laws requiring public schools to post "In God We Trust."[645] He argued, since it is the national motto (only since 1956), it was, therefore, conceptually different than the Ten Commandments. He developed appropriate posters, to be sold, to facilitate the effort. Prior to the assault on the schools, "In God We Trust" was added to the new design of the Georgia State flag in 2001. The original United States motto "E Pluribus Unum," meaning "From Many One," was entirely secular. It was not until the mid-nineteenth century the overtly religious motto began appearing sporadically in currency.

The 1980 Supreme Court decision in *Stone v. Graham* seemed definitive in excluding the Ten Commandments from government settings, including public schools. This perception was reinforced when the Supreme Court in 2001 refused to hear an appeal from a lower court ruling. It disallowed a government granite-monument display of the Ten Commandments in Elkhart, Indiana. Instead, showing typical fundamentalist perseverance, many cases involving displays have sprung up all over the country. The justification usually provided contends the Ten Commandments are the basis of American secular law, but it is a position lacking historical support. Perhaps the most conspicuous incident in this context was the unveiling of a 5,280-pound granite display. It was placed in the rotunda of the Alabama Judicial Building in Montgomery, home to the State Supreme Court and the State Appeals Courts.[646] Despite challenges, the monument remains undisturbed.

Substantive developments have not lagged behind. Prior to 1996 and Charitable Choice, there was a sharp and generally accepted distinction as to how public funds were distributed to religious organizations. There was no problem in tax money going to "religiously-affiliated" organizations such as Catholic Charities, Lutheran Services in America, and Jewish Family Services. These organizations provided social services with funding from both private and public sources. These were provided without a religious message and with appropriate constitutional safeguards. "Pervasively sectarian" institutions, meaning churches and organizations where religious practice is included during the delivery of the social program, however, were not entitled to public funds because of the obvious violation of the First Amendment.

John Ashcroft, then Republican Senator from Missouri, succeeded in 1996 in passing several pieces of legislation. They were subsumed under the title of Charitable Choice. The gap between the "religiously-affiliated" and the "pervasively-sectarian" essentially vanished. The latter became available to receive public funds and operate without any adjustments, free from most government oversight. The new scenario created a most seductive temptation for religious organizations. They could accept public funds for the provision of social services, without the apparent risk of diluting their religious identity. But there are many problems with this development. First and foremost, it represents a violation of the First Amendment and the separation of church and state, as well as state constitutions. Beyond that, it invites the inevitable regulation of churches by government. It interferes with the religious liberty of beneficiaries by failing to provide adequate alternatives. Since government cannot or should not play favorites among religious ideologies, fringe groups would be equally entitled to receive tax aid. Voluntary, or private, contributions are likely to diminish if the church programs are already funded with tax dollars. Finally, it could become the first step toward the transfer of social services entirely from the public to the private sector.

Interestingly, over the six years since its passage, Charitable Choice has developed very slowly. Several factors have been identified. Doubt and uncertainty have resulted in the lack of implementation of the necessary fiscal mechanisms, and the overall budget has not been increased, so funds have not been generally available. Perhaps most crucial, religious organizations have remained leery of dependency on questionable funds and the government oversight that inevitably follows the granting of public money. The fact the program has hardly taken off probably also explains the lack of court challenges on constitutional grounds.

Complementing and expanding Charitable Choice is the Bush administration's "Faith-Based Initiative."[647] It was one of the first programs unveiled by Bush on taking office. The President's perception of the First Amendment and his massive commitment to the radical religious right are revealed clearly by this plan. At the time it was introduced, he commented that it is "one of the most important initiatives that my administration not only discusses but implements." He proceeded to create a new federal agency, the Office of Faith-Based and Community Initiatives.

To the Administration's disappointment, the initiative has not done well in terms of widespread enthusiasm.[648] The associated bill, the Community Solutions Act, eventually passed the House. But as of this writing, it has yet to be considered seriously in the Senate. Even expected supporters, such as Pat Robertson, raised qualms at the prospect of "unorthodox" denominations getting their share of the "faith-based" pie. Another setback was the resignation of the head of the White House Initiative, John DiIulio. He made it clear he was fed up with criticism from both the Right and the Left.[649]

The problems with the Faith-Based Initiatives closely mirror those inherent in the concept of Charitable Choice. The use of tax dollars to subsidize religious programs clearly violates the separation of church and state. Despite receiving public funds, the religious institutions involved can legally discriminate when hiring on the basis of religion. The religious freedom of the recipient of the service could easily be jeopardized, as the religious message becomes mixed within the overall effort. Given the government's obligation to monitor what it finances, religious activity would inescapably become regulated. As also mentioned previously, the incentive of the private community to contribute would be diminished by the presence of tax dollars. Given the size of the pie would be finite and probably relatively small, religious groups could and would end up fighting with one another for what may be available. Worse, some religions would be favored over others, depending on who controlled the funds and the disbursements. Although religious centers would be favored over secular providers, which is the very intent of the bill, there is no proof they offer better care or achieve more successful results. It can only be hoped the high level of concern and opposition stemming from different quarters can be maintained, leading to the ultimate demise of the program.

Finally, comes the issue of "vouchers," the funding of private education with public money. Different schemes have evolved in this struggle. The principle of using tax dollars to finance private, particularly parochial, education remains the key ingredient. Even the word "voucher," after many rejections in public referenda, has been replaced by more seductive terms like "parental choice" and "opportunity scholarship."

Public education has been the main target of the radical religious right from the beginning. This is understandable because a vibrant and effective system of public education is incompatible with the establishment of a theocracy. The radical religious right has concluded it is necessary to malign public education as a step toward the goal of weakening through the denial of funding. Despite inherent constitutional flaws and the perennial absence of popular support, school vouchers continue to be promoted in a variety of settings and in different packages. Beginning in the state of New York in 1967, there have been more than twenty-five public referenda among many of the states. Voters have, nevertheless, consistently rejected the notion of vouchers and other tax aids to religious and private schools.[650]

The case against vouchers has always been, and remains strong.[651] Beyond the primary issue of violation of the First Amendment and separation of church and state, there is no popular support as evidenced, time and again through public referenda. Vouchers will not ensure "parental choice" because private and religious school administrators, in contrast to the public school setting, will always retain the right to accept or reject applicants. There is no evidence to support the claim vouchers will improve the public school system by promoting competition in education. Though it can and should be improved, the American public school system is not failing our children and our society.[652] Even beyond the issue of choice, poor families will not be able to afford private schools with the relatively small amounts of money allocated to vouchers. As Sandra Feldman, president of the American Federation of Teachers, put it: "Vouchers do not mean reform, no matter what name you give them. What they do mean is a radical abandonment of public schools and public education."[653]

It is no accident the fundamentalists, despite repeated rejections in public referenda, continue relentlessly to push vouchers. Not everyone in favor of vouchers should be assumed to be a fundamentalist or committed to the eradication of public education, however. There is dissatisfaction with local deficits in the public school system and the slowness of our society to correct such, and many people have come to believe we are ready to try an "alternative" solution. Allowing for the dust to settle, even after undergoing cosmetic changes and deceptive packaging, school vouchers remain both a scam and a hoax. They are a scam because the true purpose has been and remains the undermining and ultimate elimination of public education. They are a hoax to the economically-deprived because they cannot deliver the seductive promise of educational opportunities on a par with wealthy families.

Despite the poor showing of vouchers in public referenda and in state legislatures, the persistent efforts of their proponents culminated in the United States Supreme Court's decision to revisit the issue 30 years after its last previous undertaking. In the case of *Zelman v. Simmons-Harris*[654], at the end of the 2002 judicial year, the Court concluded that vouchers were constitutional in a 5 to 4 decision. This came about even though 96% of the students involved in the Cleveland program were attending religious schools, and 82% of the participating schools were religious. The majority opined that the program did not intend to promote religion because the religious schools were not the only option. Justice Sandra O'Connor, the acknowledged swing vote, added that the public money assistance went to individual students and not directly to religious institutions. The minority opinion commented on the ongoing trend toward approving aid to religious schools, in the process gutting the Establishment Clause and weakening the wall of separation.[655]

Although there were positive elements to be found in the decision, separationists had to come to grips with the fact that the issue of constitutionality, at least for now, had been disarmed. The decision, as expected, opened the flood gates in states and municipalities. Within two months it was reported that legislators in as many as 20 states were gearing to introduce voucher bills.[656]

Critics of the decision stressed the financial woes that would befall public education, considering it unconscionable to allocate any public money to religious institutions. They took solace in the fact that not all voucher programs would pass constitutional muster. The majority opinion suggested that future and existing programs would be struck down if they provided incentives to pick religious schools over secular ones; failed to provide genuine secular options; were not completely neutral toward religion; delivered funds to religious schools in a manner other than the independent choice of parents; and/or the purpose was to fund religious schools.

The Zelman decision resurrected for consideration and discussion a couple of earlier, seldom mentioned, Supreme Court decisions. In the 1973 Nyquist decision[657], the voucher program was struck down because it created incentives for parents to select religious schools instead of secular ones, and it provided assistance only to children attending private schools. Later in 1973, in the Sloan decision[658], the Court disallowed another program nearly identical to the one in Nyquist. The Zelman majority discussion articulated that any voucher program must provide adequate public and secular options to survive constitutional scrutiny.

With the issue of constitutionality removed at the federal level, voucher opponents turned their focus to the states. A review of state constitutions revealed that in at least 37 of them there is language that bars tax funds for sectarian institutions. In most of them, the critical language resides within sections labeled "Blaine Amendments." As expected, these sections have become targets of the radical religious right and other voucher proponents, under the primary argument that they reflect nineteenth century anti-Catholicism. The strategies for doing away with the Blaine Amendments include "persuading state courts to interpret them narrowly, having federal courts declare them in conflict with the First Amendment, and persuading voters to repeal them through ballot referenda."[659]

It did not take long, after the Zelman decision, for a court in Florida to declare the state's existing voucher program unconstitutional.[660] Though technically statewide, it was operational only in Pensacola and involved only approximately 50 students. It was found to be in violation of Article I, Section 3, of the Florida Constitution. It states that, "No revenue of the state or any political subdivision or agency thereof shall ever be taken from the public treasury directly or indirectly in aid of any church, sect or religious denomination, or in aid of any sectarian institution." It is only a matter of time before this case, or a similar one from another state, is tested before the United States Supreme Court.

Two publications from the group Americans for Religious Liberty have exposed the activities of fundamentalist Christian schools and the related home schooling movement.[661] They show how the fundamentalists' primary educational goal is to protect their youth from the diversity of contemporary American society. Fundamentalist texts promote sectarianism, religious intolerance, anti-intellectualism, disdain for critical thinking and science, and conservative political extremism. If the American populace were made aware of what is going on, the socio-political opposition to school vouchers would rise sharply.

Educational taboo

The teaching of history has become a highly-charged debate topic. Since history reflects change and development, often through conflict, it is not surprising different factions view events differently or, at least, want them to be depicted differently. By and large, history is still being reenacted by the "winners," those who survived and rose to control. Nevertheless, the rest have become more vocal in promoting their perspectives as well. Textbook publishers report increased pressure from a rapidly-expanding number of interest groups. Resolution of the conflicts and the ultimate choice of what gets presented and how is still controlled by those in power. But cracks are beginning to appear in the once adamant monolith. Conflict can also lead to the avoidance of a controversial issue. This has been seen with the scientific theory of evolution, under attack by ideologies threatened by its findings.

The First Amendment, and its corollary, the separation of church and state, seem to be experiencing a similar fate as evolution. In some instances, teachers and curricula have tended to avoid and minimize such issues, in anticipation of controversy. Organizations interested in the promotion and protection of the First Amendment such as Americans United For Separation of Church and State, the American Civil Liberties Union, and People For The American Way have become concerned, and rightly so, with the low degree of awareness of the basic concepts among both students and the public at large. Even politicians, during campaign speeches and media interviews, tend to avoid the issue beyond vague reassurances they support the separation of church and state. On specific questioning, they often prove to be poorly informed. Or worse, they seem to favor perspectives not in keeping with the secularity of the state. Accordingly, many progressive organizations favor the creation of educational materials and the related preparation of teachers. This is so the Constitution and the Bill of Rights can be presented in a vibrant and effective manner at different stages of the public school curriculum.

Although I strongly favor such efforts, I have come to recognize the dilemma is thornier. The deficits are not going to be corrected simply by better materials or more thorough lesson plans. As I travel and interact with citizens around the country, I have concluded we live in at least two disparate universes. More correctly, there exists a vast continuum and the poles at either end are what this discussion is focusing on. At one end of the continuum, we have multicultural, pluralistic settings like New York City or Los Angeles. A child in that setting, unless artificially isolated, is exposed to many ethnic and religious traditions. More importantly, the child learns to interact, and be comfortable without sacrificing his or her own identity. The child learns respecting and being respected is the name of the game. He or she also learns there are areas and rules of common exchange, which are different than, but not necessarily in conflict with, the individual tradition of each member.

People who grow up in that milieu tend to be universal and tolerant. The only problem, sometimes, is they have difficulty empathizing with the prejudice and limited outlook of those who were not as fortunate as they were in being exposed to diversity. In this context, the First Amendment does not need any undue promotion. Its precepts without formal elaboration operate on a daily basis. In fact, they provide both the glue and the solvent to render the society viable and productive. We know all too painfully the price paid by everyone when the ingredients are not in the mix. This has been seen in the Middle East, Northern Ireland, and the Balkans.

At the other end of the spectrum, we have homogeneous, monolithic situations. These are found in small and middle-sized communities in the South and parts of the Midwest. In these enclaves, conformity is the norm, and differences are viewed with suspicion and discomfort. There may be minority members such as the Chinese-American family that runs the downtown restaurant, a Jewish-American physician or merchant, or an Asian-American government employee; but they are marginalized. They are identified by their ethnicity. They are accepted or at least tolerated as long as they do not push the invisible boundaries established for them. Non-believers are viewed as even more on the fringe, and they often choose to lie low to minimize conflict. In this context, the First Amendment and the concept of separation of church and state seem so out of place as to be irrelevant. Any attempt to bring them to the fore will result in an aggressive response. The community will not take lightly to anything perceived as a challenge to the status quo and its way of life. What is really at issue is the fact that (their) religion and socio-political intercourse have become hopelessly entangled. Any call for the review of basic principles and assumptions is translated as an attack on their religious essence, and such will not be tolerated. The following incident provides a dramatic illustration.[662]

In Rhea County, Tennessee, Bible instruction had been going on for fifty-one years in kindergarten through fifth grade in three elementary public schools. The district ignored decades of Supreme Court precedents against religious instruction in public schools. The program entitled "Bible Education Ministry" was operated by students from Bryan College, a Bible-based college founded after the Scopes trial. The program was offered thirty minutes each week during regular school hours, without parental consent.

The Freedom From Religion Foundation in April 2001, filed a federal lawsuit on behalf of John Doe and Mary Roe, parents of children in the school system, challenging the practice. Plaintiffs in such cases have learned to remain incognito, given the anticipated backlash from the community.

United States District Judge R. Allan Edgar concluded readily that the practice was unconstitutional. He equated the classroom activities to what might be found in "a Sunday school class in many of the Christian churches in Rhea County." He said, "the government, through its public school system, may not teach, or allow the teaching of a distinct religious viewpoint." He concluded the Bible Education Ministry had "both the purpose and effect to endorse and advance religion in public schools." Comparing the situation to the 1948 *McCollum v. Board of Education* case, he commented the current matter represented an even stronger violation of the Establishment Clause.

The town's response is critical to understanding the complete equation. The Rhea County School Board, encouraged by an angry crowd of 300, voted unanimously to appeal the decision. A school board member explained, "We want to teach our children that the Bible is the truth. Our only course is an appeal." A member of the audience called for the impeachment of Judge Edgar, and another was even more emphatic, proclaiming, "whoever took it [the Bible] out should be strung up."

Thus, as illustrated so vividly, the protection and promotion of the First Amendment are not easy tasks. It would be complex even under relatively ideal conditions. As it is, we have a large segment of the population for whom the success of this 200-year experiment has little relevance. Worse, it stands as a barrier to the religious ideology which calls for moving in the direction of a theocracy. In such a climate, the task of imparting both the letter and the spirit of the law to succeeding generations remains very challenging. In fact, the current intense tendency to bypass or nullify the First Amendment may outweigh in effort and enthusiasm the commitment among the rest of us to preserve it.

CHAPTER 7

INERRANCY TURNED POLITICAL

by Herb Silverman

I do guerrilla warfare, I paint my face and travel at night. You don't know it's over until you're in a body bag. You don't know till election night.[663]

Ralph Reed

"Antidisestablishmentarianism" was the gold standard for those who used to compete in spelling bees. It achieved its exalted status for purportedly being the longest word in the English language. No one knew or cared what it meant. If people thought about it at all, they probably assumed any meaning attached to it had long since outlived its usefulness.

So what does the word mean, and why should anyone care? In the nineteenth century, the Free or "Nonconformist" churches, that is, the non-Anglican Protestant denominations in England, often sought to disestablish the Church of England. Those who favored the Church of England were called antidisestablishmentarians. The antis put down the rebellion of those who sought separation of the English state from the English church.

In contrast, in 1776 the soon-to-be United States not only declared independence from England, but also declared something even more radical—that "Governments are instituted among Men, deriving their just powers from the consent of the governed." Americans asserted the right of the people to form their own government, one with limited powers. They rejected kings crowned by bishops to rule through "divine right." They had no Church of the United States to disestablish.

However, the federal government did not initially prohibit states from establishing their own state churches. Prior to the Constitutional Convention of 1787, most states required their own pledges of allegiance to Christianity, if not to a particular sect. Voting and office-holding privileges were reserved only for members of the "correct" sect. Then Article 6 passed unanimously at the Constitutional Convention, prohibiting

174

religious tests for federal office. Nearly all states soon followed the federal lead.[664]

Nonetheless, there have always been people who falsely maintain that the founders intended to establish a Christian nation. Some have tried to pave the way to official establishment. For example, in 1941 a "Christian Nation" amendment to the Constitution was introduced in Congress. It stated explicitly that all laws of the United States should be subject to the "Word of God and his son, Jesus Christ."[665] Though the proposed amendment failed to pass in 1941, it has reappeared with regularity.

In the 1960s, John Anderson was elected to Congress on a platform supporting the amendment, a position he subsequently repudiated when he ran for president as a moderate in 1980.[666] Most members of today's religious right see making the United States into some form of Christian nation as a primary goal. However common the impulse to want others to share one's own beliefs, the Christian Right does more than desire it. They believe God mandates them to accomplish this and that it is their duty to obey.

During George Bush's administration, former Assistant Attorney General Charles J. Cooper, appointed during the Reagan years, argued in the Supreme Court case, *Lee v. Weisman* 1991, concerning prayers at middle-school graduations, "that the Constitution did not keep a state from designating an official religion so long as no one was forced to practice" it.[667] The intent of the case was clear. It was an attempt to set precedents to gravely change the secular face of states and, therefore, the face of America.[668] The notion of proclaiming an official religion that no one is compelled to practice is fraught with danger. Nevertheless, it is a scene the Christian Right tries to paint for those who may not favor forcing their religion on others, but who would gladly have their own religion elevated to such status.

Contrary to what many Americans believe, Christian fundamentalists today have great political strength. To challenge the religious right, their political goals must be understood, and the variety of tactics they employ must be recognized. Americans must familiarize themselves with not only the Christian Right's well-publicized national achievements, but also their large number of local political victories that affect states, counties, school boards, and cities. By realizing the magnitude of the problem, citizens may become energized enough to take action.

It is easy to minimize religious intrusion in others' lives when people are only aware of matters touching them directly. For example, it may be hard for most to fathom living in a state like Oklahoma, where all public school biology textbooks must carry a disclaimer against evolutionary theory, saying, "No one was present when life first appeared on Earth. Therefore, any statement about life's origins should be considered theory."[669] However, violations such as this are taking place throughout the country in neighboring states and communities.

The Christian Right cannot continue to be ignored with the hope they will eventually tire. Their political strength stems in part from the anger and resentment they hold toward a society that seems unable or unwilling to recognize and accommodate their wishes. As Scott Appleby, associate Professor of History at the University of Notre Dame, explains in *The God Squads*, a tiny but influential minority is "mad as hell and not going to take it anymore."[670] They are:

> the North American Christians, mad about what they see as Bible-bashing liberalism in the mainline Protestant seminaries and denominational bureaucracies, mad about indifference or hostility toward Judeo-Christian values in the entertainment and news media, mad about Supreme Court decisions banning prayer in public schools, and mad about the social revolution led by radical feminists.[671]

The following pages will describe the tactics some fundamentalist leaders use to acquire political influence, and how the religious right has politically maligned and impaired the American public school system. An examination on the tensions within the religious right explores whether political compromise can co-exist with a fundamentalist theology. I will then relate my personal and political struggle with the religious right in my home state of South Carolina. The chapter concludes by reviewing the political objectives of the religious right, how they hope to achieve these objectives, and how their tactics may effectively be countered.

Different lyrics, same tune

Why have so many fundamentalist religious leaders formed politically-active organizations? Who are they, and how successful have they been? To begin, consider the Reconstructionists, arguably the most fanatical of the Christian Right groups. According to them, says William Martin, author of *With God on Our Side*, "Christians have a mandate to rebuild . . . all of human society," and "they contend that the Bible . . .

offers the perfect blueprint for the shape a reconstructed world should take."[672]

Reconstructionists are also known as Dominionists, as in Genesis 1:28, which calls on them to: "Fill the Earth and subdue it and have dominion over every living thing that moves upon the Earth."[673] As "agents of God's unfolding plan," they are working to establish a theonomy, or "rule of God," which leaves no room for toleration of other points of view.[674] According to Martin, "a theonomic order would make homosexuality, adultery, blasphemy, propagation of false doctrine, and incorrigible behavior by disobedient children subject to the death penalty, preferably administered by stoning."[675] Since these ethical principles reflect the will of an immutable God, Reconstructionists reason, they apply to all people, in every era. R.J. Rushdoony, the founding father of Reconstructionism, regards pluralism as a heresy, since "in the name of toleration, the believer is asked to associate on a common level of total acceptance with the atheist, the pervert, the criminal, and the adherents of other religions."[676]

Frankly, it is highly unlikely that Reconstructionists will suddenly seize political power. Their ideas are simply too extreme. Leaders of the religious right have been cautious about showing any interest in this radical movement. Still, Reconstructionists have clearly been influential. Fundamentalist ministers Jerry Falwell and D. James Kennedy have endorsed Reconstructionist books. An anonymous member of the religious right undoubtedly spoke for many when he confessed, "Though we hide their books under the bed, we read them just the same."[677] While most religious right activists have discarded the more unpalatable aims of Reconstructionists, they have embraced their underlying theory that the Bible provides a blueprint for running government. Jay Grimstead, leader of the Coalition on Revival, expressed the sentiment of many conservative Christian leaders when he argued that while they may not be in full support of a theonomy, it is still their desire to rebuild a Bible-based America.[678]

Conservative Christians, who for much of American history cared more about saving souls than electing politicians, were galvanized to political action in the 1970s. The Supreme Court's 1973 *Roe v. Wade* abortion decision may well have triggered that turning point. In 1979 Reverend Jerry Falwell, a Southern Baptist televangelist, formed the Moral Majority. This religious right organization held the view that American morality was lost and must be found. Falwell urged Christians to uphold their moral duty by endorsing political candidates with conservative religious beliefs and traditional patriotic values.

In his book, *Listen America!,* written to articulate the new organization's rationale and purpose, Falwell characterized the Moral Majority as "pro-life, pro-family, pro-moral, and pro-American."[679] In particular, Falwell listed abortion, pornography, homosexuality, divorce, and secular humanism as the major evils threatening America. He urged Christians to learn how government works, from the precincts to the presidency, and then to contact public officials. Falwell, himself, claimed to have previously struggled and resisted political involvement. He had criticized other ministers who had participated in the civil rights movement. However, Falwell changed his mind, he says, because:

> I never thought the government would go so far afield, I never thought the politicians would become so untrustworthy, I never thought the courts would go so nuts on the left. We have defaulted by failing to show up for the fight.[680]

Falwell's political involvement through the Moral Majority often consisted of sending out incendiary fundraising letters. In one reporting that gays had been granted permission to lay a wreath in Arlington Cemetery, Falwell referred to changing the Tomb of the Unknown Soldier into "The Tomb of the Unknown Sodomite!"[681] Another of his favorite tactics was sending provocative questionnaires to be answered and returned by supporters, along with a donation. He then sent the responses to members of Congress. Typical of the slanted questions was: "Do you approve of American flags being burned in liberal and radical anti-American demonstrations?"[682] No distinction was made between approval of an act and approval of the right to political dissent. Nor was any nuance evident in questions about unisex bathrooms, selling pornography to children, and banning any form of prayer in school.

Although the Moral Majority may not have had the strength it often claimed (some would say that the Moral Majority was neither moral nor a majority), it paved the way for other organizations. The Moral Majority died in 1989, after playing a critical role in politicizing religious conservatives. What did religious right leaders learn from Jerry Falwell's mistakes with the Moral Majority? In *Close Encounters with the Religious Right*, Rob Boston points out that Falwell seemed to believe he could change America from the top down. After helping elect Ronald Reagan to the presidency in 1980, Falwell sat back and waited for all he wanted to be handed to him.[683] Now, most religious right leaders see the way to bring about real change is from the bottom up. Accordingly, they focus on local politics as well as state and federal races.

Enter the Christian Coalition. Born in 1989 under the leadership of Pat Robertson, the organization was by no means a mere reincarnation of the Moral Majority. It was well financed and media savvy. From its inception, Stephen L. Carter, author of *God's Name in Vain* , said:

> the Christian Coalition has been a force in the Republican Party. With its member churches, its ability to drum up letter-writing campaigns as well as votes, and its stated goal of training 10 political activists in every electoral district, of any size, in the United States—a projected 1.75 million activists—it has been, for many conservative candidates, a welcome source of energy and on-the ground-troops . . . and a group nobody wants to have as an enemy.[684]

According to Rob Boston, assistant director of communications for the organization Americans United for Separation of Church and State, the:

> Christian Coalition spends most of its money and efforts on state and local politics. The group is seeking to take over the Republican Party from the ground up and has been extremely successful in some counties and states. The group is a continual headache for GOP moderates striving to return the party to a more centrist position.[685]

Pat Robertson's views are anything but centrist. As a presidential candidate in 1988, he predicted:

> When the Christian majority takes over this country, there will be no satanic churches, no more free distribution of pornography, no more abortion on demand and no more talk of rights for homosexuals. After the Christian majority takes control, pluralism will be seen as immoral and evil and the state will not permit anybody to practice it.[686]

Robertson lost the 1988 Republican presidential nomination to George Bush, but he was an honored guest at the Bush inauguration. On the last evening of inaugural festivities, Robertson received the "Man of the Year" award from a conservative college political organization known as Students for America. Robertson shared the platform with the group's founder and president, a young man named Ralph Reed. This encounter proved fortuitous for both men. Impressed by Reed's political acumen and religious convictions, and by sophistication unusual for someone only twenty-eight years old, Robertson appointed Reed the executive director of the Christian Coalition.

The young and wholesome-looking Reed painted a kinder, gentler, and less-threatening public image of the Christian Coalition than had Robertson. Reed was a frequent guest on television talk shows. Without using the divisive "Christian nation" rhetoric of Robertson, Reed emphasized that it was important for religious conservatives to get involved in the electoral process.[687] In 1990, under Reed's leadership, the Christian Coalition distributed 750,000 "voter guides" in North Carolina just before Election Day. Subsequently, Reed took some of the credit for Jesse Helms' reelection to the Senate. The Christian Coalition also had their troops swamp key senators with phone calls in support of Supreme Court nominee Clarence Thomas during his confirmation hearing in 1991.[688] The pragmatic Ralph Reed found out, perhaps with mixed emotions, the extent to which Christian conservatives dominated the 1992 Republican National Convention, as Vice President Dan Quayle called out to a roomful of delegates, "Who do you trust?" Reed expected to hear "George Bush." But the delegates yelled back, "Jesus!"[689]

In 1994, Quayle spoke at an event hosted by televangelist D. James Kennedy. The participants recited a pledge of allegiance—but not the one familiar to most Americans. This pledge said: "I pledge allegiance to the Christian flag, and to the Savior, for whose Kingdom it stands, One Savior, crucified, risen and coming again, with life and liberty for all who believe."[690]

After a string of successes, Reed stepped into one of his few public relations disasters when he described the tactics he used to achieve political victory: "I do guerrilla warfare, I paint my face and travel at night. You don't know it's over until you're in a body bag. You don't know till election night."[691] This comment clearly represented Reed's philosophy. During the 1992 campaign, he told the Montana Christian Coalition to heed the advice of ancient Chinese philosopher Sun Tzu: "The first strategy, and in many ways the most important strategy, is secrecy. . . . We're involved in a war. It's not a war fought with bullets, it's a war fought with ballots."[692]

The frequent use of military metaphors by many Christian Coalition leaders made it easy for journalists and critics to associate the organization with a warlike character. Shortly after the 1992 election of Bill Clinton, Reed wrote a memo to Christian Coalition leaders recommending they substitute sports metaphors for war metaphors.[693] But there was no indication the Christian Coalition intended to drop its stealth tactics. The religious right knew their extreme views on issues like abortion, birth control, and public education were not mainstream. They could not win elections in moderate communities by trumpeting the beliefs that energized their base. Antonio Rivera, a New York Christian Coalition political advisor, described this stealth strategy in 1992: "You keep your personal views to yourself until the Christian community is ready to rise up, and then wow! They're gonna be devastated."[694]

In 1995, Reed met with Republican presidential nominee Bob Dole, who welcomed the Coalition's Contract with the American Family, the official public platform of the Christian Coalition. Referred to as a "family values" contract, it was loaded with religiously intrusive proposals. One was the Religious Equality Amendment, which stated:

> Nothing in this Constitution shall be interpreted to prohibit the citizens of the United States from practicing religion in public places nor to prohibit the states from facilitating the practice of religion by their citizens.[695]

Allowing states to facilitate religion, however, would chip deeply into the wall between church and state. The Contract was also criticized for promoting secular issues that appeared to be simply conservative in nature, rather than Christian. Reed defended goals of lowering tax rates and the federal budget deficit by saying religious conservatives linked to the Christian Coalition care about such matters.[696] And Robertson did not hide his goal of having the Christian Coalition take over the Republican Party. When told in 1995 that the Coalition was dominant in about half the states and had a significant presence in many others, Robertson urged that more work needed to be done. He insisted, "I want 100 percent."[697]

Ever since its inception, questions had been raised about whether the overt political involvement of the Christian Coalition was at odds with the organization's tax-exempt status. Rob Boston argued against the tax-exempt designation. He said the Coalition was "essentially a far-right political action committee dedicated to getting the most conservative Republicans possible elected to public office."[698]

At one strategy session when Robertson laid out plans for how the Coalition could elect Republicans, Robertson knew his comments were not strictly aboveboard. He quipped, "If there's any press here, would you please shoot yourself?"[699] Americans United obtained a taped copy of the remark and turned it over to the Internal Revenue Service. Shortly thereafter, in June of 1999, the IRS denied the Christian Coalition tax-exempt status. However, on July 2, "six right-wing Republican senators wrote to Attorney General Janet Reno," reports Boston, "and demanded that she launch a criminal investigation of Americans United for allegedly trying to intimidate religious voters."[700]

Lately, the Christian Coalition has lost some of its influence, especially following the resignation of Executive Director Ralph Reed in 1997. But the organization continues to be active. The coalition moved its national headquarters from Virginia to Washington D.C. as part of its strategy. In the year 2000, Robertson claimed the Coalition distributed 70 million voter guides during national elections.[701] On July 5, 2000, the Charleston *Gazette* reported Pat Robertson had joined Jerry Falwell in his "$18.6 million drive to mobilize 35 million Bible-believing Christians to elect George W. Bush president."[702]

Both Falwell and Robertson have influenced countless numbers of Americans through media saturation, but they have both opened themselves up to ridicule with periodic outlandish statements that might play well only to Christian conservatives. Jewish groups took umbrage when on January 14, 1999, Falwell told a group of pastors in Kingsport, Tennessee, that the Antichrist is Jewish, and probably walking the earth today.[703] Falwell said, "Is he alive and here today? Probably, because when he appears during the Tribulation period, he will be a full-grown counterfeit of Christ. Of course, he'll be Jewish. Of course he'll pretend to be Christ."[704]

However theologically justified these views are to Falwell and others in the religious right, such pronouncements prove troublesome when seeking political support from a more mainstream audience. Two days after the September 11, 2001, terrorist attacks on the New York World Trade Center, Robertson told Falwell, who appeared on Robertson's 700 Club:

> We have allowed rampant secularism and occult, etc., to be broadcast on television. We have permitted somewhere in the neighborhood of 35 to 40 million unborn babies to be slaughtered in our society. We have a court that has essentially stuck its finger in God's eye and said we're going to legislate you out of the

schools. We're going to take your commandments from off the courthouse steps in various states. We're not going to let little children read the commandments of God. We're not going to let the Bible be read, no prayer in our schools. We have insulted God at the highest levels of our government. And then we say, 'why does this happen?' It is happening because God Almighty is lifting His protection from us.[705]

This comment tarnished Falwell's reputation even among Christian conservatives. People noted how these words could just as easily have come from the lips of Osama bin Laden.

To the amusement of many, Pat Robertson has no problem mixing theology with meteorology. In a "700 Club" program in 1985, he ordered, in the name of Jesus, Hurricane Gloria to turn away from the Virginia coastline and head to the Northeast. The hurricane did eventually move away from Virginia—and whacked Long Island. In 1995, while running for the presidency, Robertson proudly pronounced the incident as extremely important to his political plans, "because I felt that if I couldn't move a hurricane, I could hardly move a nation."[706]

Not as well known as Falwell or Robertson, but considerably more polished, is James Dobson, founder of Focus on the Family. Although a radio psychologist, his daily program generates substantial political activity. As Boston observes, "Dobson's views are just as extreme, but he presents them in a non-threatening, 'family-friendly' package."[707] While Robertson and Falwell earn high negatives in public opinion polls, respondents regard Dobson as a kind, gentle, indulgent uncle.

In 1999, the Focus on the Family radio show was aired 18,000 times a week in more than 4,000 facilities. It reached an audience estimated to exceed five million listeners.[708] Dobson is clearly the radio version of Pat Robertson. In addition, Dobson's fourteen books have sold more than sixteen million copies, and his organization publishes ten different magazines and newsletters. Moreover, Dobson knows exactly how to wield his power, by threatening to pull out of the Republican Party if the party leaders do not meet his demands.

In a letter circulated to supporters on April 3, 1998, Dobson ordered it was time for the Republicans to "fish or cut bait," and added:

They have to understand that we will abandon them if they continue to ignore the most important issues. The threat must be real for us to have integrity, and I am determined to deliver on the promises to campaign against them if nothing changes. But I'm praying that won't be necessary.[709]

The following month top GOP leaders established a "Values Action Team" to report weekly to Dobson and other religious right leaders.[710]

The Family Research Council (FRC), founded in 1983 by Gary Bauer, serves as the political wing of Focus on the Family. John M. Swomley, Professor emeritus of Social Ethics at St. Paul School of Theology, examined the danger posed by the FRC. He explained this body "was purposely designed to keep Dobson one step removed from direct political involvement " to protect the tax-exempt status of Focus on the Family.[711] The FRC is a Washington-based group, while Focus on the Family maintains chapters in some state capitals where they can center on grassroots organizing. Like Pat Robertson in 1988, Gary Bauer attempted unsuccessfully to become the Republican presidential nominee in 2000.

What kind of candidate does Dobson, who heads a "nonpolitical" organization, overtly support? Consider abortion opponent Randall Terry, for one. When Terry sought to win the GOP nomination for a Congressional seat in New York in 1998, Dobson endorsed him, saying, "I wish we had a dozen more like him in Congress."[712] Terry is an extreme anti-abortionist who called pro-choice Supreme Court justices "enemies of Christ." He compared them to Hitler and Stalin. As was pointed out in a previous chapter, at a training session for those willing to harass and threaten women's clinic employees, Terry said, "Intolerance is a beautiful thing. We're going to make [abortionists'] lives a living hell."[713]

Dobson, himself, is not known for tolerance, and he has even attacked the Girl Scouts for promoting "humanism and radical feminism." The cause of his wrath? Delegates at the 1994 Girl Scout convention, recognizing the diversity of their organization, voted overwhelmingly to make a reference to God optional in the organization's oath. The Girl Scouts did not drop the oath; they simply wanted to make girls of all backgrounds feel welcome to join.[714]

Thus far we have focused exclusively on religious right Protestants, who are disproportionately associated with white evangelical churches such as the Assemblies of God and the Southern Baptist Convention. Many of these groups do not consider Roman Catholics to be true Christians, and Catholics have been understandably reluctant to ally with Protestants of the religious right. In fact, they have frequently been bitter enemies.

In the nineteenth century, many Catholics were opposed to Bible reading in public schools, at least to the passages usually selected. Catholics objected to the Protestant version of the "Lord's Prayer," which differed from the similar Catholic prayer known as the "Our Father." In 1859, an eleven-year-old child of Catholic parents in Boston was beaten for refusing to read the Ten Commandments from the King James Bible. He knew his Catholic Douay Bible had a different version. The teacher was taken to court, but the judge dismissed all charges.[715] Also, in 1843, a three-day riot erupted in Philadelphia. The city's board of education had allowed Catholic children either to be excused from mandatory religious exercises or to use their own version of the Bible. In response, furious Protestants burned Catholic churches and even homes. Thirteen people were killed.[716]

These incidents eventually led Catholics to establish their own private schools to avoid religious coercion through the tyranny of the majority. Consequently, it is ironic that some conservative Catholics have joined the contemporary movement for a school prayer amendment, which would make other groups feel just as uncomfortable as they once felt.

Even so, mandatory school prayer is not the most energizing issue on which conservative Catholics and Protestants agree. Their passions intensify over opposition to abortion. With this in mind, in 1975 Catholic bishops organized an ambitious political campaign to take control of judicial seats, Congress, state, and national political offices. According to Catholic writer Timothy A. Byrnes, twenty major Catholic organizations participated in this effort. The focus of the Catholic campaign was to gain enough Supreme Court seats to reverse *Roe v. Wade*. Their plan stated: "Efforts should be made to reverse the decision, to restrain lower courts from interpreting and applying [Supreme Court decisions] more aggressively and more absolutely than the Supreme Court."[717] This campaign gained strength during the Reagan and Bush years. Even as late as 1998, after six years of the Clinton administration, more than seventy percent of federal judges and at least four Supreme Court justices were anti-abortion.[718]

Just as conservative Protestants learned to make effective use of the media, so did conservative Catholics. The Catholic League for Religious and Civil Rights is one of the most misnamed and determined organizations of the religious right. Its main objective is to protect the Catholic Church, the Vatican, and the papacy from "activity, language, speech, publication, or media presentation" the League might consider offensive.[719] William Donohue, the Catholic League's leader, has opposed freedom of speech and the press, women's and gay rights, and affirmative action.[720] The Catholic League claims "the support of all the U.S. cardinals and many of the bishops."[721]

Canon 1369 of the Code of Canon Law justifies the Catholic League's existence:

> A person is to be punished with a just penalty, who, at a public event or assembly, or in published writing, or by otherwise using the means of social communication, utters blasphemy, or gravely harms public morals, or rails at or excites hatred or contempt for religion or the Church.[722]

Donohue revealed the secret of the Catholic League's success in its December 1995 issue of the journal *Catalyst*. He wrote:

> We specialize in public embarrassment of public figures who have earned our wrath and that is why we are able to win so many battles: no person or organization wants to be publicly embarrassed, and that is why we specialize in doing exactly that.[723]

The Catholic League has attacked many news programs, newspapers, and other media sources for being even the least critical of the Pope or Catholic Church. It has gotten Ann Landers' advice column dropped from a newspaper, and national advertisers dropped from television stations. As Rob Boston put it, the Catholic League exists, "primarily to scream bloody murder any time anyone dares to criticize the political goals of the Roman Catholic Church."[724]

In fact, a tactic employed by most religious right groups is to decry "anti-Christian bigotry" when there is any criticism of their goals. The technique has effectively energized their base, whether or not they really believe the charge. This could be one of the reasons for increased attendance at Protestant evangelical churches across the U.S., while attendance at mainline Protestant churches has decreased. With evangelicals and Catholics joining forces on issues like abortion, the religious right has become politically stronger than the religious left.[725]

"Saving" public schools

When and why did public education become the whipping boy of the religious right? In the 1960s, the Supreme Court ruled against permitting Bible reading in public schools and mandated racial integration in public schools. Conservative Protestants, unlike Catholics, did not have an established parochial school system. Primarily to evade court-ordered requirements for public schools, private schools began to open in the South. Although the religious right wanted prayer in public schools, there were many things they wanted out, including sex education, drug education, evolution, and so-called pornographic books.

In *Holy Terror: The Fundamentalist War on America's Freedoms in Religion, Politics and Our Private Lives,* Conway and Siegelman argue, "Many parents saw in fundamentalist schools a way to shield their children from a changing world—as they were trying to shield themselves."[726] The authors suggest that for the religious right, "the most dangerous substances in public schools are ideas, specifically any notions that violate their unbending interpretation of the Bible."[727]

One of the most ludicrous comments during the Vietnam War was in an Associated Press story filed by Peter Arnett about the Tet offensive of 1968. He quoted an unnamed American major as saying, "It became necessary to destroy the town in order to save it."[728] This "nothing is worse than communism" belief coincides with the "nothing is worse than public schools" belief of many within the religious right. Jerry Falwell remarked he was "looking forward to the day when all schooling in America is run by churches."[729]

Howard Philips, during his 1992 presidential campaign as the candidate of the U.S. Taxpayers Party (now known as the Constitution Party), attacked the idea of public education because "inevitably government conveys anti-Christian premises about the nature of God and man."[730] And Reconstructionist author Gary North explained the importance of destroying public schools. "Until the vast majority of Christians pull their children out of the public schools," North pointed out, "there will be no possibility of creating a theocratic republic."[731]

The religious right would like to "save" our schools (pun intended) by providing vouchers for parents who wish to send their children to private schools. Since the vast majority of private schools are religious, the vouchers would primarily support church-run schools. Voucher proponents argue public schools would become more efficient and responsive to the needs of the children if they had to compete with private schools for tax dollars. But besides violations of state-church separation, adoption of this policy would seriously erode the limited amount of funding available for public schools. In addition, competition works best only when playing fields are level. Private schools may select students, while public schools must accept all the expensive-to-educate children with special needs. The voucher plank has become a fixture of Republican Party platforms through many presidential election conventions.[732]

Besides advocating vouchers, the Christian Coalition's 1996 Contract with the American Family called for a Parental Rights Act to "reaffirm parents' right to direct the education, medical care, discipline, and religious upbringing of their children."[733] What are the implications of this innocuous-sounding contract? Religious right activists could effectively prevent public school teachers from using critically acclaimed books that a minority of parents deemed pornographic or too controversial. Medical care related to school could mean "abstinence only" programs would represent the entire sex education curriculum. Condoms would be mentioned only to emphasize their failure rates, and they would be unavailable to sexually active students. Absolute parental right to discipline could be offered as a "spare the rod, spoil the child" justification for child abuse. And parents might be granted the right to withhold medical treatment from children with diabetes and other deadly illnesses.

Permitting prayer in public schools is high on the religious right agenda. Of course, students are allowed to pray silently in public schools. Wherever tests are taken, you are likely to find students praying. (Though prayer may be perfectly permissible, most teachers would agree that studying is more effective!) Not allowed are government-sponsored prayers. Yet millions of people continue to believe students are prohibited from ever praying while on school grounds.

Rob Boston says myths persist about children being scolded by teachers and hauled to the principal's office in disgrace for saying a prayer over lunch. Pat Robertson mentioned such a story about five-year old "Shannon" in Kingsville, Texas on his December 4, 1992, "700 Club" television program. Local reporters looked into the case. They could not even find a girl named Shannon at the school. When confronted, Robertson had no evidence. Boston added, "The religious right has failed to produce one bona fide instance of a violation of a student's right to pray in public schools."[734]

To listen to the religious right, all hell broke loose after the Supreme Court took God out of the classroom in 1963, when the court ruled government-sponsored prayers were unconstitutional. People who claim this court decision led to a rise in violence, drug addiction, and other societal ills, would benefit from taking an elementary statistics course.

There they will learn to distinguish between correlation and causation. No one disputes, for example, the high correlation between students with matches in their shirt pockets and students who develop lung cancer thirty years later. However, should it be deduced that matches in shirt pockets cause lung cancer? Can anything be concluded from the increase in drug abuse since 1954, when the words "under God" were added to the Pledge of Allegiance?

The Supreme Court decision banning government-sponsored prayer in public schools may have energized the religious right, but sanctioned prayer in public schools was never as widespread as they would have us believe. In a 1960 survey, two years before the first prayer case reached the U.S. Supreme Court, only five states had laws requiring daily Bible reading in public school. In twenty-five states, Bible reading was optional and in eleven, government-sponsored Bible reading was unconstitutional. The remaining states had no laws on the books one way or the other.[735]

Proposed school prayer amendments have periodically been introduced in Congress. In 1982, President Reagan supported an amendment for "voluntary" school prayer. A White House briefing paper explained: "States and communities would be free to select prayers that have already been written, or they could compose their own prayers."[736] Though a majority of senators favored the amendment, it did not receive the necessary two-thirds endorsement. A 1998 school prayer amendment also fell short of the needed two-thirds majority.[737] Practically speaking, it is easier to change local public schools through local school board action than through national legislation. Locally is where the "tyranny of the majority" can be most effective. This is why Ralph Reed of the Christian Coalition has talked about school board seats being more important than congressional seats.[738]

Rob Boston points out some frightening statements by elected school board members. A La Mesa/Spring Valley, California, school board member in 1990 said, "We want to have it like it was 100 years ago, when God, the Ten Commandments and prayer was the focus of the schools."[739] A Vista, California, school board member in 1992 told the *Wall Street Journal* she thought public school teachers should tell students about Christ and lead them in religious exercises. She went on to say, "It would be wonderful to see the scripture read in schools so that children learn the truth. This is our heritage. Anyone who comes into this country is welcome, but we shouldn't be diluted [sic] by others' beliefs."[740]

There are also back-door attempts to proselytize unsuspecting students. Benny Proffitt, president of First Priority of America, has been working to establish religious clubs in public schools. Under his plan, local churches join forces to train students and fund their activities. Using the Equal Access Act to gain a foothold in schools, students are instructed to seek converts and regularly report the number of conversions to First Priority. According to Proffitt, there are 3,000 such schools spread over 200 communities. These schools seem to be in violation of the Equal Access Act, which states, "non-school persons may not direct, conduct, control, or regularly attend activities of student groups."[741] Legal organizations like the American Center for Law and Justice, a group related to Pat Robertson, and the conservative Rutherford Institute, regularly send representatives to address school boards and "explain" the rights of students to engage in religious activities in public schools. According to Boston:

> These missives are designed to intimidate school officials with threats of lawsuits, while the legal 'advice' they contain is really designed to circumvent Supreme Court decisions on issues like state-sponsored prayer in public schools.[742]

Enter science into the political and educational arena. Arguments about possible conflicts between science and religion are as old as science, itself. Fundamentalists 500 years ago found Biblical justification to insist that the Earth was flat; 400 years ago, they kept an unmoved Earth at the center of the universe; and 100 years ago, they tried to replace the irrational number pi (the ratio of the circumference of a circle to its diameter) with the more Biblically justified whole number 3. [I Kings 7:23]

Today, fundamentalists attack the teaching of evolution in our public schools, calling it only a "theory." However, it is important to realize scientists do not use the word *theory* the way laymen do in casual conversation, as in "I have a *theory* that . . . ." Scientists elevate a hypothesis or conjecture to theory status only after a system of assumptions, accepted principles, and rules of procedure are devised to analyze, predict, or otherwise explain specific phenomena. Well over ninety-nine percent of all biologists agree there is substantial documentation that life forms change over long periods. They agree current forms of life have arisen from previous forms and that fossils represent the remains of creatures living in the distant past.

Despite what the religious right would have us believe, the theory of evolution is not controversial within the scientific community. It is backed by our best scientific minds, including the 2,000 members of the National Academy of Sciences, with more than 160 Nobel Prize winners among them. The National Association of Biology Teachers, comprised of more than 8,000 science educators and scientists, states on its web site: "Nothing in biology makes sense except in the light of evolution."[743]

Refinements and additional insights are certainly needed to complete the theory of evolution. Still, reputable scientists readily accept its basic framework. Evolution is as established as the theory of gravity, which will also require significant breakthroughs to understand completely. Gravity, however, has not become politicized. If evolution were replaced with "creation science," fossils would be seen as the remains of Noah's flood and geologic time would be viewed as a scientific delusion. Physicists would also have to dismiss the concept of a constant speed of light, since under the creationist idea, the Earth and universe are only 6,000 years old. The measurement of the distance light travels in a year indicates the Earth is approximately 4.6 billion years old, and the universe is approximately 15 billion.

The religious right has waged a long and, unfortunately, successful media campaign to mold public perception about the theory of evolution. A significant number of Americans think it either should not be taught in our public schools, or should be taught along with so-called "Scientific Creationism." But science is not democratic. If a million people believe a wrong thing, it is still a wrong thing. Scientific Creationism is an alternative to Zeus or Krishna, not to Darwin. "Creation science" should no more be taught as an alternative to evolution than should the "stork theory" be taught as an alternative to reproduction.

The religious right's condemnation of evolution has managed to frighten and confuse so many educators and administrators, some public schools now avoid the subject of evolution. They seek to dodge the controversy, or use textbooks limiting evolution to a mere paragraph or two. Boston says, "Creationists are responsible for the dumbing down of an entire generation of American students and have done great damage to science education in this country."[744] I do not doubt the sincerity of creationists. They want the whole truth and nothing but the truth taught in the classroom, just as evolutionists do. As Carter points out, "For evangelicals in particular, all the Bible is encompassed within a single heading, and that heading is truth."[745] But this version of "truth" is not science, and it has no place in a science curriculum.

Our society empowers parents to raise their children as they wish, so long as they do not inflict serious damage. Courts often have trouble determining when the parental right to use punishment as discipline crosses the line into physical or emotional abuse. Although children are required to partake in some kind of schooling, parents are granted much latitude on this matter. They can home-school their children or send them to fundamentalist schools, where students may hear the theory of evolution defined as a belief that humans are nothing but "rearranged pond scum."[746]

I find it painful as an educator to see any student complete school without studying even the rudiments of the theory of evolution. The desire by fundamentalists to also prevent public school children from learning about evolution is potentially the most harmful thing they can do to society as a whole. I want to thank British scientist Richard Dawkins for informing me about Nicholas Humphrey's excellent essay titled "What Shall We Tell the Children?"[747] In it, Humphrey argues that society has a duty to protect children from ignorant and bigoted parents who sabotage their children's right to the best education available.

Today we may be astounded by the scientifically illiterate geocentric battles of the Middle Ages. Future generations likely will look back with equal amazement at our twenty-first century "evolution battles."

The art of religious politics

Politics is the art of negotiation and compromise, while fundamentalism espouses an uncompromising and absolutist worldview. So it makes sense to wonder how deeply imbedded in politics can or should fundamentalists become. We will consider the divisions between the pragmatists and the purists within the religious right over whether to focus on the practical politics of this world, or the saving of souls for the next. The case of former President Ronald Reagan offers a good starting point.

On the surface, Republican candidate Reagan does not seem to be the kind of person the religious right would have enthusiastically supported for the 1980 presidency. He was divorced. He had been, for the most part, an absentee father whose grown children were unlikely role models for those trumpeting "family values." As governor of California, Reagan had signed liberal abortion bills and opposed legislation that would have barred gays from teaching in public schools. He achieved prominence as a Hollywood actor and had not even been a regular churchgoer. Moreover, he was running against incumbent President Jimmy Carter, a born-again Southern Baptist Sunday school teacher.

Reagan benefited from an approach exercised in a previously successful Republican campaign. Richard Nixon had become president in 1968 largely through a "Southern strategy" that had applied divisive racial politics to convince George Wallace Democrats to vote for a Republican. Sidney Blumenthal, in describing the "religious right" Republican strategy employed against Carter in 1979, said Reagan used social issues to separate the evangelicals, mostly Southern Baptists, from their traditional allegiance to the Democratic Party.[748]

This tactic scored a major victory at the Southern Baptist Convention of 1979. Morton Blackwell and Ed McAteer, Republican Party operatives, had cooperated with fundamentalist forces to engineer "a stunning takeover of the nation's largest Protestant denomination."[749] The takeover was designed to bring Southern Baptists into the Republican Party. According to Appleby, fundamentalists replaced moderates in seminaries and missionary boards. They focused their attention on the Republican Party at local, state, and national levels.[750]

The communication skills that Reagan, the actor, had developed so effectively in Hollywood also helped Reagan, the politician. While campaigning on August 21, 1979, at the National Affairs Briefing in Dallas, a convention bringing together some of the leading conservative political and religious figures, Reagan declared, "You can't endorse me, but I can endorse you."[751] This struck a unique chord, explained Ed Dobson, a close aid to Jerry Falwell:

> I don't think people understand that the average fundamentalist felt alienated from mainstream American culture. That was a significant moment, because the candidate came to us; we didn't go to the candidate.[752]

At a press conference that same day, Reagan urged that the Biblical story of creation be taught in public schools as an alternative to the theory of evolution. He claimed evolution was increasingly discredited by scientists. Reagan also complained that the Supreme Court had "expelled God from the classroom," and noted "everybody in favor of abortion had already been born."[753] Another speaker at this convention was Dr. Bailey Smith, newly-elected president of the Southern Baptist Convention. He made no pretense of tolerance when he proclaimed: "God Almighty does not hear the prayer of a Jew." His explanation afterward was that he did not mean his statement to be anti-Semitic—he was just as intolerant of Muslims, Buddhists and Hindus! Smith said:

> For how in the world can God hear the prayer of a man who says that Jesus Christ is not the true Messiah? That is blasphemy. It may be politically expedient, but no one can pray unless he prays through the name of Jesus Christ.[754]

The elation felt by evangelicals over the election of President Reagan in 1980 soon lost some of its luster. In a meeting with religious ministers in 1979, Reagan had promised that the number of evangelical Christians in his administration would be proportional to their strength in the population.[755] However, the administration learned that forty percent of the country considered themselves born-again Christians, and very few had previously participated in government. It then became clear this was a promise Reagan would break. He did appoint James Watt, a member of the Assemblies of God, as Secretary of the Interior, but made few other high-level appointments among the born-again.[756]

Even more troubling to the religious right was an announcement by the Reagan administration shortly after his election "that serious consideration of the 'social agenda' would have to be deferred for at least a year, to give the new administration time to focus on economic recovery."[757] The religious right quickly learned that getting into bed with the political right could lead to broken hearts. Their issue was not the traditional guns vs. butter, it was God vs. butter. It was religious absolutism vs. political compromise.

Cal Thomas, a syndicated columnist and vice president of the Moral Majority, called politics "a great seducer." He spoke of traveling around the country to different churches and seeing prominently displayed pictures of the local pastor with Ronald Reagan. Thomas worried about the ability of some pastors to speak truth to power because, "Ronald Reagan became the surrogate messiah."[758] Many religious leaders were troubled by what political dabbling could do to their religion. Such concerns over the years led Cal Thomas to assert that religious right activists had erred by placing too much emphasis on politics when they should be saving souls.[759]

Not everyone on the religious right agreed. Reverend D. James Kennedy, head of Coral Ridge Ministries, views such talk as heresy.[760] Kennedy had invited Thomas to be a leadoff speaker at Kennedy's 1999 "Reclaiming America for Christ" conference. After Thomas's book appeared, Kennedy summarily replaced him on the program with

Republican House Majority Leader Dick Armey. Thomas even complained to the *Washington Post* about how the Right, not the Left, had censored him.[761]

Cal Thomas had certainly not been a liberal humanist over the years. In his syndicated January 2, 1995, column that I read in the Charleston *Post and Courier*, he expressed dismay over the views of a theology student at Emory University. He wrote, "One might ask what good it does to study theology if the subject doesn't point the student to an authority higher than his or her own mind?"

I responded in a letter to the editor that:

> Mr. Thomas, along with most of the religious right, apparently does not understand the difference between an education and indoctrination. A rational inquiry into transcendent religious questions like the nature and existence of a deity leads different people to different conclusions. There is more to an education than the memorization of a body of facts or a catechism.[762]

In some sense, when the Soviet Union "evil empire" was no longer around to demonize, many in the religious right began focusing even more on the culture war they saw within the United States. In his 1994 book, *Character & Destiny*, Reverend D. James Kennedy asserts that America was once a Christian nation. However, he argues, "the hostile barrage from atheists, agnostics, and other secular humanists has begun to take a serious toll on that heritage." He continues, "Our job is to reclaim America for Christ, whatever the cost." He is certain victory will be achieved: "Christians did not start the culture war but we are going to end it. That is a fact, and the Bible assures us of victory."[763]

A couple of years earlier, at the 1992 Republican convention, conservative presidential candidate Pat Buchanan also spoke on the same theme: "There is a religious war going on in this country. It's a cultural war as critical to the kind of nation we shall be as the Cold War itself. This war is for the soul of America."[764] The religious left had also long been active in working for cultural changes, especially in advocating civil rights and a decent standard of living for all. The cultural and political issues most identified with the religious right were, and still are, abortion, pornography, homosexuality, and prayer in public schools.

Ralph Reed, former Executive Director of the Christian Coalition and currently President of Century Strategies, a political consulting firm, is both a Christian conservative and a practical politician who has tried to cast a wider net. He mentioned in 1996 the difficulty the Christian Coalition had in recruiting blacks. It was because white evangelical Protestants, especially in the South, had been on the wrong side of the most central struggle for social justice in the twentieth century, the struggle for civil rights. He said, "They preached against it, they organized against it, they used their pulpits to argue that the mixing of politics and religion by black ministers like Martin Luther King was wrong."[765]

The religious right continued to struggle with civil rights during the Republican primary campaign of 2000, when most candidates competed for votes from the religious right. In one debate, George W. Bush scored points when he said his favorite philosopher was Jesus Christ. By February of 2000, the field had narrowed to two—George W. Bush and John McCain. While campaigning in the politically crucial South Carolina primary, Bush accepted an invitation to speak at Bob Jones University, a controversial fundamentalist school in the state. The University's web site contained the following judgment about Roman Catholicism:

> The Roman church is not another Christian denomination. It is a Satanic counterfeit, an ecclesiastic tyranny over the souls of men, not to bring them to salvation, but to hold them bound in sin and hurl them into eternal damnation. It is the old harlot in the Book of Revelation, the mother of harlots."[766]

Bush's spokesperson, Mindy Tucker, was asked why he spoke at the school, which also did not allow interracial dating. Tucker gave an honest response: "The governor doesn't agree with that policy, but this is a school that has a lot of conservative voters, and it's a common stop on the campaign trail."[767] Competing candidate John McCain criticized Bush's visit to Bob Jones and lost the South Carolina fundamentalist vote and the South Carolina Republican primary. McCain never recovered, and Bush easily captured the Republican nomination.

The religious right has made and continues to make significant political inroads. At a prayer breakfast during the 2000 Republican convention, Roman Catholic Father Frank Provone of Priests for Life spoke:

> There never has been a national election more important than the one we face this year. It is not going to be business as usual, particularly in the churches. We need to reaffirm again and again that we as believers who look forward to the world to come . . .

have our citizenship in heaven. . . . We are called to testify to the truth and one of the places we testify to the truth is the voting booth. . . . The church does not dictate the policies of the nation. The church proclaims the truth of God to which these policies must conform.[768]

President George W. Bush certainly pleased the religious right with his choice for attorney general. The American Civil Liberties Union (ACLU) commented:

The mere fact that the nation's new Attorney General John Ashcroft received a 100 percent rating on every Christian Coalition voting scorecard from the time he entered the U.S. Senate in 1995 should be enough to send a shudder down the spine of anyone who cares about the separation of church and state.[769]

The ACLU pointed out that Ashcroft had steered his "entire political career" in one direction. He was trying to institute sectarian religious practices and beliefs into United States laws.[770] President Bush and Ashcroft have mentioned Antonin Scalia and Clarence Thomas as models for the type of justices they would like to appoint to the Supreme Court. Both Scalia and Thomas have proven their anti-gay and anti-abortion biases in their Supreme Court voting records.[771]

President Bush has established a federal office to implement the funding of religious organizations providing social services. This is an alarming example of where the president stands on separation of church and state and where he intends to go with it. But most worrisome of all is the likely intent of the Bush administration to replace retiring Supreme Court justices with others in the Scalia-Thomas mold.[772]

The candidate without a prayer

In 1990, I had a personal and political encounter with the religious right. Born in Philadelphia, educated there and in New York, I moved to South Carolina in 1976 to teach at the College of Charleston. Before 1990, I was vaguely aware of living in the "Bible Belt," but blissfully unaware of what it really meant or how it could affect me. After all, as a mathematics professor, my cultural life was wrapped around the wonderfully insulated world of academe. I was about to learn how the influence and effectiveness of the religious right would significantly change my world forever.

Why would a liberal, Yankee, atheist Jew, who had never before sought political office, suddenly become a South Carolina gubernatorial candidate? My political saga began when a colleague at the College of Charleston pointed out a clause in the South Carolina Constitution that, "No person shall be eligible for the office of governor who denies the existence of the Supreme Being."

Article VI of the U.S. Constitution prohibits religious tests as qualification to any public office. So, I consulted a local attorney, who worked pro bono for the South Carolina affiliate of the ACLU. I asked him how this obviously unconstitutional provision could be removed. The attorney told me the only way to challenge it would be through an actual candidacy by someone who publicly declared him or herself an atheist. In fact, he said, the very best candidate would be me—in a race for governor of South Carolina!

After giving this surprising suggestion much thought, I agreed to run. I assumed, in my political naïveté, the state attorney general would simply consent to bring South Carolina into compliance with federal law. I even found that the United Citizens Party, a small party that rarely ran candidates for any office, was willing to nominate me. Of course, I neither expected nor wanted to be elected.

Much to my amazement, my announced candidacy drew national attention because it seemed so unusual. South Carolina Governor Carroll Campbell reacted by declaring that the state Constitution was fine as it was because the country was founded on Godly principles. However, the first political fence I had to mend was with my astonished and disapproving mother. She had read an Associated Press story about my candidacy in the *Philadelphia Inquirer*. I had to admit that reading her morning newspaper was not the best way to find out that her only son was a gubernatorial candidate—and an atheist!

I never thought my constitutional challenge would reach so far geographically. And, like many nonbelievers, I wanted to spare family members the potential discomfort such a revelation could bring. After I calmed my mother down, she admitted she was not so distressed about my actually being an atheist. She was more worried about the possible damage to my reputation by such an open and public admission.

I told a reporter that I knew of no acknowledged atheists holding public office anywhere in the country, but I expected there were "closet atheists" in South Carolina and elsewhere. An AP story in the Charleston *News & Courier* on May 3, 1990, printed responses by South Carolina legislators. Representative Lenoir Sturkie called my statement, "political maneuvering and a bunch of hogwash." He added he knew of no atheists in the state legislature. Representative Larry Martin assured the citizenry that more than ninety percent of the legislators were "very active in their local churches above and beyond their belief in God." Martin, a Southern Baptist, also offered to pray for me.[773]

Meanwhile, the South Carolina Election Commission noticed a story printed in the *News & Courier*. The story had alleged "irregularities" in the way I obtained the nomination of the United Citizens Party. On May 15, the Election Commission voted 3-2 that this should be investigated by the State Law Enforcement Division (SLED). The following day, the *News & Courier* ran an uncomplimentary editorial about my alleged misdeeds under the headline "Panel Wants Silverman Inquiry." Neither the election commission nor the newspaper offered me an opportunity to defend myself against any charges, although I had informed SLED of my willingness to cooperate and provide them with appropriate documentation.

After hearing nothing about the investigation for eight weeks, I again called SLED. I was told the investigation was nearly complete and my input would not be needed. A few days later, the election commission issued a report that irregularities had been found by SLED and therefore, I would not be allowed on the ballot. It seems one of the United Citizens Party leaders had been badgered by law enforcement officers about why he was supporting an atheist. Eventually, he said he did not understand the document he was signing when I received the party nomination. I had witnesses who could have proved otherwise. My ACLU lawyer said I had a legitimate grievance with the election commission, but he pointed out our case would not be jeopardized if I campaigned as a write-in candidate, which I agreed to do.

I campaigned across the state, appearing in as many "Meet the Candidate" forums as I could persuade to invite me. I always explained that I viewed my case as a civil rights issue. After a forum, the audience often had a chance to speak with the candidates over refreshments. At one such event in the city of Spartanburg, people were keeping their distance from me, as invariably happened. But as I was leaving, one man approached me and hurriedly whispered he was a high-school principal and just wanted to let me know how brave he thought I was to say what I did. He then quickly walked away.

I also appeared on radio talk shows. I would typically be introduced as a "so-called" atheist, or an "admitted" atheist. I wondered what the reaction would have been if another guest had been introduced as a "so-called" Presbyterian, or an "admitted" Southern Baptist. Christian conservative callers would often ask if I worshipped Satan, since I "had to believe in something." However, the oddest comments came from callers who assumed I must feel free to rape, murder, or commit all sorts of atrocities because I did not believe in a judging God. I told those callers that, with such an attitude, I hoped they maintained their belief in a God—for the sake of society!

I received many condemnatory and proselytizing letters from the religious right. On the rare occasions a return address was included, I wrote back and explained my point of view. I was learning that my campaign was needed not simply to change an unconstitutional state provision. More important was my attempt to change the hearts and minds of my fellow South Carolinians.

My day in court came on October 5, 1990, a month before the election. The state Attorney General had refused to declare the religious test for public office unconstitutional. Instead, he sent three lawyers to challenge me on four grounds: mootness, because I was denied nomination by a party; standing, because I was not a legitimate candidate; ripeness, meaning there was no need to decide the case at the moment; and the Eleventh Amendment, regarding restrictions on suing state officials.

I thought it ironic that the *News & Courier* had recently ended an editorial with, "If Mr. Silverman truly is trying to teach tolerance rather than atheism, as he says, then he will think twice about legal challenges that needlessly consume taxpayer dollars."[774] In truth, the state was spending thousands of dollars to enforce an obviously unconstitutional provision.

On judgment day, Judge David Norton dismissed the case on grounds it was not ripe because I had little chance of winning. Norton had just been appointed to the U.S. District Court of South Carolina upon nomination by Senator Strom Thurmond. In effect, he refused to rule on the constitutional issue unless I won the election—which, of course, I did not.

A few months later, I discovered that South Carolina's Constitution prohibited atheists from holding any public office. My lawyer told me I could challenge this by applying for a notary public license. A virtually identical provision of the Maryland Constitution had been struck down in 1961 by the U.S. Supreme Court in *Torcaso v. Watkins*. If South Carolina were to grant me a notary public license, it would be an admission by the state that religious tests could no longer be a qualification for public office.

My attorney expected this notary campaign to be shorter and more successful than my gubernatorial campaign. Shorter, it was not! South Carolina is normally one of the easiest states to become a notary. All applications are routinely approved by the office of the governor. I paid my $25 fee in October of 1991, but crossed out the phrase "so help me God" on the application. I also mentioned that the U.S. Constitution prohibits religious tests as a qualification for public office.

Secretary of State James Miles returned my application on the grounds I had not filled out the form properly. My lawyer then sent it directly to Governor Carroll Campbell, who rejected it. When we asked why, a spokesperson for his office replied it would be far too burdensome to give reasons for every negative decision. Later, in a deposition taken from Secretary Miles in 1994, he was forced to disclose that 33,471 notary applications were approved from 1991 to 1993. Mine was the only one denied in that period. To my knowledge, I am the only person in the history of South Carolina to be rejected as a notary public.

Governor Campbell left office in January 1995, still claiming immunity from giving a deposition in which he might be compelled to state under oath the reason for denying me the notary. Then we got help from a most unlikely source. My ACLU lawyer argued successfully in circuit court that if the lawyers of Paula Corbin Jones could depose President Clinton, then former Governor Campbell could no longer avoid being deposed.

In an ironic coincidence, John Whitehead, founder of the politically conservative Rutherford Institute, defended Paula Jones in her case against Clinton. In his book, *The Second American Revolution*, Whitehead had blasted the U.S. Supreme Court for striking down religious requirements for public office in the 1961 *Torcaso v. Watkins* case. This decision was the basis for my case. In that ruling, Whitehead wrote, the Supreme Court, "rejected Judeo-Christian theism as the religion and foundation of the United States."[775] Whitehead is correct in his assertion. The Supreme Court affirmed we are, indeed, a secular nation in which religious tests for public office are unconstitutional.

My lawyer took an eighty-six-page deposition from Governor Campbell on March 3, 1995. Among his many convoluted responses, the governor argued why it might be permissible to deny office based on religious beliefs:

Would it be right to have somebody running for public office that was avowed to overthrow and destroy the United States of America, and they didn't believe in a supreme being but they believed in a foreign government, and they call that a religion?[776]

On August 2, 1995, the presiding judge of the Fifth Judicial Circuit in the Court of Common Pleas said my petition to be a notary met all the legal requirements. He requested that the governor act on my application within thirty days. Former governor Carroll Campbell had successfully resisted granting me a notary while in office. So, the decision now resided with his successor, Governor David Beasley. He had been elected in 1994 with strong Christian Coalition support. A born-again Christian, Beasley hoped to see creationism incorporated into the public school curriculum.

Secretary of State James Miles urged state officials to appeal the Circuit Court decision because he did not think the provision represented religious discrimination. He said, "I believe that language is appropriate because I'm a Christian."[777] Unwilling to go quietly, even after losing a judicial reconsideration appeal, Governor Beasley then appealed to the South Carolina Supreme Court.

A headline in the renamed Charleston *Post & Courier* on October 31, 1995, read, "Gov. David Beasley wants the S.C. Supreme Court to decide if office seekers should be forced to *believe* in a Supreme Being."[778]

I responded to an inquiring reporter that I understood how I could be forced to *say* I believe (torture would work!). But Governor Beasley did not clarify how I could actually be forced to *believe*. My point was that it is proper for government to regulate some behavior, but it can never regulate belief. In interviews, I could not resist mentioning that the state considered me qualified to be a professor of mathematics at a public institution, yet it deemed me lacking high enough ethical and moral standards for the office of notary public. Perhaps the value of religious indoctrination over reason and scientific inquiry might help explain the dismal condition of education in South Carolina today, where SAT scores have been among the lowest in the nation for many years.

The state Supreme Court heard my case in October 1996. A local reporter asked me why I thought Governor Beasley was appealing to the state Supreme Court. I said I was under the assumption that Governor Beasley, who had a law degree, knew religious tests for public office were unconstitutional. "By trying to exclude nonbelievers," I said, "I think he is simply playing to the religious bigotry of a segment of his constituency."

In the same article, Gary Karr, the Governor's press secretary, responded that he "denies in the strongest terms that Governor Beasley is a religious bigot and thinks it is a shame that Dr. Silverman would attack the governor's religious beliefs like that."[779]

Good news for me came on May 27, 1997. The state Supreme Court unanimously affirmed the Circuit Court's holding that the South Carolina Constitution violated the First Amendment and the Religious Test Clause of the United States Constitution. Ironically, I shared top billing in the local paper the next day with the person whose lawsuit paved the way for our deposition of Governor Campbell. The two side-by-side headlines in the Charleston *Post & Courier* were: "Atheist wins fight against 'God clause'" and "High court says Jones is clear to sue Clinton."

The May 30 Spartanburg *Herald-Journal* opinion page said:

> Silverman may not be a completely sympathetic figure as he pursues office just to make a point for atheist rights. But he should not be disqualified from the political life of the state solely because of his religious beliefs or the lack thereof.[780]

Nevertheless, Governor Beasley still had a tough call to make. He did not want to be the first governor of South Carolina to grant a notary commission to an acknowledged atheist. However, he was reluctant to appeal to the U.S. Supreme Court for a couple of reasons. His lawyers had concentrated on the states' rights argument that state officials had sworn to uphold the state constitution without regard to previous U.S. Supreme Court decisions. How could they then ask the federal government to interfere with the unanimous decision of the highest court in the sovereign state of South Carolina?

In addition, South Carolina had recently squandered a substantial amount of taxpayer dollars attempting to keep women out of The Citadel, a South Carolina military college for men only. More litigation was anticipated for having recently posted the Ten Commandments in the Charleston County Council chambers. Conservative state officials did not want to be criticized for wasting even more taxpayer dollars on what would obviously be another costly and fruitless appeal of my case. Finally, on August 8, 1997, Governor Beasley mailed me my notary commission.

Though I had hoped in 1990 for quick affirmation of an atheist's right to hold public office, the protracted engagement added undeniable benefits to my life. I received considerable media attention in South Carolina, which afforded me the opportunity to publicize a point of view not often heard in the Bible belt. After each such appearance, I received enthusiastic phone calls and mail from people who thought they were the only ones in South Carolina with those beliefs. This encouraged me to help found the Secular Humanists of the Lowcountry, a vibrant community of local freethinkers who meet monthly. Best of all for me, personally, I met my wife, Sharon Fratepietro—in church! When I was running for governor in 1990, she heard me speak at the local Unitarian Church. She offered to help in my campaign, and we have been together ever since.

Recently, one of my mathematics students, unfamiliar with my case, saw my notary sign prominently displayed in my office and asked if I'd had to go to law school to become a notary. I told him it was not quite that simple. Law school would have taken only three years. It took longer for me to receive my notary commission than my Ph.D. in mathematics! Of course, my right to become a notary should not have taken seven years or happened the way it did, but in many ways it was well worth the wait.

Although the religious right was ultimately unsuccessful in preventing me from becoming a notary public, my case indicates the influence they can exert over politicians. None of the political leaders in South Carolina, and certainly not the lawyers advising them, believed they could prevail legally if I continued to pursue my case. Yet, those same politicians demonstrated they would rather waste time and money on a lost cause than risk the wrath and lose the votes of a well-organized religious right.

Theocracy or democracy?

What are the political objectives of the religious right? After conducting a wide variety of interviews, Conway and Siegelman summarized the answers from leaders in the movement:

> To Christianize America, to fill all government positions with Bible believing Christians, to gain ascendancy over the national media, to have fundamentalist beliefs taught as science in public schools, to dictate the meaning of human life and ultimately to convert every person on earth.[781]

In short, they would like to replace our secular democracy with a fundamentalist theocracy.

Still, there is a tension within the religious right community about whether a theocracy would be preferable to a democracy. Christian Reconstructionist Gary North called the Constitution a "secular humanist" document and called for scrapping it outright in favor of a new governing document based explicitly on the Bible—or at least his interpretation of it.[782] This is a minority view, even among the religious right. Nonetheless, Christian Right adherents generally view theonomy, or Rule of God, as an ideal to work toward through the democratic process.

While a democratic society can easily accommodate differences of opinion, a theonomy cannot. Few Americans would argue that the U.S. Constitution is an infallible document, as the religious right views the Bible. The framers understood the need for change and set forth mechanisms for achieving it. On the other hand, the religious right accepts the Bible, from Genesis to Revelation, as inerrant and unamendable. This leads to conflicts with the religious right when scientific or humanistic advances make it desirable to incorporate new information and change our worldview and behavior. It is especially so when such changes seem to conflict with their Biblical worldview. Evolution, which no literal reading of the Bible can support, is a notable example.

Like the Bible, the Constitution once condoned slavery. But the Constitution has been amended to make slavery illegal. Many nineteenth century fundamentalists could easily quote Biblical passages (Genesis 9: 25, Timothy 6:1-2, Titus 2:9-10, Ephesians 6: 5) to defend the institution of slavery. The Southern Baptist Convention came into existence in 1845 because of its support for slavery. Now, all but the most radical elements of the religious right can either ignore or drastically reinterpret Biblical passages to affirm their opposition to slavery. Homosexuality is another issue the mainstream culture has begun to regard through twenty-first century eyes, despite objections from the religious right.

Most religious right organizations assume there is a "correct" Christian position on particular issues. However, the majority of Christians in this country are not fundamentalists, and even they have significant denominational differences. For example, every society, secular or theocratic, condemns murder. Nevertheless, human interpretations of murder differ, even for those who live according to their holy books. Christians do not agree on whether murder includes euthanasia, suicide, abortion, war, capital punishment, and now, stem cell research.

Christian Right groups insist only their version of the truth is correct. It then becomes easy to dismiss Christians who disagree with them as not being "true" Christians. Taking it one step further, any criticism of extreme fundamentalist political objectives is painted as an assault on religion. This "victimization" tactic becomes a useful political tool to energize the religious right. Conservative strategist Paul Weyrich says he advised Republican leaders in 1994 "to describe Clinton's attacks on the Christian

Right as an attack on religion itself."[783] Haley Barbour, former chairman of the Republican National Committee, told the *Washington Times* that the Democrats "think Christian-bashing is the only acceptable form of religious bigotry left. . . . It's offensive to every religious group in the country."[784] Sometimes it is difficult to ascertain whether we are listening to political pandering or a virulent strain of religious bigotry.

In trying to counter the religious right, President Bill Clinton in 1994 told a National Prayer Breakfast audience that "we should all seek to know and do God's will even when we differ."[785] Michael Kinsley questioned comments about how Christians were shamed into retreating to their closets. He asked, "Are those who pray regularly forced to keep it a 'shameful secret'? Not in any America I know."[786]

And how does the religious right hope to achieve its objectives? Although they frequently complain about "liberal" control of the media, the religious right does quite well on the airwaves. They maintain 24-hour-a-day television and radio programming on a variety of networks. Moreover, many religious right broadcasters have learned to progress effortlessly from theological to political points. Political statements made on religious broadcasts generally are not scrutinized or challenged by the mainstream media.

As Mallica Dutt observes, "What gives the religious right its power is a clear vision of the kind of society it wishes to create."[787] In part, because of their effectiveness with media, the religious right is currently much better organized than the political left. They vote in greater proportion to their numbers and they communicate with their elected representatives. According to Appleby, fundamentalist leaders often manipulate religion to meet their political ends. They are well versed in political processes and mass-marketing techniques. They seem to thrive "because secular modernity seems exhausted of solutions to social problems."[788]

George Grant, a far right activist, explains how concentrating on single candidates can help gain control: "Since only about sixty percent of the people are registered to vote and only about thirty-five percent of those actually bother to go to the polls, a candidate only needs to get the support of a small, elite group of citizens to win."[789]

This strategy has proved successful in many local and congressional elections. Ed Dobson and Edward Hindson, in their book, *The Seduction of Power,* reveal:

> Conservative evangelicals have shown a great ability to make the
> political system work for them. . . . Right wing evangelicals have

learned very quickly how to get voters registered, platforms adopted, and candidates into office.[790]

Further, the religious right has made strategic alliances. Fundamentalists who do not have a strong interest in a particular fundamentalist goal will often coalesce with those who do. This way they earn support from fellow fundamentalists on other issues of importance to themselves. With the polarization of religion in America, conservative Jews, Mormons, Christian fundamentalists, and many Catholics now team up on issues like opposition to abortion.[791] Politicians, especially Republicans, have come to see the religious right as an important constituency.

How can the tactics of the religious right be neutralized? First, it must be recognized that political success for this small but vocal and influential minority relies on the apathy of others. Americans must become informed, involved, and better organized. Those not on the religious right are generally more flexible and can accommodate a broader range of opinions. This should make it easier for diverse groups to work together.

That chimpanzees have a genetic structure more similar to humans than to gorillas is a surprising discovery. If a "religious" gene were ever discovered, I expect its structure for a liberal religionist would be more similar to that of an atheist than a conservative religionist. Fundamentalists in different religions have more in common with each other than they do with the liberal wings within their own religions. On a plethora of political issues such as church and state separation, abortion rights, gay rights, and others, liberal religionists and nontheists are natural allies. More cooperation can and should effectively counter the well-organized religious right.

The religious right has not been averse to spreading erroneous information on issues like public school hostility toward Christianity, church and state separation, and the charge that the U.S. was founded as a Christian nation. If left unchallenged, more people will begin to believe the inaccurate assertions. This requires paying attention to the propaganda of the religious right and learning which statements are misleading.

One need not master all the esoteric details before responding. Neutrality toward religion in public schools is not anti-Christian. It is not necessary to read about the original intent of the framers of the U.S. Constitution, or what theological beliefs they held. What matters is that this country was not founded as a Christian theocracy, but as a secular state which guarantees freedom for all. One can point to Article 6 of the U.S. Constitution, prohibiting religious tests for public office. In addition, there is the First Amendment's separation of government from religion. These are the only mentions of religion in the Constitution. No deities appear anywhere in the U.S. Constitution, which makes it a "godless" document.

If someone argues that his or her church is being discriminated against because it cannot endorse political candidates, it is not necessary to cite dozens of legal justifications. Just mention that this country fought a revolution against taxation without representation, not for representation without taxation. If churches were willing to give up their tax-exempt status, they would certainly be allowed to endorse candidates.

All sides agree on the importance of influencing future generations. This is why the clash over educational philosophy is so crucial. Should public institutions teach critical thinking skills and encourage ethical and scientific development? Or should they follow a rigid code that demands absolute obedience? These irreconcilable differences ensure the struggle will endure for as long as there is a religious right.

The United States is fortunate never to have had a religious war, although religious conservatism has long been a force in American society. The influence of the religious right ebbs and flows, but its strength and potential must never be dismissed. The religious right is a minority, though an energized and outspoken one. Americans must remain vigilant to assure that this minority will not intrude on the liberties of those who look, act, or think differently from the way they do. Curt Sytsma understood this persistent problem and illustrated it well in his poem "A Humanist Manifesto," which can be found in the introduction of Corliss Lamont's book, *The Philosophy of Humanism.*

A Humanist Manifesto

In every age, the bigot's rage requires another focus,
Another devil forced on stage by hatred's hocus pocus.
The devil used to be a Jew and then it was the witches,
And then it was the Negroes who were digging all the ditches.
The devil once was colored pink and labeled Communistic,
Now, all at once, in just a blink, the devil's Humanistic. [792]

CHAPTER 8

WINNING THE 'BATTLE ROYAL' PARALLELS AND SOLUTIONS TO THE GROWING DANGER

by Edward M. Buckner

He that is not with me is against me.

Jesus, according to Matthew 12:30 (King James Version)

If a man abide not in me, he is cast forth as a branch, and is withered; and men gather them and cast them into the fire, and they are burned.

Jesus, according to John 15:6 (King James Version)

As the preceding chapters demonstrate, fundamentalism presents real dangers to the lives and liberties of all Americans. It is not merely an academic problem or a problem for people who find fundamentalism a little strange or irrational. At risk are women, children, fair elections, society as a whole, the rights of Americans to reproductive choices, their freedom to choose sexual partners, freedom of religion, the freedom for all kinds of dissent, and their rights to privacy and to die with dignity.

Therefore, the very existence of the American secular society is at risk. The dangers to secularism ebb and flow. And it is certainly possible to find historical examples of greater threats to freedom and secularism than we now face, even in the history of the U.S. and certainly elsewhere, such as during the Middle Ages. But the beginning of the twenty-first century seems to be fraught with perils, many of them growing more frightening.

In a single sentence, the editor of *The Fundamentals*, Curtis Lee Lawes, summed up, probably partly unintentionally, both the backward-looking and the militant stance of most fundamentalists: "We suggest that those who still cling to the great fundamentals and who mean to do battle royal for the fundamentals shall be called 'Fundamentalists.'"[793] The fear of modernism hinted at by the word "cling," combined with the military imagery of doing "battle royal," accurately describe the challenge for anyone interested in finding solutions to the problems of fundamentalism. Military imagery in the writing and speeches of fundamentalists remains prevalent, despite being identified by Ralph Reed as bad for public relations.[794]

The core reasons fundamentalists are dangerous—and extraordinarily hard to counter—are that fundamentalists:

- are absolutist and unyielding in their certainty they are right
- are sure an all-powerful, all-knowing God is directing them
- are part of churches demanding strict obedience to doctrine and expecting unquestioning loyalty
- are more emotional than rational in maintaining their beliefs than others, and,
- since Curtis Lee Lawes first used the term and for centuries before that, are aggressive, militaristic, militant in their approach—in short, willing to be violent in the course of doing "battle royal."

It should be immediately added that not all fundamentalists have all these characteristics in equal measure, nor do fundamentalists even all agree on exactly what constitute the "fundamentals." Certainly some non-fundamentalists, including some non-believers, have some of these traits. But, the above is a fair summary of fundamentalism in general.

New Testament verses such as those introducing this chapter are typical of the passages of allegedly sacred texts that the most dangerous followers of any religion turn to. They take these literally and seriously, as the adherents destroy lives. Jesus' reported declaration that there can be no middle ground, no neutrality, often stands in the way of defending a secular society, which is the only long-term solution for the problems of fundamentalism. John 15:6 is not used as often now. But it was a terrifyingly dangerous verse during the Inquisition and could easily become as dangerous again.

One of the most basic beliefs of fundamentalists is that moral prescriptions for human behavior are unchanging and unchallengeable. These prescriptions are believed to have come straight from a perfect, immutable God. This makes for an almost impenetrable defensive shell, a key reason for the intractable nature of these problems. If, after all, one or a group is certain that directions for living are coming unfiltered from an all-powerful, all-knowing God, how can others hope to argue against such orders? If an absolute foundation, a rigid code, is considered desirable, then the pressure to accept a particular one is strong even if the evidence it actually came straight from a divine source is lacking. This is a major reason fundamentalist leaders teach that secularists are a grave threat. It is because of secular tentativeness, the relativity of secular standards, the inability to declare that moral standards are connected to an absolute foundation or to fundamental supernatural truths.

To solve any problem, the critical first step is to understand exactly what the problem is, the purpose this book is dedicated to. If, as Curtis Lee Lawes suggested, Americans are in a "battle royal," a leading item on the agenda should be to identify allies and opponents correctly. It should be taken into account the lessons to be learned from experiences outside of one's own, such as those seen in Islamic-controlled societies. The crucial battle is not between fundamentalists and "liberal" or "mainstream" religious believers nor is it between fundamentalists and irreligious people. Rather, the fight most crucial is between fundamentalists and secularists. That is the one for which secularists must be prepared to do serious battle, if only as a necessary defense to liberty for all.

Secularists constitute the main audience for this book, for they are the only hope for combating the perils of fundamentalism. They are all those people, some religious and some not, who understand that secular control of government and society is necessary. Secularists are those who are capable of looking beyond their own beliefs or lack of beliefs. They understand that those who have, or who pretend to have, religious authority cannot be allowed to govern society.

Fundamentalist Islam: different problems, different solutions?

Islamic fundamentalism has been brought forcefully to the attention of Americans since September 11, 2001. Much of the rest of the world was already aware of the dangers even before the events of that horrible day. Because the word "fundamentalism" is a Christian invention, Muslims object to its application to Islam.[795] Despite this, it seems reasonable in many regards to expand its use to cover any who believe the fundamentals of their faith require doing "battle royal."

Since September 2001, the fundamentalists making the news most often have been Islamic, but they have not been the only ones. Not only Islamic fundamentalists, but Israeli Jewish fundamentalists, have contributed to the rigidity, horrors, and intractability of problems in the

Middle East.[796] Fundamentalist Hindus and Muslims in India killed more than 800 in early 2002 alone. They apparently burned or hacked to death innocent, uninvolved people, including many women and children on both sides, in religious warfare in Gujarat state in western India.[797] Christian and Muslim fundamentalists have brutally murdered each other at least since the Crusades. One of the more recent examples of this is in the Maluku province of Indonesia. There, 9,000 have been killed in religious warfare, including women and small children who have been stabbed, burned, or shot, just in the last three years.[798] Another recent example is in Nigeria, where over 100 people have died in rioting in "Kaduna, a northern city of several million people with a history of Muslim-Christian violence," over disputes about the claimed insult to Islam of holding the Miss World pageant there in December 2002.[799]

A brief summary of non-Christian fundamentalism, especially Islamic fundamentalism, is appropriate. This is because there are many things in common among those of all religions who are willing to be literalist and militant, to engage in a "battle royal" for their religions. Fundamentalist Muslims, like fundamentalist Christians, can easily find support for their militancy and absolutism in a literal reading of their scriptures.[800] For the Islamic literalists, verses from the Qur'an serve that purpose:

> Say to the Infidels: if they desist from their unbelief, what is now past shall be forgiven; but if they return to it, they have already before them the doom of the ancients! Fight then against them till strife be at an end, and the religion be all of it Allah's.[801]

> Kill those who join other gods with Allah wherever you may find them.[802]

Since this book concerns primarily Christian fundamentalism, only an overview of Islamic fundamentalism and of possible solutions for it will be considered. There is no implication intended here that Christian and Islamic fundamentalism are precisely parallel. Nor are their dangers exactly the same. But the brusque dismissal by Christian fundamentalists of any parallel presented is also unwarranted. When fundamentalism of any sort reaches its most fanatical stage, the dangers to individuals and society are acute and the need for solutions urgent.

The best sources for in-depth understanding of Islam from the perspective of a non-Islamic believer are probably books published by Prometheus Books. These include several by Ibn Warraq, especially *Why I Am Not A Muslim*.[803] Consider the threats that have come from contemporary Islamic fundamentalists. This best shows the real paradox for any who want to protect religious liberty for all, including for fundamentalists. The fundamentalist variations of Islam show, vividly and frighteningly, what dangers a rigid, absolutist religion of any kind can produce. As Lawrence Davidson wrote in *Islamic Fundamentalism*, "Any ideology (Islamic or otherwise) that claims a monopoly of truth, and sees its content as divinely posited, is unlikely to tolerate political opposition."[804]

Bernard Lewis has described Islam, at earlier periods of history, as being strong, even dominant. Islamic scholars are divided on "What Went Wrong." He noted:

> It was bad enough for Muslims to feel poor and weak after centuries of being rich and strong, to lose the position of leadership that they had come to regard as their right, and to be reduced to the role of followers of the West. But the twentieth century, particularly the second half, brought further humiliation. . . .[805]

There are, according to Lewis, scholars who blame Islamic fundamentalism for the great decline. But there are many others, mostly fundamentalists, who are convinced otherwise. They are certain the problems and losses in Islamic lands are directly attributable to abandoning true, foundational Islam in favor of modernism. These fundamentalists stand in sharp contrast to those for whom, says Lewis, a "principal cause of Western progress is the separation of Church and State and the creation of a civil society governed by secular laws."[806] Lewis argued forcefully for the idea that Islamic culture has lost its once-great power and effectiveness. He says it is for precisely the opposite reasons identified by the fundamentalists; the reduction of power came because of the loss of crucial freedoms.[807]

Ibn Warraq concluded *Why I Am Not a Muslim* with a chapter called "Islam in the West." It offers a firm call to Western cultures to have the courage of their values and to not be afraid to defend those values. He warned against interpreting Western liberalism as supporting a simplistic multiculturalism that essentially declares all cultural values are equally valid. Warraq insisted Islamic fundamentalists should not be allowed to exploit Western values while they attempt to overthrow them.

As Warraq wrote, "despite all the shortcomings of Western liberal democracy, it is far more preferable to the authoritarian, mind-numbing certitudes of Islamic theocracy."[808] He offered no specific solutions beyond education. He did offer his clarion call for fighting forthrightly against those fundamentalists of the Islamic faith intent on battle royal. He concluded *Why I Am Not* with war imagery: "Therefore, the final battle will not necessarily be between Islam and the West, but between those who value freedom and those who do not."[809] The authors of this book firmly agree with Warraq: this is a battle. And it will not be won unless we have the courage to oppose anti-secularism, anti-American, anti-freedom fundamentalists, wherever they exist. However, we urge exclusively nonmilitary, nonviolent action.

As already noted, both Islamic and Christian fundamentalists would hotly deny their similarities. Islamic defenders might point out that past Christian absolutism and extreme orthodoxy has proven every bit as dangerous to human beings and society as the worst extremes of Islamic fundamentalism. In Iran, Pakistan, and Afghanistan, secularists did not prevail. In other more democratically-run nations such as Turkey, secular society increasingly comes up against Islamic and other religious fundamentalists. If given their way, Turkish fundamentalists would have religious rule.

Many Americans, out of concern for human welfare, express concern with events halfway around the globe. But why, outside of the legitimate concern for human welfare, should Americans care? Because scores of parallels identified between Christian, Islamic, and other fundamentalisms must be acknowledged. These parallels have been addressed by journalists since September 11. Yet, probably for defensive reasons, Christian fundamentalists, and Americans in general, often fail to see the connection and denounce the comparisons.

This lack of vision was demonstrated most profoundly when evangelical columnist Gregory J. Rummo recently wrote, "calling Christians 'Taliban' is slander." This reference to the Taliban, contrary to Rummo's perception, has generally been made in a comparative sense. The purpose has been to point out the likeness between Christian and Islamic fundamentalists and has been limited in reference to Christian fundamentalists and extremists. It has not been a catch-all for Christians in general. "So what are the differences," Rummo asked, "between the Taliban and America's Christian conservatives?" According to Rummo:

> The Taliban are Islamic extremists who use the Koran to justify repressive and reprehensible practices on members of their own

faith while declaring jihad against all who oppose them. They have been rightly characterized as 'misanthropic, misogynist, triumphalist [belief in the superiority of a religious creed], millenarian, anti-modern, anti-Christian, anti-Semitic, terroristic, jihadistic, and suicidal.'[810]

With the exception of "anti-Christian," which could easily be replaced with 'anti-Muslim' and 'anti-secular humanist,' the characteristics described by Pipes and Rummo are quite similar to those observed in Christian fundamentalists. This has been revealed time and again throughout this book. Christian and Islamic fundamentalists have nearly identical characteristics—and for the most part hold the same myopic views as to what constitutes morality. Christian fundamentalists read about the atrocities in Islamic-controlled nations. Yet, they see only the extreme, oppressive forces that have grasped control. They fail to see the parallels between their own beliefs and those of the other fundamentalism.

Like Christians, Muslims are not all the same. What sets Islamic fundamentalists apart from liberal Muslims is that Islamic fundamentalists interpret the Qur'an literally[811] just as the Bible is interpreted by Christian fundamentalists. There are two main Islamic groups, the Shi'ites and the Sunnites. The Sunnites are the overwhelmingly larger and more liberal of the Muslims. The Shi'ites are divided into several sects[812] and are the smaller, more conservative and extreme of the Muslims. As observed in Christian fundamentalism, some Islamic sects are politically active and some keep to themselves.

In the South Asian subcontinent, the two most important Islamic fundamentalist movements take very different approaches, according to Mumtaz Ahmad of the Fundamentalism Project. At a 1989, Jamaat-i-Islami Pakistan national conference in Lahore, Pakistan, Qazi Hussain Ahmad, president of the movement stated in his inaugural address:

> We are gathered here to reaffirm our pledge to Almighty Allah that we will make Pakistan a truly Islamic state, a state where Shariá [the way of life set forth by the Qur'an] will reign supreme, a state based on justice for the people and accountability of the rulers, a state which will be a model of Islamic power for the rest of the Muslim world.[813]

At the same time, only thirty miles away, a million Muslims gathered at the international conference of Tablighi Jamaat. This very different event found people in tents. According to Ahmad, they were "either praying or reciting the Qur'an or listening to each other's testimonies of faith and spiritual reawakening." The enis (president) of the Tablighi Jamaat, Maulana Inamul Hasan, said in his farewell address:

> Go and take the eternal message of Islam to the four corners of the globe. Remind your brethren of their religious duties, remind them of the day of Judgment; and call them to the remembrance of the Almighty Allah, to submission to His will and obedience to Prophet Muhammad (peace be upon him).[814]

The Tablighi Jamaat movement is most concerned with the morality and spirituality of individuals. It asks "them to fulfill their religious obligations," points out Ahmad, regardless of the nature of the state. Paralleling Christian separatists, they believe their duty will be fulfilled by closely adhering to the Muslim faith and by showing others the way. The Jamaat-i-Islami, on the other hand, believes it is its duty to enforce its fundamentalist views on all of society. It therefore, wants to establish an Islamic state "with the Qur'an and Sunna (the way of the Prophet) as its constitution and the Shariá as its basic law."[815]

More telling of the views of more extreme Islamic fundamentalists, similar to those of the Christian Right and specifically Christian Reconstructionists, is that of Maulana Maududi. An Islamic fundamentalist, he inspired the Pakistani Islamization. This is the process of reviving the Shariá (Islamic law) in Pakistan, as narrowly interpreted by Islamic fundamentalists. He argued that:

> Unlike a Secular state, its duty is not merely to maintain internal order. . . . Rather its first and foremost obligation is to establish the system of Salat [prayer] and Zakat [alms tax], to propagate and establish those things which have been declared to be "virtues" by God and His Messenger, and to eradicate those things which have been declared to be "vices" by them. In other words, no state can be called Islamic if it does not fulfil [sic] this fundamental objective of an Islamic State. Thus a state which does not take interest in establishing virtue and eradicating vice and in which adultery, drinking, gambling, obscene literature, indecent films, vulgar songs, immoral display of beauty, promiscuous mingling of men

and women, co-education, etc. flourish without let or hindrance, cannot be called an Islamic State. An Islamic Constitution must declare the above mentioned objective as the primary duty of the State.[816]

These goals and obsessions differ little from those of many other fundamentalist religions, most evidently, Christian fundamentalism.

Notably, Islamic fundamentalists took credit for one of the largest revolutions of modern history in Iran in 1979. The conservative religious leader, Ayatollah Khomeini, led an Islamic regime to replace Iran's semi-secular government. Religious symbols and slogans were used by the new conservative government, as has swept America since September 11. A focus on gender relations and female sexuality also became markedly pronounced in Iran. As is prescribed by Christian fundamentalists, domesticity and motherhood were stipulated for Iranian women "based on divine rules." The promotion of marriage became the emblem for solving society's problems. Family planning came to be seen as an evil, just as it is by Christian fundamentalists, and was severely affected. Supplies for birth control "became erratic" and unaffordable because of disapproval by conservative religious leaders. This ultimately resulted in substantial population growth.[817]

Islam provides direction to the Islamic fundamentalist "for every aspect of life—culture, politics, economics and personal behavior," says Richard Swift, editor of *The New Internationalist*. Islamic fundamentalists adhere to the Shariá Law, he explains, "which represents the direct rule of Allah over society." They are militantly puritanical (professing a pure moral code) and egalitarian. They oppose drugs, alcohol, homosexuality, women's rights, abortion, premarital or extramarital sex, and are suspicious of wealth. Islamic fundamentalists take extreme measures. They censor and even dismember to ensure such "manifestations of 'the modern world'" are not practiced.[818]

The effects of Christian fundamentalism on women in America have not reached the severity witnessed in Islamic-controlled countries. This is because America's democracy is currently intact. Still, the degree to which women can be affected by fundamentalism is staggering. Domestic violence may not be as readily accepted in America. Regardless, it is still present to a large degree in Christian fundamentalist homes and in many cases, even to the severities that have been demonstrated in Middle Eastern Islamic societies.

Similar to views endorsed by Christian fundamentalists, women in Pakistan and elsewhere are looked upon as merely property. Their duty is to serve and be treated as a husband sees fit. Many Pakistani women believe just as those in Christian fundamentalist homes do—that they deserve such treatment. At the very least, they know there is nothing they can do to prevent it.[819] In October 2001, a study by the Punjab Women Development and Social Welfare Department reported:

> some 42% of women accepted violence as part of their fate, while over 33% felt too helpless to stand up to it; only 19% protested and only 4% took action against it. The perpetrators of such violence were male relatives (53%), husbands (32%) followed by other women (13%) and other relatives (2%). The report stated that only some five per cent of rape and 'honour' crimes were reported.[820]

As in America, however, such violence often goes far beyond abuse. In Lahore, a woman was burned to death in April, 2000, by her husband. In the hospital, just before passing away, she told her family her mother-in-law had helped her husband beat her. The punishment was for giving "birth to a baby girl after two years of marriage." She "had also refused to consent to her husband marrying a second wife."[821]

In many Islamic countries, honor killings are a widespread practice. This is true in Iran, and even Turkey, a country that is relatively democratic, but which has increasingly been affected by Islamic fundamentalism. Husbands and male relatives commonly murder women for bringing shame to the family. This can result simply by refusing a forced marriage. The killers often defend their actions by referring to the Qur'an or Islamic doctrines. They are likely to receive reduced sentences or none at all. In a documentary, *Crime of Honour*, broadcast on Cinemax, footage was shown of a woman and a man who was presumed to be her lover. They were "huddle[d] in the middle of a street covered only in a white sheet and [being] stoned until death."[822] Stoning is the form of death penalty favored by Christian Reconstructionists.

Since the Taliban took power in Afghanistan in 1996, women were beaten on the street regularly by religious police "for infractions like wearing white socks," which qualifies as "fashionable" or "charming" clothing. This is something an earlier decree by the Ministry for the Promotion of Virtue and the Prevention of Vice insisted would prevent women from going to heaven. Women were also brutally beaten for going into public without their burkas, the "head-to-toe" garments used to cover their faces. A ban had also been placed on women working outside the home, except for select healthcare positions. This resulted in nearly one million widows being turned into the streets to beg. Women's healthcare suffered because male physicians were not allowed to thoroughly examine women lest the doctor risk imprisonment. Because of the rulings affecting women's healthcare and other oppressive measures, the average life expectancy of Afghan women is now only forty-four years.[823]

The Christian Right's lack of concern for women's welfare and their hostility toward women in general can be easily identified. First, they oppose measures protecting women from the immense suffering they are subjected to in other parts of the world. Second, they call for divorce law and welfare reforms to make divorce more difficult to obtain in America, and third, they oppose reform in countries where divorce is difficult if not impossible to attain. These are yet two more examples of their disregard for women.

The tragic treatment of women in many Middle Eastern countries has finally come to light. Therefore, it is beyond irresponsible that the U.S., under the Bush administration, failed to sign international measures for their protection. Despite the Taliban's recent flight from Kabul, women have not been relieved of the risk of being beaten by their husbands. A reporter for *Time*, Richard Lacayo, as reported in the December 3, 2001, issue, was told by a mother of seven, "My husband says the Koran tells him he can control his wife however he wants." She said she has read the Qur'an and found this to be an untruth. Yet, if she disobeys him, she is helpless and has been beaten on many occasions.

The perverseness placed on women's sexuality by Christian fundamentalists extends to other fundamentalisms and cultures as well. The only difference is that in Islamic fundamentalism it is seen to a more far-reaching degree. In African and Middle Eastern nations, nearly two million girls are genitally mutilated each year. Infibulation, the severest form, consists of removing part or all of the clitoris and labia minora. Then there is the "cutting of the labia majora to create raw surfaces, which are then stitched or held together in order to form a cover over the vagina."[824] A small opening is left for urination and menstrual flow. The procedure is performed anytime between infancy and adulthood, without any pain relief. It is usually "carried out using broken glass, a tin lid, scissors, a razor blade, or some other cutting instrument" and often leads to death or lifelong health or psychological problems. Upon first intercourse, a woman must endure painful dilation and often must be cut, generally by her husband, before penetration can take place.

Genital mutilation is not done exclusively for religious purposes. Gender identity, cultural identity, and beliefs pertaining to hygiene play a large role. Nonetheless, religion is often a factor. Although most Muslims do not practice the ritual, sayings of the Prophet Muhammad are cited by those Muslims who do, as the reason for the practice.

There is also the dimension of female sexuality and an obsession with purity, similar to Christian fundamentalists, playing a crucial role in genital mutilation. As a Kenyan woman argued, "Circumcision makes women clean, promotes virginity and chastity, and guards young girls from sexual frustration by deadening their sexual appetite."[825]

As has been most clearly seen since the World Trade Center collapse, "jihad" is a primary focus of the more extreme Islamic fundamentalists. This concept is thoroughly studied in Pakistan's madrasahs (religious schools). The meaning can range from the harmless "personal struggle" to the most lethal—"holy war." Professor Syed Minhaj ul Hassan, of Peshawar University, said many Muslim students are taught they will be welcomed by virgins into heaven if they die for Islam.[826]

Christian fundamentalists also talk of being at war. But for many it is a political and social rather than a physical war. A large assemblage of others are preparing and arming themselves through a vast number of militias. And like the heavenly welcome anticipated by Muslim extremists, there are also the millennial beliefs held by Christian fundamentalists. While they do not include a heavenly welcome by virgins, they do anticipate the chosen being raptured while the rest of humanity faces immense suffering and warfare.

The Christian fundamentalist fear of uncensored ideas being taught in school also has its counterpart in Islamic fundamentalist societies. For example, as part of its Islamisation campaign, Jamaat leaders in Kashmir, "ransacked libraries in the educational institutions," says O.N. Trisal. They also "ordered bans on books which did not correspond to their brand of knowledge about man and his world." The Kashmir University library saw the loss of more than 2,000 books. This included, points out Trisal, "all the books on Hindu philosophy, Milton's 'Paradise Lost' and George Bernard Shaw's plays, and books by many other world renowned writers . . ."[827] Teachers affiliated with the Jamaat shut down courses on Darwin's theory of evolution in medical institutions. This was because it was not in keeping with fundamentalist Islamic tenets.[828] Much of this same literature or ideas have been subject to censorship by Christian fundamentalists for years. In the Sudan, lectures were monitored to make sure they were in accordance with fundamentalist tenets. Dr. Farouk Ibrahim el Nur, a member of the Faculty of Science at Khartoum University was arrested for this crime. He was tortured, "in an effort to force him to recant his belief in Darwinian evolution."[829] This, of course, was before the closing of universities by the National Islamic Front, the country's most influential fundamentalist party during the late 1980s.[830]

Most disturbing, in Pakistan, Mohammad Younas Sheikh, "is one of perhaps dozens of educators accused by their students" of blasphemy as was noted in the *Washington Post* on May 17, 2002. The sentence for blasphemy in Pakistan, just as Christian Reconstructionists would respond, is execution. Sheikh was convicted of a religious crime even though his comments did not reject or ridicule Islam or the Prophet Muhammad. Rather, he pointed out a contradiction in what Islamic fundamentalists see as an Islamic truth. Sheikh had responded to a question by one of his students that Muhammad could not have been a prophet or a Muslim before the age of 40 because Islam had not previously existed. He now awaits his execution. What is most ironic is the blasphemy cases took place "under Pakistan's president, General Pervez Musharraf, Washington's partner in the 'war on terror.'"[831]

Restrictions on the practice of other religious beliefs have been documented throughout American history and around the world today. Wherever there is "official religion," restrictions and religious persecution may ensue. For example, in Malaysia, where Muslims are sixty percent of the population, Islam is the official religion. The Malaysian Constitution "gives citizens the right to freely profess, practice, and propagate their religion." However, "this right is restricted in practice."[832] While there are no restrictions on Muslim places of worship, other religions must seek government approval to establish such a place. Christian materials are tightly restricted. Apostasy is punishable by fines or else imprisonment to religiously rehabilitate the offender.

In Bosnia, the state constitution guarantees religious freedom, but lacking a provision for church-state separation, there is little meaning behind it. Catholics, Orthodox, and Muslims each dominate certain areas of the country and persecute minority religions.[833] It is tempting to view the Middle East as unique by imagining it as a part of the world that has always been out of step with modern society. But, this is not the case. Because of the petroleum industry, the Middle East saw modernization in the twentieth century, and its traditional ways of life subsided. Secularization gave rise to the first wave of modernization in the Middle

East, and religion became a private, rather than a public matter. Along with this secular society arose equality for women. But, as with Christian fundamentalism in America, the late 1960s in the Middle East was marked by a rise in Islamic fundamentalism. The rights of women were reversed as subordination to men again became emphasized.[834]

Perhaps the strongest example of Islamic fundamentalism run amok and its ability to prevail under democratic rule occurred in Algeria beginning in the early 1990s. Professor James A. Haught described the horrors that befell Algeria thereafter. In 1990, the one-party governing group in Algeria was pressured into holding multiparty elections at the city level. The Islamic fundamentalists won handily, gaining control in over half the Algerian cities. Fundamentalists quickly intensified their longstanding insistence on establishing a state based on the Shariá. This is a state where violations of religious law would lead to floggings, amputations, and even executions.

By the early 1990s, terrifying violence was spreading rapidly in Algeria, and martial law was imposed. As Haught noted:

> When the parliamentary election was reset for late 1991, the fundamentalists campaigned on the slogan: 'No constitution and no laws. The only rule is the Koran and the law of Allah.' . . . About 300,000 secular-minded Algerians marched through Algiers chanting 'no to fundamentalism.'[835]

The overwhelming victory of the fundamentalists in the parliamentary election resulted in a military take-over and voiding of the election. Representative democracy was destroyed. And the only alternative to military rule was a theocracy. The murders and rioting cost thousands of lives. As Haught observed, "Today, religion in Algeria is as gory as it was 3,000 years ago."[836]

Secularism is *the* solution

Secularism is quintessentially the American way. Therefore, as seen, it should be defended as such. It stresses religious freedom and respect for religious belief or lack of belief. At the same time, it insists that worldly matters (whether or not there are any other kind) must be decided without primary reliance on any one set of theological authorities. Secularism recognizes social complexity and the desirability of a scientific approach and of tentativeness. It understands the desirability and the inevitability of myriad influences on society and the positive riches of cultural diversity.

Ironically enough, secularism insists on defending the rights, including the religious rights, of fundamentalists on the same grounds as the rights of others. Unfortunately, fundamentalists do not support cultural diversity. They often consider pluralism and diverse views as heresy and intolerance as overtly desirable.

Fundamentalists also demonstrate consistent fear of the non-religious as the most direct threat to the idea that religion-based control of society is mandated by God. Fundamentalists usually condemn religious secularists at least as fiercely as they do irreligious secularists in fundamentalist writings and in the curricula of schools fundamentalists control. This includes condemning "liberal" religious ideas.[837] Indeed, at times liberal believers that are at odds with fundamentalism stir more fear and thus more anger in fundamentalists than do the irreligious.[838]

Religion stirs emotions, sometimes for good and sometimes for ill, but separating the emotional effects of religion from the power centers in a society is crucial for long-term sustainable peace. As Atlanta newspaper columnist Colin Campbell has noted, "Religion can be murderous, as well as civilizing and life-sustaining." Campbell concluded that the framers of the U.S. Constitution recognized this sometimes-paradoxical nature of religion in establishing a secular society. American history is also replete with examples of the need to be alert to the dangers of religious extremism.[839] As described in detail in earlier chapters, the "murderous" aspects of religion are not always aimed at nonbelievers, or people of other religions. Since obedience to authority is valued as perhaps the highest virtue by fundamentalists, violence designed to compel obedience is considered not only acceptable, but desirable.

The most basic solution for the dangers of fundamentalism is to have and maintain a secular society, but the means for accomplishing that are complex and never certain. The basic solution can be reached best by a combination of:

- political commitment
- support for public schools
- support for genuine scientific investigations of all matters
- efforts to engender public respect for science and rationality, for critical thinking, and appropriate skepticism regarding all truth claims
- broad educational efforts of all kinds—formal and informal, institutional and society-wide

- a constant alertness about the need to defend the wall of separation between church and state
- an awareness of the emotional needs of human beings, including fundamentalists, and
- consistent, thoughtful, respect for the rights of all to religious liberty.

More than a matter of life and death

What fundamentalists fail to see is that being absolute is justified only if reality is absolutely simple and if one is absolutely right. They fail to recognize that millions of past believers have been quite sure they were right and that they were carrying out God's wishes about things current fundamentalists now reject or disagree about. They also seem not to notice that hundreds of millions of current fundamentalists worldwide disagree with each other.

Carrying out divine directives has often proven deadly. This was evidenced in the infamous Inquisition,[840] the trial and horrifying execution of Michael Servetus in 1553,[841] slavery in the American South before the Civil War,[842] Hitler's holocausts,[843] the persecutions of "witches," pogroms, the Crusades, and thousands of other examples. Nor, as has been made clear throughout this book, are the dangers safely in the historical past. The recent news story of a Christian mother in Tennessee, unhappy about a Bible course being removed from a public school curriculum at a judge's direction, provides a tiny but clear example. She declared, "Whoever took it out should be strung up."[844] In our secular society, a fundamentalist like that is, usually, unable to act effectively on her instincts and preferences—but the danger nevertheless lurks, even if she were merely an isolated example. Unfortunately, she is not. The danger is acute for people who are personally trapped by fundamentalism. This is so whether it is their own fundamentalism or that of their parents or spouses. It is also severe for the larger society wherever fundamentalist social or political power is strong or growing.

Americans must deal with the damage caused to individuals and to society by fundamentalists' beliefs and practices. For individuals, solutions need to be developed to help people to escape these extreme beliefs and prevent them from turning to fundamentalism again. For the broader problems, broader solutions are needed. Sociologists, psychologists, and government representatives must study this epidemic more systematically and intensely. They must seek solutions, not mere understanding;

otherwise, the devastating effects of fundamentalism will continue and are bound to increase.

For fundamentalists starting to move away from their personal fundamentalism, there is some hope, although resources ebb and flow. For example, Fundamentalists Anonymous was founded in 1985 by Richard Yao and James J. D. Luce. By 1987, its membership exceeded 30,000, and it continued to rise thereafter.[845] However, there is apparently no current public telephone number, website, or address for the group. So, its continuing existence is in doubt. According to Rod Evans and Irwin Berent, there were some attempts to establish similar groups for Muslims as early as 1988.[846] There is a current website, operated by the Institute for the Secularisation of Islamic Society (ISIS), http://www.secularislam.org/. It promotes rationalism and secularism within Islamic societies.

Individuals seeking alternatives and escape from fundamentalism can find help in books, on the Web, and through organizations criticizing fundamentalism. These include the Council for Secular Humanism, the Freedom From Religion Foundation, and others. There are also Web pages run by religious people eager to help fundamentalists. For example, http://home.earthlink.net/~jcmmsm/ Groups/index.html is a useful site by former Seventh Day Adventist James C. Moyers. It directs former members of restrictive religious groups to many resources, religious and secular, including books and other Web pages. A site by Jeff Van Vonderen, http://www.spiritualabuse.com/, is a conservative Christian site for Christians suffering from "spiritual abuse" by fundamentalists.

A good example of a book specifically designed as a self-help work for this individual need is *Leaving the Fold: A Guide for Former Fundamentalists and Others Leaving Their Religion* by Australian psychologist Marlene Winell.[847] Another useful website for former Christian fundamentalists is "Walk Away," a part of the Institute For First Amendment Studies, http://www.ifas.org/wa/index.html. The site describes itself as "a place where former fundamentalists can read the stories of other people who have left fundamentalism behind." Also of help to former fundamentalists is "Families in Reason," http://www.yourpreacher.com/FIR.html.

For those suffering from fundamentalism, sources like the above are helpful only if they are known. So, secularists should support a wide variety of information sources and organizations. Those groups that provide emotional support for former fundamentalists or the children or spouses who are at risk are of particular importance. As the chapter in this book on women makes clear, addressing emotions involves more than merely providing solace and comfort. Fundamentalist men succeed in oppressing fundamentalist women largely by playing on the emotional needs of the women whether consciously or unconsciously. Countering oppression requires emotional education for female victims, as well as ongoing emotional support. While the primary focus should be the more general task of establishing and maintaining a secular society, it should also be remembered education occurs at the individual level.

The plight of fundamentalists and possible solutions for them deserve and will receive more attention in this chapter. Before returning to the individual level of treatment, it is necessary to summarize the larger problem. As Kimberly Blaker pointed out, "Fundamentalism is in no way a weak or dying force in America. Although it is not always obvious at first glance, this movement is all around us and likely to continue growing."[848]

Frederick Clarkson, in *Eternal Hostility: The Struggle Between Theocracy and Democracy*, made clear the struggle continues and is widespread. He argued, forcefully and effectively, that "the threat posed by the Christian Right comes not from a few extreme elements but from well-organized cadres, both political and paramilitary, dedicated to overthrowing democracy."[849] Clarkson's recommended responses in his concluding chapter, "Defending Democracy,"[850] were among the most thoughtful and well-supported approaches available, although they were mostly aimed at political activism. His wise prescriptions are not in conflict with the conclusions presented here.

The advice found in Robert Boston's *Close Encounters with the Religious Right: Journeys into the Twilight Zone of Religion and Politics* was similar and equally sound. As his subtitle implied, Boston was also chiefly concerned with the threat of fundamentalists in the political arena. Like Clarkson, he recommended political activism. He also suggested research into the organizations and strategies of the politically active fundamentalists. He said a constant campaign is needed to expose and publicize fundamentalist values counter to the U.S. Constitution. The ideals that have provided the greatest strengths of American society are also necessary. His chapter, "What's to Be Done?"[851] is especially valuable in combating the political dangers presented by fundamentalists.

The "Church of Love" versus the "Church of Law"

Not surprisingly, people who consider themselves as religious, but not fundamentalist tend to see threats from fundamentalism in a somewhat different light than do non-religious people. Religious observers often focus on fundamentalism as primarily dangerous to religion. It is likely to lead religious people astray. Karen Armstrong, author of the best-selling *A History of God: The 4000-Year Quest of Judaism, Christianity and Islam*, attacked fundamentalists primarily as having oversimplified what she saw as the rich and necessary truth of religions and of God. She wrote, for example, "In all its forms, fundamentalism is a fiercely reductive faith."[852] Armstrong concluded *History* with:

> Human beings cannot endure emptiness and desolation; they will fill the vacuum by creating a new focus of meaning. The idols of fundamentalism are not good substitutes for God; if we are to create a vibrant new faith for the twenty-first century, we should, perhaps, ponder the history of God for some warnings and lessons.[853]

In Armstrong's more recent book, *The Battle for God*, she warned, "It [fundamentalism] represents a widespread disappointment, alienation, anxiety, and rage that no government can safely ignore." She added that, there has been little success in dealing with the problem of fundamentalism.[854] Armstrong argued the answer to this is not coercion or suppression. Such only leads to retaliation and greater extremism. "Fundamentalists see conspiracy everywhere and are sometimes possessed by a rage that seems demonic,"[855] Armstrong noted. We must keep in mind, she explained, fundamentalism and its theologies and ideologies are a result of fundamentalist fears. Secularists find excitement in the modern world, but it "seems Godless, drained of meaning, and even satanic to a fundamentalist."[856]

From a psychological standpoint, the paranoid and extreme thoughts of vengeance common among fundamentalists "would undoubtedly be diagnosed as [a] disturb[ance]," says Armstrong. Therefore, reasoning is an unrealistic way to resolve the fears they hold. So, solutions must start by recognizing "the depth of this neurosis. . . ."[857] Fundamentalists, she points out, preach exclusion, hatred, and sometimes violence. Yet, secularists have also played a role in the rise of fundamentalist rage by, if not secular hostility, at least a lack of respect for religion and its followers. Therefore, secularists should start by learning to empathize with fundamentalists' needs, fears, and anxieties.[858] Empathy for and acceptance of the rights of fundamentalists are necessary and desirable. Whatever Armstrong's views, it should not mean sitting back and watching them transform our government into a theocracy or even one that tramples the rights of others.

Randall Balmer, Professor of Religion and a "colonial historian,"[859] was raised in an evangelical household. He confessed he has neither embraced it altogether nor rejected it altogether, given what he found to be "a tradition that is at once rich in theological insights and mired in contradictions."[860] In "Winning the Country Back: The Ironies of the Religious Right," in his book *Blessed Assurance*, Balmer reported at some length on the dangers of fundamentalism and the religious right. This included in such diverse arenas as the rights of women and religious liberty.

Balmer noted that fundamentalist Baptists have turned their backs on Baptist heritage when they oppose the separation of church and state. Balmer presented an interesting conclusion why this has happened:

> My only guess is that they no longer believe they can compete in the free marketplace of religion. That is, they feel so overwhelmed by the successive waves of multiculturalism the United States has seen in the twentieth century that they seek some kind of advantage.[861]

This summarizes succinctly both the need to convince fundamentalists of the value of separation of church and state and the great difficulty in so convincing them.

Bishop John Shelby Spong, the famous and controversial Episcopalian bishop, has insisted that fundamentalists are a serious threat to understanding the Bible. They are a threat, he wrote, deserving to be taken seriously, and a threat to religion itself. As Spong argued, mainline Christians must respond to fundamentalists or "the ignorance of mainline Christians will increase and the absurdity of fundamentalist Christians will reach a new crescendo." He described the approach of fundamentalists as holding the Bible in the "clutches of a mindless literalism."[862] Spong has consistently presented fundamentalism as a real and serious threat to sound Christianity. He has not been shy about his criticism of fundamentalism. For example, he wrote, "A major function of fundamentalist religion is to bolster deeply insecure and fearful people."[863]

Fundamentalists are a real threat to both "liberal" Christians and to any others who realize that only a secular society will be stable and protect the religious liberty of fundamentalists, mainline believers, and the non-religious. Lloyd J. Averill described himself as "a Christian of evangelical liberal persuasion."[864] He condemned fundamentalists as essentially un-

American, noting fundamentalists are hostile to the genuine American political heritage even as they distort what it is. He also described fundamentalists, despite claims of being conservative in their views, as being eager in fact for radical change.[865]

Averill is a good example of an important truth. Secularists should not turn their backs on religious Christians as allies in the attempts to solve the problems fundamentalism presents. Averill did not agree with some features of separation of church and state that some strict separationists would want. Still, he argued effectively for an ongoing commitment to the basic ideal of religious liberty as quintessentially American.[866]

Liberal Episcopalian Bruce Bawer, in *Stealing Jesus: How Fundamentalism Betrays Christianity*, wrote: "Behind the fundamentalists' strident assertions of certitude was, in most cases, a grievous spiritual emptiness."[867] "If you want to destroy the idea of a Church of Love once and for all," said Bawer, "you would target the real Jesus and attach his name instead to a vengeful, bloodthirsty monster. This is what legalistic Christianity [fundamentalism] does at its most extreme."[868]

Bawer's conclusions were similar to Armstrong's. And he offered more of an impassioned plea for a return to true, loving, open-ended Christianity (the "Church of Love") than any general solutions to fundamentalism. Still, Bawer, like Averill, Balmer, and Spong, is an example of a Christian who fundamentalists would likely target as their enemy in the "battle royal," as much as they would target non-religious citizens.

Another Christian writer, the Roman Catholic Lorene Duquin, stressed that fundamentalism is emotional and difficult for Catholics, even Catholic leaders, to contend with. She complained fundamentalists are so rigid and pre-programmed that arguing with them verges on being useless. Rage and emotional considerations cloud fundamentalists' judgment and rationality.[869]

She quoted a "Msgr. William Gallagher" as saying:

> I have all the answers to the things that the Fundamentalists preach . . . but in most cases I'm not dealing with people who are open to exploration of the truth. They have been trained to believe standard answers and criticism. They won't move from it. You can say anything you want, but it doesn't do a bit of good because

they don't enter into the discussion with openness and good will.[870]

Some may find the Monsignor's complaint ironic. It is not difficult to argue that Catholics also, "have been trained to believe standard answers and criticism." But his complaint summed up a major difficulty for all who want to counter fundamentalism.

Humanist perspectives

A variety of solutions or analyses of the difficulties of finding solutions for the threats from fundamentalism was included among the essays in *Neo-Fundamentalism: The Humanist Response*.[871] Vern Bullough's essay on Islamic fundamentalism in this work was written at least a dozen years ago. But it accurately predicted the great difficulty secularists would have contending with Islamic fundamentalists in the Soviet Union and elsewhere. He predicted then that secularists would find Islamic fundamentalism especially hostile to religious liberty. And the problems generated would be thereby intractable.[872]

In the same collection, Alberto Hidalgo Tuñon also expressed pessimism about countering fundamentalism. He explained:

> philosophical and scientific criticism can do little to erode the great social influence of fundamentalism supported by powerful pressure groups—sometimes entire churches and political parties—by the sympathy of the mass media and, particularly, by popular gullibility.[873]

Philosopher Paul Kurtz, in the opening essay of *Neo-Fundamentalism*, provided the broadest prescriptions for solving the threats of fundamentalism of all sorts. It is advice that still deserves to be followed. He implored:

> I believe that it is important that we embark on a major educational outreach worldwide, but especially in the third world—Latin America, Africa, and Asia. We cannot remain content to espouse our principles politely in the quiet cloisters of our own societies, but must meet head on the massive challenges in the developing countries of the world.[874]

He added that secularists should refuse to "mute their strong critiques of the Bible, the Qur'an, the Book of Mormon, and other so-called sacred documents." Secularists should not hesitate to proselytize against the proselytizers.[875] Wrote Kurtz:

> We need to make sense out of the universe in which we live. But we can do so only by testing our hypotheses and theories by the rigorous methods of science. We can only do so if we recognize that the high priests of the past are inadequate to the task. It is not the theologians or mystics who will point the way, but the astrophysicists and astronomers.[876]

Gerald A. Larue stressed, in that same collection, secularists must be committed to genuine education in the broadest sense—not limited to what happens in schools, but education across all the institutions of society. He urged defeating the "ultra-right-wing efforts" of fundamentalists. By spreading sound information and analysis as widely as possible, this can be done. Such an effort should include information on the methods by which secular conclusions are reached, analyses of our ethical understanding, a constant awareness of fundamentalist threats, and consistent refusal to give in to fundamentalist pressures.[877]

The solution to the dangers of fundamentalism many would like best to see is universal rationality. Thus, universal rejection of fundamentalism of all stripes should be sought. As Kurtz has quipped, "Religion is all right, so long as you don't take it too seriously."[878] Fundamentalists are precisely those who do take it too seriously. Trying to convince them not to can play directly into the hands of fundamentalist leaders. Many tell their followers any opposition is the work of the devil. If universal rationality is ever to be achieved, education in the broadest possible sense is what will make it happen, as both Kurtz and Larue have argued.

However, it is irrational, alas, to believe all humans will adopt rational, fulfilling lives any time in the near future. Real, practical antidotes are needed for the very painful dangers that fundamentalism presents. Therefore, solutions must be more limited than attempting to achieve complete universal rationality, even while striving for something close to it. Americans must not sell themselves and society short. Goals must be quite broad, while recognizing they will be far from easy to effect and sustain.

The solutions that have worked, moderately well, are still the best ones available; they are a secular society and religious freedom. But these solutions are under great pressure. They cannot be expected to persist as solutions unless ongoing efforts to maintain and strengthen them are continued. A secular society, with religious freedom for all, will persist, but only one way. It must be secured by a consensus and a constitution demanding religious neutrality from the government at all levels. The emotional power of religion, for good or ill, must be scrupulously kept separate from the great practical power of government. Only then can fundamentalism be prevented from ruining humanity.

Views from other windows (anthropologists, philosophers, demographers, and former fundamentalists)

The great popular anthropology writer, Marvin Harris, in *Our Kind: Who We Are, Where We Came From, Where We Are Going*, denies all things about religion are so far understandable in anthropological terms. He holds out hope, however, for eventually explaining all the workings of religion.[879] In addition, he summarizes much of what is now understood in ways that suggest possible insights about fundamentalists. He argues, for example, human understanding of and development of religion, while always complex, has always involved exchanges. It has not merely been obedience to the perceived directives from supernatural beings.

According to Harris:

> one impulse has been salient since the beginning of animistic thought [the first stage of what Harris identified as religion rather than mere superstition]. Our kind has always wanted gods and other spirit beings to provide us with certain kinds of benefits. . . . Most frequently, the sought-after benefits have been quite tangible and mundane: recovery from illness, success in trading ventures, rains to water parched crops, victory on the battlefield. Requests for immortality, resurrection, and eternal bliss in heaven may seem less crass, but they nonetheless involve the gods in the delivery of goods and services. Even when sought-after benefits consist of nothing more than help in acting and thinking in conformity with the wishes of the deity or in achieving inner peace, however lofty our motives, it is a service that we seek. Has there ever been a religion that did not ask what the gods could

do for the humans as well as what the humans could do for the gods? I don't think so.[880]

To persuade a fundamentalist to give up his absolutism, for the sake and freedom of others, there has to be a powerful exchange available. Emotional needs must be addressed as well. If fundamentalists are to be persuaded to limit the ways in which they do "battle royal," secularists must at least find ways to engage them in real debate. They and their allies will not change nor be deterred. That is, unless exchanges of ideas can occur. Philosopher Keith Parsons has remarked, in *Why I Am Not A Christian* (his title intentionally echoed the earlier famous book by the same title by Bertrand Russell), on the difficulty of such debate:

> Can belief argue with unbelief or only preach to it? When worldviews clash, is rational debate possible, or only a hostile exchange of epithets and rhetoric? Positions too far apart cannot find enough shared ground even to begin a debate, and there is no question that believers and unbelievers often simply talk past one another.[881]

Parsons concludes, "fruitful communication is possible." Although he adds, with a parenthetical qualification: "I think that Christians and nonbelievers share enough background beliefs, values, and standards to engage in fruitful debate . . . (though some of the wilder effusions of creationists and fundamentalists tempt me into doubt)."[882] Parsons' comments about believers and Christians apply equally well to the needs for and the difficulties of exchanges between fundamentalists and secularists.

The state of religion in the world and in the U.S. is complex, and there is every indication that the complexity—and the dangers—will only increase. Toby Lester noted, in an essay, that the religious landscape is changing. In fact, so much so that "what is now dismissed as a fundamentalist sect, a fanatical cult, or a mushy New Age fad could be the next big thing."[883] Lester quoted David Barrett, editor of the *World Christian Encyclopedia*. Barrett concluded there are "nine thousand and nine hundred distinct and separate religions in the world. And they are increasing by two or three new religions every day."[884]

Lester also noted what British sociologist Colin Campbell wrote many years ago about fundamentalist growth. Campbell said secularization itself could well be an important force in generating hardier varieties of fundamentalist religions to flourish. This could result from reduced influences of "established" religions.[885]

The number of religions continue to increase, and fundamentalists gain more power worldwide. Therefore, the problems caused by fundamentalism will increase, and the difficulties in solving those problems will expand. City University of New York staff Barry A. Kosmin, Egon Mayer, and Ariela Keysar carried out a recent study, "American Religious Identification Survey 2001." Their findings suggested that only sixteen percent "described their outlook as secular or somewhat secular."[886] The context was, however, to ask respondents to choose between being religious and secular—not between fundamentalism and secularism as defined in this book.

Their study did not measure the number or percentage of Americans who consider themselves to be fundamentalists. But it seems reasonable to conclude the number is no higher than thirty-seven percent. That is the figure who reported themselves as "religious" as opposed to "somewhat religious" (thirty-eight percent), "somewhat secular" (six percent), or "secular" (ten percent). Another nine percent were tabulated as "Don't Know" or "Refused."[887] Respondents were also asked for identification with specific religions in this survey. In response to this item, 14.1 percent identified themselves as having "No Religion." A small proportion of these chose a label such as "atheist," "agnostic," or "humanist." Another 5.4 percent surveyed refused to answer.[888]

The transition of moving away from fundamentalism can be emotional and difficult. Several collections of essays have made this clear. Dan Barker, a leader of the Freedom From Religion Foundation, started his career as a fundamentalist preacher well before he was an adult. Many of the essays in his *Losing Faith in Faith*[889] described the sometimes-painful trip away from the fundamentalist life. In *Leaving the Fold: Testimonies of Former Fundamentalists*,[890] Edward Babinski presented more than thirty personal tales of former fundamentalists, including Barker, who then became liberal religionists or non-believers. And *Amazing Conversions: Why Some Turn to Faith and Others Abandon Religion*[891] described transitions both towards and away from fundamentalism as well as other religious worldviews. A slightly oversimplified summary of the thesis of the latter would be that moving to religion is more likely to be based on emotion. On the other hand, leaving religion, especially fundamentalist religion, is more likely to be an intellectual, rational journey.[892]

The detailed testimonies of former fundamentalists show the paths leading them away from fundamentalism were quite diverse. Idiosyncratic aspects were seen throughout. No summary of those stories can really do justice to the depth and richness found in books like *Leaving the Fold: Testimonies of Former Fundamentalists* or *Losing Faith in Faith*. The reader who wants the full story must go to those sources. However, there were some commonalities. They included the authors' fears as they faced up to what just did not, in the end, make good sense. Many grappled with the need for social support, which was sometimes available from unexpected sources. Other times it was painfully denied from sources they had expected to be able to rely on. Usually, there was also real relief and a sense of self-empowerment from the realization that escape was possible.[893]

Two examples from *Leaving the Fold: Testimonies of Former Fundamentalists* will at least suggest some of the complexities of these transitions for individuals. David Montoya went from being a fundamentalist Baptist to being a Baptist pastor of a different sort in Kansas. His struggles with fundamentalism were quite personal and painful, both for him and for his wife. This was not unlike most of the others offering testimonies. But Montoya also experienced a different order of difficulty. There was backbiting, vicious politics in the Southern Baptist Convention. It was all done in the name of Jesus and of defending the Bible by fundamentalists. Montoya is still worried about fundamentalism. He wrote of:

> the creeping darkness that seems to be enveloping America and the rest of the world, a darkness that is becoming ever more diabolical as it seeks to merge its religious-political system with the political system of secular government.[894]

Another example of a former fundamentalist is Farrell Till, who testified in Babinski's book. Till was a fundamentalist Church of Christ preacher, a believer in the inerrancy of the Bible, but also a serious student of the Bible. He continued to study the Bible while he represented his church as a missionary in France, to "free people there from the heresy of Catholicism." This led him, after a long struggle, to realize that Biblical inerrancy is in fact not defensible. He left Christianity and his church and became an agnostic. Still, he continued to study the Bible diligently and is now editor of *The Skeptical Review*, a journal devoted exclusively to examining Biblical literalism. Till is probably the nation's leading expert on the impossibility of maintaining that the Bible is literally inerrant. He shared:

> I became concerned about the resurgence of Christian fundamentalism and the trend in government to curry its favor. Events in Iran and other Middle Eastern countries demonstrate what can happen once religious fundamentalists gain political control.[895]

All of these transition testimonies and analyses suggest that leaving fundamentalism behind will be difficult for individuals and societies. All of them also strongly support solutions including education and social support networks. Finally, they support a spirited defense of the separation of church and state at every turn.

Secularism as solution: the American way

Anthropologists believe religion seems to be a basic human need. Thus, it is not easy to rationally question or change religiously-based beliefs. Philosophers advise of the great difficulty of even being able to hold a useful exchange between fundamentalists and rationalists. Those converted tell of the wrenching emotional journeys to change. "Mainstream" or "liberal" believers seem to be at a loss for solutions to fundamentalism. Journalists, demographers, and religious historians say religiosity, especially fundamentalist religion, is exploding, rather than fading. It certainly is, at least as compared to other, calmer periods in our history.

From every quarter it is learned that fundamentalism is likely to persist and probably even likely to flourish. Even those who fear it the most and are most eager for solutions agree that no solution may be available, certainly no simple one. Yet, what makes turning away from fundamentalism so difficult? The social pressure of family and friends plays a crucial role. It may reach hysteria because of a certainty that "the backslider" will be doomed to hell following death. There is also the painful upheaval that can often result. Because of the supreme importance fundamentalists place on their religious views, the person fleeing fundamentalism may be forced into moving his home or even divorcing a fundamentalist spouse. There is also the need to find all new interests and friends. Formerly, as a fundamentalist, those interests had likely revolved almost exclusively around church activities and members.[896]

Reiterated, the solutions, though difficult to achieve, will come only by defending a secular society. That defense must consist of a whole series of related approaches. Secularists must engage politically and must be willing to pay attention to and actively commit to political solutions. Public education, from kindergarten through college, has to have active support. And secularists must expose the consistent opposition of fundamentalists to public schools. As noted in earlier chapters, opposition to public education is widespread. It is yet another example of the anti-American nature of fundamentalism. General, ongoing education of the public must include effective use of the broadcast media by secularists. It is specifically necessary to counter the extensive use of these media by fundamentalist organizations.

Genuine science, unfettered by religious barriers or anyone's insistence on predetermined conclusions, has to be supported. Serious, sustained efforts to increase the public's respect for science and for reason must be undertaken. As a part of that, critical thinking skills and healthy skepticism have to be championed and encouraged. This is both in schools and in the media. And, finally, violations of church-state separation must be effectively held in check.

We cannot forget that human beings, including fundamentalists, have complex emotional and social needs. These needs must be met. Respect for religious liberty demands respect and freedom for those who hold fundamentalist ideas even as we combat their beliefs. This, also, must be remembered.

For secularism to succeed, a commitment has to be made to broaden educational efforts of all kinds—formal and informal, institutional and society-wide. Secularization cannot be maintained if all the elements above are not understood and acted on.

It is well worth noting, as described in the earlier chapter on social implications, that fundamentalist organizations themselves commonly declare their devotion to "religious liberty." Many of these organizations are quite simply using a sort of double-speak. Their only interest in and commitment to religious liberty is on behalf of those who agree with them, their fellow fundamentalists. Their loud concerns about religious liberty are most often thinly-disguised efforts to use government power to defend their own religious ideas. As covered in an earlier chapter, many fundamentalist leaders repeatedly claim conservative Christians' liberties have been violated. But they never manage to show actual evidence of such.

Logic and experience indicate that all humans tend to believe they are right about their religious views. Even agnostics are often sure they are right about the impossibility of anyone knowing; as one bumper sticker put it, "Militant Agnostic: I Don't Know and You Don't Either!" The key question is therefore not who is right about religion. Nor is it how to succeed in persuading others who is right. Rather the question is how to live with each other in disagreement. It may not be necessary to persuade a fundamentalist to give up most of his fundamental religious beliefs. It may only be necessary to persuade him or her to join everyone else in agreeing on a prior value: liberty. But this borders on being an unattainable goal. Fundamentalists are often convinced it is sacrilege even to talk of a value higher than being fierce defenders of the fundamentals. Those imbued with the absolute certainty of their conclusions and the belief those conclusions come from God will never be easy to persuade of the importance of liberty for all.

Persuasion and education are, however, the only solutions with a chance to succeed. Where changes of mind cannot be accomplished, it is crucial that laws defending separation of church and state be enforced. Religious fundamentalists, like members of any other group, must be made to understand, preferably through education, that religious liberty is either for all or for none. As Thomas Jefferson wrote, nearly 200 years ago, "It behooves every man who values liberty of conscience for himself, to resist invasions of it in the case of others; or their case may, by change of circumstances, become his own."[897] Every member of society must be educated about the truth and importance of Jefferson's statement. This is important whether one is a fundamentalist or a thorough secularist.

For individual fundamentalists who are suffering because of their beliefs, there are answers if the sufferers are willing to seek them. There is a more general solution for many of the dangers posed by fundamentalism that can work even for most fundamentalists while they remain fundamentalists. It is the great American solution of which President John Adams wrote:

> Although the detail of the formation of the American governments is at present little known or regarded either in Europe or in America. . . . [i]t will never be pretended that any persons employed in that service had interviews with the gods, or were in any degree under the influence of Heaven, more than those at work upon ships or houses, or laboring in merchandise or agriculture; it will forever be acknowledged that these

governments were contrived merely by the use of reason and the senses.[898]

The United States established the first significant secular government designed to lead the first truly secular society in history. In spite of this, many of its citizens and leaders, then as now, were religious individuals. Being so diplomatic that basic truth is avoided cannot be afforded. Those who are unswervingly devoted to fundamentalism are hostile to democracy. Thus they are literally un-American.

Reaching individual victims of fundamentalism, such as women trapped in abusive marriages, or children who cannot protect themselves, will never be easy. Yet, in a firmly defended secular society that strongly supports education in critical thinking, even those victims will have a chance. The exact reasons the U.S. came under attack in September 2001 may never be known. But it is likely at least part of the reason is that the U.S. is a secular nation. It is a modern nation and therefore perceived to be a direct threat to fundamentalist Islam. A less likely but still possible reason may be the inaccurate perception, despite Christian fundamentalist claims, that the U.S. is a "Christian nation."

A secular government that does not make religious decisions for its citizens is one based on ideas like those of Thomas Jefferson as he acknowledged:

> The legitimate powers of government extend to such acts only as are injurious to others. But it does me no injury for my neighbor to say there are twenty gods, or no god. It neither picks my pocket nor breaks my leg.[899]

As Michael Buckner wrote, in "The UnChristian Roots of the Fourth of July:"

> The theory of government presented in the Declaration of Independence . . . represents a radical break with Judeo-Christian traditions that went back thousands of years. Government, it asserts, derives its powers not from the will of God but from the consent of the governed. From being an instrument of God's wrath, government is demoted to an invention of human beings, to be altered at the will of its creators. Our Constitution goes even further than the Declaration in its godlessness, not even bothering

with a ceremonial invocation of God or 'Divine Providence' in vesting ultimate authority in 'We, the people.'"[900]

This solution, a secular society with an insistence on honoring the rights and beliefs of religious fundamentalists along with those of everyone else, is the American value most worth defending, bragging about, and spreading. The idea belongs to no religion, but it benefits all except those who insist on utter absolutism. It tolerates all except those who will tolerate no disagreement whatever.

So, is the solution to persuade fundamentalists to give up their religion? Well, it would help. It is difficult to imagine, after all, secular humanists killing those who disagree. But, no, it is certainly not that simple. Most modern Christians do not take the Bible seriously or literally when it says that nonbelievers should be destroyed. Many Muslims, likewise, do not take their sacred texts that seriously or simplistically. Fanaticism can be inspired by ideas other than religion—leaders as diverse as Stalin and Pol Pot proved that—but mass murderers have one thing in common: certainty. It is a blind fanatical devotion to ideas, devotion so strong the fanatics are willing to kill and die for them.

America's power and strength is first in its people, but it is also in the inventing of and persisting in devotion to a secular government, one where all can take religion or irreligion as seriously as they wish, short of enlisting the government on one's side or killing those who disagree. A secular society is not one where no religion is allowed; it must be instead one where all religions and philosophies have to compete in the marketplace of ideas for individual support.

A secular society, not a fundamentalist society, is the only kind where religious freedom is available for all or secure for any. All who are in the majority at any particular historical moment should share in a commitment to minority rights, if only because tomorrow they may no longer be in the majority. Secular means neutral regarding religion. That can be difficult for followers of any religion, or even the irreligious, to accept.

Jesus is reported to have said, in Matthew 12:30, "He that is not with me is against me." Nevertheless, official neutrality is the only way to avoid seriously risking a return of the Holy Crusades, pogroms, oppression, persecution, and, almost certainly, terrorism as well. These calamities will befall fundamentalists as well as committed secularists, and the need to educate everyone on this is urgent and continuing. Those who understand that need must not wait for others to do the work, which includes political action in support of education and secularism.

As has previously been noted, the education that has to occur must be both broad and specific. It must include an unabashed, unrelenting counter to the false propaganda of the fundamentalists themselves. It must also include a clear and accurate indictment of those fundamentalists who think they are above the law, who believe the rights of others are inferior to their own, and who are willing to use violence to further their own beliefs.

It will never be easy, but Americans must not rest. We must not fail to persuade everyone, fundamentalist, secular humanist, and everyone in every other category, that a secular society with firm separation of church and state is necessary. The cost of failure is severe. People who are absolutely sure about the need to protect the fundamentals of their religion can do terrible things. They can even do things like flying airplanes loaded with jet fuel and innocent passengers into buildings that symbolize and empower secular societies, buildings filled with people freely living peaceful lives.

Notes

Chapter 1 Notes

[1] James C. Dobson, Children at Risk, 27.

[2] Philip Smucker and Michael Stachell, "Hearts and Minds," U.S. News & World Report, 15 October 2001, [online] [cited 15 October 2001]; available at http://www.usnews.com/usnews/issue/011015/ideas/taliban.htm.

[3] James Dobson, Parenting Isn't For Cowards (Word Publishing, 1997), 104, cited in Albert J. Menendez, Three Voices of Extremism: Charles Colson, James Dobson, D. James Kennedy (Silver Spring, MD: Americans for Religious Liberty, 1977), 52.

[4] Dobson, Parenting, 106.

[5] "'White Rose' Activists Preach Violence Against Abortion Clinics, Gays," Church & State April 2001 [online] [cited 20 October 2002]; available at http://www.au.org/churchstate/cs4016.htm.

[6] "'White Rose."

[7] "'White Rose."

[8] David C. Trosch, letter to Congress, 16 July 1994, quoted in Maxine Parshall, "The 'Reverend' David C. Trosch to 'Dear Congressman,'" Perspectives Fall 1994, 1-3.

[9] Barbara M. Jones, Libraries, Access, and Intellectual Freedom: Developing Policies for Public and Academic Libraries (Chicago: American Library Association, 1999), 84-85.

[10] Kimberly Blaker, "U.S. breeds its own religious extremists," San Francisco Examiner, 20 September 2001.

[11] Bill Baird and Joni Scott, "A test of our resolve: the religious right's attack on freedom," The Humanist, (September/October 2000, cited in WilsonSelect Plus_FT [database online] [cited 4 June 2001]), 14-21, quoted in Kimberly Blaker, "U.S. breeds its own religious extremists," San Francisco Examiner, 20 September 2001.

[12] Blaker, "U.S. breeds."

[13] "Catholic Church Blamed for Backing 'Clones' of Islamic Terrorists," The Catalyst November 2001, 11.

[14] "Catholic Church."

[15] "Catholic Church."

[16] "Catholic Church."

[17] "Catholic Church."

[18] "Catholic Church Blamed for Backing 'Clones' of Islamic Terrorists," The Catalyst, Catholic League for Religious and Civil Rights website, 21 September 2001 [online][cited 22 September 2001]; available at http://www.catholicleague.org/01press_releases/pr0301.htm#CATHOLIC%20CHURCH%20BLAMED%20FOR%20BACKING%20"CLONES"%20OF%20ISLAMIC%20TERRORISTS.

[19] Michael Stoll, letter to anonymous, 14 November 2001.

[20] A freelance production assistant who briefly did some work for Mag Rack shared this information when we spoke over the phone. It is noted that, according to a letter from Mag Rack in response to my attempts to follow up with the freelance production assistant, the freelancer did not have the authority to speak on behalf of Mag Rack, Rainbow Media, or "American Catholic," nor did the freelancer claim to have been speaking on any of their behalf during our telephone conversation.

[21] Michael Connor of Mag Rack, the video-on-demand service from Rainbow Media that includes "American Catholic," letter to the author 22 October 2002.

[22] "Palm Beach Post Justifies Anti Catholicism," The Catalyst, March 2002 [online][cited 1 March 2002]; available at http://www.catholicleague.org/catalyst/2002_catalyst/3-02.htm#NAPA%20VALLEY%20MUSEUM%20DISPLAYS%20DEFECATING%20POPE.

23 "Catholic League's 2001 Annual Report on Anti-Catholicism," [online] [cited 17 October 2002]; available at http://www.catholicleague.org/2001report/media2001.html.
24 Michael Stoll, letter to Kimberly Blaker, 25 February 2002.
25 Jones, Libraries, 84-85.
26 "About AD/HD," Children and Adults with Attention-Deficit/Hyperactivity Disorder website [online] [cited 19 May 2002]; available at http://204.29.171.80/framer/navigation.asp?charset=utf-8&cc=US&frameid=1565&lc=en-us&providerid=262&realname=CHADD&uid=1725424&url=http%3A%2F%2Fwww.chadd.or g%2F.
27 Andrew Adesman, "Does My Child Need Ritalin?" Attention! April 2001, 38.
28 T. Dwaine McCallon, "If he outgrew it, what is he doing in my prison?" National Attention Deficit Disorder Association website [online] [cited 25 April 2002]; available at http://add.about.com/gi/dynamic/offsite.htm?site=http%3A%2F%2Fadd.org%2Fimages2%2Fpr ison.htm.
29 "CHADD Applauds International Consensus Statement on AD/HD issued by Nation's Leading Clinicians," Children and Adults with Attention-Deficit/Hyperactivity Disorder website [online] [cited 25 April 2002]; available at http://chadd.org/press.cfm?cat_id=10&subcat_id=29&press_year=2002&press_id=27
30 "General Information," The Mackinac Center for Public Policy website [online][cited 22 February 2002]; available at http://www.mackinac.org/join/default.asp?ID=1542.
31 "Purpose & Mission," The Mackinac Center for Public Policy website [online][cited 22 February 2002]; available at http://www.mackinac.org/1662.
32 Curt Guyette, "Non-Partisan – Not!" Metrotimes.com [online] [cited 25 April 2002]; available at http://www.johnengler.com/002.html.
33 James Ferency, Mackinac Center for Public Policy Watch [online] [cited 25 April 2002]; available at http://scnc.mindnet.org/~ferencyj/forward.html.
34 Terry L. Coomer, "Is Ritalin the Answer?" For the Love of the Family Ministries website [online] [cited 27 June 2002]; available at http://www.churchpages.org/fortheloveofthefamily/articles/isritalintheanswer.htm.
35 "Known Funding of the Mackinac Center," The Mackinac Center for Public Policy Watch website [online] [cited 27 January 2002]; available at http://scnc.mindnet.org/~ferencyj/funding.html.
36 "Known Funding."
37 "The Mother Jones 400: Richard M. DeVos Sr. (with Helen)," MotherJones.com, 5 March 2001, [online] [cited 28 January 2002]; available at http://www.motherjones.com/web_exclusives/special_reports/mojo_400/12_devos.html.
38 "The Mother Jones 400."
39 "Council for National Policy: (CNP) and Scientology," Cephas Ministry Inc. website [online][cited 27 January 2002]; available at http://newsletters.cephasministry.com/ncp8.html.
40 "A Pledge to Children and Families," Citizens Commission on Human Rights website [online][cited 27 January 2002]; available at http://www.cchr.org/educate/aptcaf1.htm.
41 "A Pledge."
42 Mary Eberstadt, "Why Ritalin Rules," Policy Review, Heritage Foundation website [online] [cited 27 June 2002]; available at http://www.heritage.org/policyreview/apr99/eberstadt_print.html.

Chapter 2 Notes

43 "Terry Preaches Theocratic Rule 'No More Mister Nice Christian' is the Pro-Life Activist's Theme for the '90's," The News-Sentinel (Fort Wayne, IN), 16 August 1993, quoted in B. A.

Robinson, "Reacting to Religious Diversity: Religious Exclusivism, Pluralism, and Inclusivism," Ontario Consultants on Religious Tolerance website [online] [cited 28 May 2002]; available at http://www.religioustolerance.org/rel_plur.htm.

[44] Jeffrey S. Victor, "Forecasting the Future of Religion: The Next 50 Years," The Humanist May/June 1996, 21.

[45] Richard J. Gelles and Ann Levine, Sociology: An Introduction, 5th ed. (New York: McGraw-Hill, 1995), 470.

[46] Gelles, Sociology, 465.

[47] Richard Swift, "Fundamentalism: Reaching for Certainty," New Internationalist August 1990. Replicated in SIRS CD-ROM, 7.

[48] Swift, "Fundamentalism," 7.

[49] Victor, "Forecasting," 21.

[50] Associated Press, "Political Religious Extremists Reject the King James Version of the Bible," Marriage Project-Hawaii website [online] [cited 22 April 2002]; available at http://members.tripod.com/~MPHAWAII/Religion/KingJamesBible.htm.

[51] Cheryl Mullenax, "Akhenaten, Visionary or Heretic?" Akhenaten, The Sun King website [online] [cited 5 March 2002]; available at http://www.angelfire.com/ny/akhenaten/index1.html.

[52] Swift, "Fundamentalism," 4.

[53] Michael Lienesch, Redeeming America Piety & Politics in the New Christian Right (Chapel Hill, NC: University of North Carolina Press, 1992), 247-48.

[54] Field, "Oliver Cromwell, Hero or Villain?" Schoolhistory.co.uk website [online] [cited 28 March 2002]; available at http://www.schoolhistory.co.uk/year8links/civilwar/Cromwellheroorvillain.

[55] "The Mayflower Compact," The University of Oklahoma Law Center-A Chronology of U.S. Historical Documents website [online] [cited 16 April 2002]; available at http://www.law.ou.edu/hist/mayflow.html.

[56] "The Mayflower Compact," The History Place-American Revolution website [online] [cited 16 April 2002]; available at http://www.historyplace.com/unitedstates/revolution/mayflower.htm.

[57] "The Constitution of the United States of America," The University of Oklahoma College of law-A Chronology of U.S. Historical Documents website[online] [cited 21 March 2002]; available at http://www.law.ou.edu/hist/constitution/.

[58] Edward M. Buckner and Michael E. Buckner, eds., Quotations That Support the Separation of State and Church, 2nd ed. (Atlanta: Atlanta Freethought Society, 1995), 3.

[59] Alan Brinkley, American History: A Survey, Volume I: To 1877, 9th ed. (New York: McGraw-Hill, Inc., 1995), 86-7.

[60] Brinkley, American History, 86-7.

[61] William Martin, With God on Our Side: The Rise of the Religious Right in America (New York: Broadway Books, 1996), 2.

[62] David S. Noss, A History of the World Religions, 10th ed. (Upper Saddle River, NJ: Prentice Hall, 1999), 518.

[63] Noss, A History, 518.

[64] Brinkley, American, 86-7.

[65] Brinkley, American, 86-7.

[66] Brinkley, American, 86-7.

[67] Martin, With God, 3.

[68] Martin, With God, 3.

[69] Martin, With God, 3.

[70] Martin, With God, 3-4.

[71] Brinkley, American, 188-89.

[72] Martin, With God, 4.

[73] Martin, With God, 4-5.

[74] Martin, With God, 4-5.

[75] Michael S. Horton, "The Legacy of Charles Finney," in Premise [electronic journal], (Vol.II No. 3 27 March 1995 [cited 5 April 2002]); available at http://capo.org/premise/95/march/horton-f.html.

[76] Martin, With God, 5-6

[77] Martin, With God, 4.

[78] Martin, With God, 5-6.

[79] Noss, A History, 521.

[80] Lienesch, Redeeming, 247-248.

[81] Lattin, "Apocalypse," 4.

[82] Noss, A History, 522.

[83] Noss, A History, 522

[84] Noss, A History, 522.

[85] Lattin, "Apocalypse," 32-38.

[86] Scott Appleby, "Unflinching Faith: What Fires Up the World's Fundamentalists?" in U.S. Catholic, December 1989, 1, quoted in "Fundamentalism and Its Motivation," Sphaira-A Symbol of Unity website [online] [cited 24 February 1998]; available at http://incolor.inetnebr.com/mdavis/fundmntl.htm.

[87] Lattin, "Apocalypse," 3.

[88] Jim Strayer, Telephone interview by author, 2 June 2002.

[89] John Shelby Spong, Rescuing the Bible From Fundamentalism: A Bishop Rethinks the Meaning of Scripture. (New York: HarperCollins, 1992), 15

[90] Gary Leak and Brandy Randall in the Journal for the Scientific Study of Religion (1995) quoted in Michael Franklin and Marian Hetherly, "How Fundamentalism Affects Society," in The Humanist, 1 September 1997, 26.

[91] Leak, Journal.

[92] "The Rapture: Hoax or Hope?" Ontario Consultants on Religious Tolerance website [online] [cited 6 April 2002]; available at http://www.religioustolerance.org/rapture.htm.

[93] "The Rapture."

[94] "The Rapture."

[95] B. A. Robinson, "Millennialism: Competing Theories," Ontario Consultants on Religious Tolerance website [online] [cited 6 April 2002]; available at http://www.religioustolerance.org/millenni.htm.

[96] Lattin, "Apocalypse," 8.

[97] Martin, With God, 7.

[98] "They Said What?!? The Religious Rights Quotes," The Humanist Society of Gainesville website [online] [cited 15 March 2002]; available at http://www.lipsio.com/gainesvillehumanists/quotes.htm.

[99] Martin, With God, 7.

[100] Charles B. Strozier, Apocalypse on the Psychology of Fundamentalism in America (Boston: Beacon Press, 1994), 120.

[101] Strozier, Apocalypse, 121.

[102] Mark Twain, Letters from the Earth, ed. Bernard DeVoto (Greenwich, Conn.: Fawcett Publications, 1970).

[103] Robinson, "Millennialism."

[104] Edward Hindson, "What Will It Be Like To Be Left Behind," The Tim LaHaye School of Prophecy website [online] [cited 14 May 2002]; available at http://www.schoolofprophecy.com/left_behind.html.

[105] Martin, With God, 353-54.

[106] Robinson, "Millennialism."

[107] Strozier, Apocalypse, 120.

[108] Swift, "Fundamentalism," 8.

[109] Gelles, Sociology, 459.

[110] Victor, "Forecasting," 22.

[111] Swift, "Fundamentalism," 2.

[112] Gelles, Sociology, 470.

[113] Gelles, Sociology, 470-71.

[114] Lattin, "Apocalypse," 5.

[115] Strozier, Apocalypse, 254.

[116] Norman F. Furniss, The Fundamentalist Controversy, 1918-1931 (Hamden, CT: Archon, 1963), 35.

[117] Gelles, Sociology, 470-71.

[118] Appleby, "Unflinching Faith," 1.

[119] Scott R. Appleby, "The God Squads," in Notre Dame Magazine, summer 1995, Replicated in SIRS CD-ROM, 11.

[120] Rob Boston, "Weekend Warriors," Church & State 55, no. 6 (2002): 7.

[121] Gelles, Sociology, 453.

[122] Kay Marie Porterfield, Blind Faith: Recognizing and Recovering From Dysfunctional Religious Groups (Minneapolis: CompCare Publishers, 1993), 71.

[123] Appleby, "The God Squads," 33-38.

[124] Appleby, "Unflinching Faith," 1.

[125] Appleby, "Unflinching Faith," 2.

[126] Flo Conway and Jim Siegelman, Holy Terror: The Fundamentalist War on America's Freedoms in Religion, Politics and Our Private Lives (Garden City: Doubleday, 1982), 4.

[127] Bruce Hunsberger, "Religion and Prejudice: The Role of Religious Fundamentalism, Quest, and Right-wing Authoritarianism," in Journal of Social Issues, 51 (1995): 121.

[128] Appleby, "The God Squads," 11.

[129] Swift, "Fundamentalism," 14.

[130] Gelles, Sociology, 469.

[131] Strozier, Apocalypse, 253.

Chapter 3 Notes

[132] Robert Thoburn, The Children Trap (1986), quoted in David C. Berliner, "Educational Psychology meets the Christian right: differing views of children, schooling, teaching, and learning," Teachers College Record Spring 1997, 159, cited in WilsonSelectPlus_FT [database online] [cited 5 June 2001].

[133] Prov. 29.15, Revised Standard Version.

[134] Michael Franklin and Marian Hetherly, "How Fundamentalism Affects Society," The Humanist, 57, September/October (1997): 25-2.

[135] 2 Kings 2.24, RSV.

[136] Prov. 22.15, RSV.

[137] Carolyn Holderread Heggen, "Religious Beliefs and Abuse," Women, Abuse, and the Bible: How Scripture Can Be Used to Hurt or Heal, Catherine Clark Kroeger and James R. Beck eds. (Grand Rapids, MI: Baker, 1996), 17.

[138] Such research that is in agreement includes that of Ellison, Bartkowski, and Segal as well as Ellison and Sherkat.

[139] Henry Danso, Bruce Hunsberger, and Michael Pratt, "The Role of Parental Religious Fundamentalism and Right-Wing Authoritarianism in Child-Rearing Goals and Practices," Journal for the Scientific Study of Religion, 36 no. 4 (1997): 497.

[140] Pam Belluck, "Many States Ceding Regulations to Church Groups," New York Times, 27 July, 2001, sec. A.

[141] "Spanking on the decline in U.S. schools," USA Today, 2 December 1996, sec. A.

[142] Eli H. Newberger, The Men They Will Become: The Nature and Nurture of Male Character, (Cambridge, MA: Perseus Publishing, 2001), 75.

[143] David C. Berliner, "Educational Psychology Meets the Christian Right," Teachers' College Record, Spring, (1997): 381-416.

[144] Rick Bragg, "Christian School Questioned Over Discipline for Wayward," New York Times, 5 July 200l, Late edition, East Coast, sec. A.

[145] Bragg, "Christian School."

[146] Charles N. Sharpe, "Pastor's Letter," Heartland Ministries, Heartland Ministries [online] [cited 6 November 2001]; available at http://www.heartland-ministries.org/pastorsletter.htm.

[147] Jill Young Miller, Atlanta Journal Constitution, 26 February 2002, Metro Edition, sec. B.

[148] Lolita Wolf, "Lolita's Predictions & Predilections," Leather Page.com [online] [cited 10 April 2002]; available at http://leatherpage.com/columns/lolita/lw000925.htm.

[149] "Got Kids? Spank Them, Group Says," Detroit News, Associated Press, Features sec., 24 Sept. 2000, [online] [cited 15 March 2002]; available at http://detnews.com/2000/features/0009/26/a03-125033.htm.

[150] James C. Dobson, "Hot Topics: Spanking," Focus on the Family website [online] [cited 25 March 2002]; available at http://www.family.org/docstudy/solid/a0014858.html.

[151] DYG, Inc., "What Grown-ups Understand about Child Development" [online] [cited 2 April 2002] http://www.zerotothree.org/executivesummary.pdf.

[152] B.D.Schmitt, "Spanking," Clinical Reference Systems, Annual 2000, 1461.

[153] Wendy Walsh, Family Relations, vol. 51, issue 1, 81-88.

[154] "Spanking Makes Children Violent, Antisocial," excerpt from the "American Medical Association News Update," 13 August 1997 [online] [cited 20 March 2002]; available at http://wwwave.org/DataBase/SPANKING_Children.htm.

[155] "The Spanking-Depression Connection," Canadian Medical Association Journal, 161, no. 7, 5 October (1999).

[156] Erica Good, "Findings Give some Support to Advocates of Spanking," New York Times, 25 August, 2001, sec. A.

[157] Harold Grasmick, Robert Bursik Jr., and M'lou Kimpel, Violence and Victims, 1991, cited in Michael Franklin and Marian Hetherly, "How Fundamentalism Affects Society," The Humanist, September (1997): 25-26.

[158] Elinor Burkett and Frank Bruni, A Gospel of Shame, (New York: Viking Penguin,1993), 6.

[159] J. Alford, M. Grey, and C.J. Kasper, "Child molesters: Areas for further research," Corrective and Social Psychiatry and Journal of Behavior Technology Methods and Therapy, 34 (1988): 4 cited in Ruth Miller, Larry S. Miller, and Miller,Mary R. Langenbrunner, "Religiosity and child sexual abuse: A risk factor assessment," Journal of Child Sexual Abuse, vol. 6, issue 4 (1997): 15-34.

[160] Michael Powell, Lois Romano, The International Herald Tribune, 14 May, 2002, Bankok edition, Section A.

[161] Jim Seghers, "Catholic Fundamentalism, What is That," Apologetic and Other Free Essays, Totus Tuus Ministries website [online] [cited 31 March 2002]; available at http://www.totustuus.com/essays.htm.

[162] Alford, "Child molesters," 4.

[163] Teresa Watanabe, "Sex Abuse by Clerics—A Crisis of Many Faiths," Los Angeles Times, 25 March 2002, sec. A.

[164] According to Hull & Burke (1991), cited in Jackie J. Hudson, "Characteristics of the Incestuous Family," Women, Abuse, and the Bible: How Scripture Can Be Used to Hurt or Heal, Catherine Clark Kroeger and James R. Beck eds. (Grand Rapids, MI: Baker, 1996), 71-72.

[165] Jackie J. Hudson, "Characteristics of the Incestuous Family," <u>Women, Abuse, and the Bible: How Scripture Can Be Used to Hurt or Heal</u>, Catherine Clark Kroeger and James R. Beck eds. (Grand Rapids, MI: Baker, 1996), 72.

[166] Hudson, "Characteristics," 77.

[167] Hudson cites Finkelhor, Herman and Hirschman, Hull and Burke, and Jehu.

[168] Hudson, "Characteristics," 77.

[169] Hudson, "Characteristics," 77 citing Cohen.

[170] Hudson, "Characteristics," 77 citing Herman & Hirschman, Trepper & Barrett, and Jehu.

[171] Ruth Miller, Larry S. Miller, and Miller,Mary R. Langenbrunner, "Religiosity and child sexual abuse: A risk factor assessment," <u>Journal of Child Sexual Abuse</u>, vol. 6, issue 4 (1997): 15-34.

[172] Miller,"Religiosity," 15-34.

[173] Miller,"Religiosity," 15-34.

[174] Miller,"Religiosity," 15-34.

[175] Miller,"Religiosity," 15-34.

[176] David Thibodeau and Leon Whiteson, <u>A Place Called Waco</u> (New York: Public Affairs, 1999), 107-108.

[177] "Why Exempt Churches from Reporting Child Abuse?" USA Today, 22 March, 2002, sec. A.

[178] Prov. 2.6 RSV.

[179] Vincent M. Wales, "Hitler, Gun Control, and School Prayer," <u>The Atheist Attic</u>, [online] [cited 22 March 2002]; available at http://www.bee.net/cardigan/attic/120101.htm.

[180] 19th Century Schoolbooks website, University of Pittsburg Library System, Nietz Full Text Database, [online] [cited 1 April 2002]; available at http://digital.library.pitt.edu/nietz.

[181] Elmer Schwieder and Dorothy Schwieder, <u>A Peculiar People: Iowa's Old Order Amish</u>, (Ames, Iowa: State University Press, 1987), 114.

[182] Debi S. Edmund, **"Different rules for public and private schools,"** <u>The Education Digest</u>, vol. 65a, Issue 3a, 1 November (1999), 2.

[183] Belluck, "Many States."

[184] "Support for Homeschooling on the Rise," <u>USA Today</u>, 30 August 2001, sec. D.

[185] Patrick Basham, "Homeschooling: From the Extreme to the Mainstream," <u>Public Policy Sources</u>, vol. 51, (Vancouver, BC: Frazer Institute, 2001), [online] [cited 30 March 2002]; available at http://www.fraserinstitute.ca/admin/books/files/homeschool.pdf.

[186] Loretta F. Meeks, Wendall A. Meeks, and Claudia A. Warren, "Racial desegregation: Magnet schools, vouchers, privatization, and homeschooling," <u>Education and Urban Society;</u>" vol. 33, Issue 1, November (2000): 88-101.

[187] Stacey Bielick, Kathryn Chandler, and Stephen P. Broughman, "Homeschooling in the United States: 1999," <u>Education Statistics Quarterly</u> (2002) [online] [cited 24 March 2002]; available at http://nces.ed.gov/pubs2002/quarterly/fall/q3-2.asp.

[188] Bielick, "Homeschooling."

[189] William Blake is very popular in religious studies. He used the imagery of the Christian lamb, easily led by the shepherd. Blake was certainly religious, and did indeed believe in angels, but a comprehensive study of his work or his life reveals this image to be a satirical reference to those too easily led.

[190] Alfred Darnell and Darren E. Sherkat, "The Impact of Protestant Fundamentalism on Educational Attainment," <u>American Sociological Review</u>, 62 (1997): 309-11. cited in Kimberly Blaker, "Christian Fundamentalism: A Growing Danger," (paper presented at the Student Scholars Conference for Students at Michigan's Two-Year Colleges, Lansing, Mich., 26 September 1998) 5.

[191] Darnell and Sherkat, "The Impact," 309-311.

[192] Azam Kamguian, "Remove God from the Schools," <u>Institute for the Secularism of Islamic Society,</u> (17 May, 2002) [online] [cited 11 June, 2002] available at http://www.secularislam.org/Default.htm.

193 Kamguian, "Remove God."

194 Mallica Dutt, "God's Guerillas," New Internationalist, August 1995, 16-17.

195 Robert Simonds, How to Elect Christians to Public Office, (1985) quoted in David C. Berliner, "Educational Psychology meets the Christian right: differing views of children, schooling, teaching, and learning," Teachers College Record, Spring (1997), cited in WilsonSelectPlus_FT [database online] [cited 5 June 2001], 3-4.

196 Simonds, How to.

197 Thoburn, The Children, 3.

198 Thoburn, The Children, 3.

199 Randy Moore, "Educational Malpractice: Why Do So Many Biology Teachers Endorse Creationism?" Skeptical Inquirer, vol. 25, no. 6, November/December, 2001, 38-43.

200 Roger Doyle, "Down with Evolution!," Scientific American, vol. 286, no. 3, March 2002, 30.

201 Katherine Gleeson, "Teens and Taboos: Fact and Fiction," ZPG Backgrounder winter 1990-91, replicated in SIRS CD-ROM, 1-7.

202 "Teenagers' Sexual and Reproductive Health," Alan Guttmacher Institute website [online] [cited 30 March 2002]; available at http://www.agi-usa.org/pubs/fb_teens.html.

203 Gleeson, "Teens and Taboos," 3-4.

204 Gleeson, "Teens and Taboos," 6.

205 Douglas Kirby, "No Easy Answers: Research Findings on Programs to Reduce Teen Pregnancy," March 1997, Washington DC: The National Campaign to Prevent Teen Pregnancy website [online] [cited 20 March 2002]; available at http://teenpregnancy.org/resources/data/report_summaries/no_easy_answers/default.asp.

206 Susan Motamed, "Condom Availability and Responsible Sexuality Education," Planned Parenthood website [online] [cited 15 March 2002]; available at http://www.plannedparenthood.org/articles/sexed.html.

207 Fritz Detwiler, Standing on the Premises of God (New York: New York University Press, 1999), 85.

208 "Group says YMCA promotes witches," Associated Press, 24 January 2002 [online] [cited 27 Feb. 2002]; available at http://www.canoe.ca/CNEWSWorldTrade/home.html.

209 "Group says."

210 Donna Harrington-Lueker, "Book Battles," American School Board Journal, February (1991).

211 Detwiler, Standing, 78.

212 John M. Swomley, "The 'Power' of Prayer," The Humanist, vol. 60, no. 1, (2000): 38, replicated in WilsonSelectPlus_FT [database online] [cited 5 June 2001].

213 Edd Doerr, Catholic Schools: the Facts (Silver Spring, MD: Americans For Religious Liberty, 1993), 149.

214 It should be noted that Catholic schools are not presented here as fundamentalist. They are given as examples of religion in education.

215 Jodie Morse, "Letting God Back In," Time, 22 October 2001 [online] [cited 3 Feb. 2002]; available at http://www.time.com/time/magazine/article/0,9171,1101011022-179476,00.html.

216 "Letting God Back In."

217 "Letting God Back In."

218 Matt. 6.5, RSV.

219 Exod. 20, 1-17, RSV.

220 Andrea J. Sedlak and Diane D. Broadhurst, Executive Summary of The Third National Incidence Study of Child Abuse and Neglect, U.S. Department of Health and Human Services Administration for Children and Families Administration on Children, Youth and Families National Center on Child Abuse and Neglect, September 1996. (Cited 20 March 2002) Available at http://www.calib.com/nccanch/pubs/statinfo/nis3.cfm.

[221]Betty Lou Bettner and Amy Lew, Raising Kids who Can (New York: Harper Perennial, 1992), 45.

[222] H. Stephen Glenn and Jane Nelson, Raising Self-Reliant Children in a Self-Indulgent World (Roseville, California: Prima Publications, 2000), 191-92.

[223] K.M. Brigman, "Churches helping families" Family Perspectives, volume 18 (1984) 77-84.

[224]Pamela Warrick, "The Fall From Spyglass Hill," Los Angeles Times 29 April 1998, sec. E.

Chapter 4 Notes

[225] "Report of the Baptist Faith and Message Study Committee to the Southern Baptist Convention," Southern Baptist Convention website [online] [cited 15 April 2002]; available at http://sbc.net/default.asp?url=bfam_2000.html.

[226] David Phinny, "Baptists tell Wives to Submit," ABCNews.com 10 June 1998, [online][cited 5 February 2002]; available at http://abcnews.go.com/sections/us/DailyNews/baptistcon980610.html.

[227] Lynn Hunt et al., The Challenge of the West: Peoples and Cultures from the Stone Age to 1640, (Lexington, MA: D.C. Heath and Company, 1995), 1:19.

[228] Richard Dawkins note to Kimberly Blaker 24 October 2002.

[229] Alan Brinkley, American History: A Survey, Volume I: To 1877 9th ed. (New York: McGraw-Hill, Inc., 1995), 291-92.

[230] "Women in American History by Encyclopedia Britannica," Britannica Online [online] [cited 8 May 2002]; available at http://women.eb.com/women/articles/coverture.html.

[231] Carole Pateman, 1988 "The Sexual Contract" http://instruct.uwo.ca/anthro/211/slavery.htm.

[232] Brinkley, American History, 291-92.

[233] Brinkley, American History, 291-92.

[234] Brinkley, American History, 291-92.

[235] Kimberly Blaker, "In Remembrance of Women's Freedom," Rochester Woman, March 2002, 23.

[236] Webster's New World Encyclopedia (New York: Prentice Hall, 1992), 981.

[237] Susan Faludi, Backlash (New York: Anchor Books, 1991), 232-233.

[238] William Martin, With God on Our Side: The Rise of the Religious Right in America (New York: Broadway Books, 1996), 162.

[239] Martin, With God, 162.

[240] Faludi, Backlash, 232.

[241] Faludi, Backlash, 235.

[242] Faludi, Backlash, 235.

[243] Faludi, Backlash, 235-36.

[244] Faludi, Backlash, 236.

[245] Faludi, Backlash, 236.

[246] Faludi, Backlash, 233.

[247] Mallika Dutt, "God's Guerillas," New Internationalist August 1995,17.

[248] John W. Wright, ed., The New York Times 2001 Almanac (New York: Penguin Putnam Inc., 2000), 400.

[249] Robert D. Culver, "A Traditional View: Let Your Women Keep Silence," quoted in David M. Scholer, "The Evangelical Debate over Biblical 'Headship,'" Women, Abuse, and the Bible: How Scripture Can Be Used to Hurt or Heal, eds. Catherine Clark Kroeger and James R. Beck (Grand Rapids, MI: Baker Books, 1996), 36-7.

[250] "The Woman's Role in the Plan of God," Biblical Viewpoints Publications published by Church of God in Christ, Mennonite [online] [cited 13 June 2001]; available at http://www.bibleviews.com/womanrole.html.

[251] "The Woman's Role," 2.

[252] Charles W. Peek, George D. Lowe, and L. Susan Williams, "Gender and God's Word: Another Look at Religious Fundamentalism and Sexism," Social Forces 69 (1991): 1206.

[253] Peek, "Gender and God," 1215.

[254] Tracey Ann Martin, "The Truth Behind. . . Promise Keepers," For NOW The Official Publication of the Western Wayne County Chapter March 1997

[255] "Myths and facts about the Promise Keepers," in National Organization for Women website [online] [cited 4 May 1998], 1.

[256] Martin, With God, 161.

[257] "The Woman's Role," 3-4.

[258] Alice P. Mathews, "How Evangelical Women Cope with Prescription and Description," Women, Abuse, and the Bible: How Scripture Can Be Used to Hurt or Heal, eds. Catherine Clark Kroeger and James R. Beck (Grand Rapids, MI: Baker Books, 1996), 86-7.

[259] J.M. Miles, The Femine Principal: A Woman's Discovery of the key to total fulfillment (1975), 42, cited in Alice P. Mathews, "How Evangelical Women Cope with Prescription and Description," Women, Abuse, and the Bible: How Scripture Can Be Used to Hurt or Heal, eds. Catherine Clark Kroeger and James R. Beck (Grand Rapids, MI: Baker Books, 1996), 86-7.

[260] Mathews, "How Evangelical," 87.

[261] Mathews, "How Evangelical," 100.

[262] Mathews, "How Evangelical," 88.

[263] Mathews, "How Evangelical," 100-01.

[264] Mathews, "How Evangelical," 100-01.

[265] Mathews, "How Evangelical," 100-01.

[266] Mathews, "How Evangelical," 101-02, quoting the surveyed women's responses.

[267] Mathews, "How Evangelical," 102, quoting the surveyed women's responses.

[268] Mathews, "How Evangelical," 103.

[269] "Christians Are More Likely to Experience Divorce Than Are Non-Christians," Barna Research Online, 21 December 1999 [online][cited 12 February 2002]; available at http://www.barna.org/cgi-bin/PagePressRelease.asp?PressReleaseID=39&Reference=D.

[270] "Christians Are More."

[271] Carolyn Holderread Heggen, "Religious Beliefs and Abuse," Women, Abuse, and the Bible: How Scripture Can Be Used to Hurt or Heal, eds. Catherine Clark Kroeger and James R. Beck (Grand Rapids, MI: Baker Books 1996), 21.

[272] John M. Swomley, Abortion and Public Policy (Silver Spring, Maryland: Americans for Religious Liberty, 1994), 418-19.

[273] U.S. Department Of Justice, U.S. Bureau of Justice Statistics, Statistics on Violence Against Women: 1995 [online] [cited 9 April 2002]; available at http://www.cfpa.org/programswomen/9704summitreport/appendix.cfm.

[274] Richard J. Gelles and Ann Levine, Sociology: An Introduction 5th. Ed. (New York: McGraw-Hill, Inc., 1995), 58.

[275] Gelles, Sociology, 58.

[276] Gelles, Sociology, 59.

[277] Gelles, Sociology, 59.

[278] Gelles, Sociology, 60.

[279] V. Michael McKenzie, Domestic Violence in America, (Lawrenceville, VA: Brunswick Publishing Corporation, 1995), 92.

[280] Michael Franklin and Marian Hetherly, "How fundamentalism affects society," The Humanist, 57, September/October 1997, 25, in WilsonSelectPlus-FT [database online] [cited 5 June 2001].

[281] Heggen, "Religious Beliefs," 16-24.

[282] Heggen, "Religious Beliefs," 17.

[283] McKenzie, Domestic Violence, 56.

[284] McKenzie, Domestic Violence, 58.

[285] Heggen, "Religious Beliefs," 18.

[286] Shirley Gillett, "No Church to call Home," Women, Abuse, and the Bible: How Scripture Can Be Used to Heal or Hurt eds. Catherine Clark Kroeger and James R. Beck (Grand Rapids, MI: Baker Books, 1996), 107-08.

[287] Heggen, "Religious Beliefs," 24.

[288] Christine E. Gudorf, "The worst sexual sin: Sexual violence and the church," Christian Century, 6-13 January 1993, 21.

[289] Franklin, "How Fundamentalism,"1.

[290] Heggen, "Religious Beliefs," 18.

[291] Faludi, Backlash, 233.

[292] Russ Bellant, The Coors Connection (Cambridge, MA: Political Research Associates, 1990), cited in "Group Watch: Heritage Foundation," February 1991 [online] [cited 10 March 2002]; available at http://www.publiceye.org/research/Group_Watch/Entries-62.htm.

[293] Bellant, The Coors.

[294] John Ashcroft, "Remove Perverse Incentives," Policy Review September 1996 [online] [cited 14 June 2001]; available at http://www.policyreview.org/sept96/symp.html.

[295] James Dobson, Straight Talk, 92, cited in Albert J. Menendez, Three Voices of Extremism: Charles Colson, James Dobson, D. James Kennedy (Silver Spring, MD: Americans for Religious Liberty, 1977), 64.

[296] James Dobson, "Revive the 'Marriage Culture,'" Policy Review September 1996 [online] [cited 14 June 2001]; available at http://www.policyreview.org/sept96/symp.html.

[297] William S. Lind and William H. Marshner, Cultural Conservative: Toward a New National Agenda, cited in Paul M. Weyrich, "Reverse an Anti-Marriage Bias," Policy Review September 1996 [online] [cited 14 June 2001]; available at http://www.policyreview.org/sept96/symp.html.

[298] Carl J. Cunio, "The Withering of Trade Union Patriarchy," [online] [cited 10 March 2002]; available at http://socserv2.socsci.mcmaster.ca/vol001.003/DOMESTIC.HTM.

[299] Lind, Cultural.

[300] David Blankenhorn, "Find the Will," Policy Review September 1996 [online] [cited 14 June 2001]; available at http://www.policyreview.org/sept96/symp.html

[301] Blankenhorn, "Find the Will."

[302] D. James Kennedy, "Praise the Two-Parent Family," Policy Review September 1996 [online] [cited 14 June 2001]; available at http://www.policyreview.org/sept96/symp.html.

[303] Kennedy, "Praise the Two-Parent."

[304] Dan LeRoy, "West Virginia Gives $100 Marriage Welfare Bonus," Women's Enews available on National Organization for Women website [online] [cited 29 January 2002]; available at http://www.now.org/eNews/aug2001/081401westvirginia.html.

[305] "Fathers Count Bill: Warm and Fuzzy or Cold and Calculated," National Organization for Women website [online] [cited 29 January 2002]; available at http://www.now.org/nnt/winter-2000/viewpoint.html.

[306] "Fathers Count Bill."

[307] Patrick F. Fagan, "How U.N. Conventions on Women's and Children's Rights Undermine Family, Religion, and Sovereignty," The Heritage Foundation Background Executive Summary 5 February 2001[online] [cited 15 June 2001]; available at http://wwwheritage.org/library/backgrounder/bg1407es.html

[308] Fagan, "How U.N.," 2.

[309] "Survey: Religion Affects Teen Sex," National Center for Policy Analysis website [online] [cited 8 May 2002]; available at http://www.ncpa.org/iss/soc/pd100301f.html

[310] Denise Golumbaski, Research Analyst, Federal Bureau of Prisons, letter to Mr. Swift, [online] [cited 7 September 1999]; available at http://www.holysmoke.org/icr-pri.htm.

[311] BOES.ORG [online] [cited 9 April 2002]; available at http://www.boes.org/urgent/gwbush02.html.

[312] Alabama Code Section 13A-12-200.2 (1998).

[313] ACLU Newswire 27 November 2000 [online] [cited 25 January 2002]; available at http://www.aclu.org/news/2000/w112700.html.

[314] ACLU Newswire.

[315] ACLU Newswire.

[316] "Churches, Political Authoritarians Support Alabama Dildo Ban," American Atheist Flashline 1 March 1999 [online] [cited 25 January 2002].

[317] "Churches."

[318] Heather Corinna, "Women shalt not pleasure in Alabama," Maxi Magazine [online] [cited 19 October 2001]; available at http://www.maximag.com/current/vibes/index.html.

[319] Maxine Parshall, note to the author, May 2002.

[320] Parshall, letter.

[321] ACLU Newswire 27 November 2000 [online] [cited 25 January 2002]

[322] Gerald C. Davison and John M. Neale, Abnormal Psychology, 7th ed. (New York: John Wiley & Sons, Inc.), 388-89.

[323] Davison, Abnormal Psychology, 388-89.

[324] Gillett, "No Church," 110-11.

[325] Gillett, "No Church," 111.

[326] Davison, Abnormal, 385.

[327] Davison, Abnormal, 387.

[328] Christopher G. Ellison and Patricia Goodson, "Conservative Protestantism and Attitudes Toward Family Planning in a Sample of Seminarians," Journal for the Scientific Study of Religion, 36, no. 4 (1997): 512-15.

[329] Ellison, "Conservative," 512-15.

[330] Ellison, "Conservative," 512-15.

[331] Janet E. Smith, "Barnyard Morality," America, 13 August 1994, 14.

[332] "105th Congress: Rolling Back Women's Rights," National Organization for Women, October 1998 [online][cited 12 March 2002]; available at http://www.now.org/issues/election/analysis1998/key.html.

[333] "105th Congress."

[334] Flo Conway and Jim Siegelman, Holy Terror: The Fundamentalist War on America's Freedoms in Religion, Politics and Our Private Lives (Garden City: Doubleday, 1982), 103.

[335] National Conference of Catholic Bishops, "Pastoral Plan for Pro-life Activities," Priests for Life website 20 November 1975, [online] [cited 14 March 2002]; available at http://www.priestsforlife.org/magisterium/bishops/75-11-20pastoralplanforprolifeactivitiesnccb.htm.

[336] National Conference.

[337] National Conference.

[338] Conway, Holy Terror, 104.

[339] Conway, Holy Terror, 104.

[340] Conway, Holy Terror, 104-05.

[341] Conway, Holy Terror, 104-05.

[342] Conway, Holy Terror, 105.

[343] Conway, Holy Terror, 105.

[344] "Major U.S. Supreme Court Rulings on Reproductive Health and Rights," Planned Parenthood website [online] [cited 6 May 2002]; available at http://www.plannedparenthood.org/about/narrhistory/court-23.html.

[345] Tanya Melich, The Republican War Against Women (New York: Bantam Books, 1996), 236.

[346] Michael Lienesch, Redeeming America Piety & Politics in the New Christian Right (Chapel Hill, NC: University of North Carolina Press, 1993), 259.

[347] Martin, With God, 355.

[348] Martin, With God, 355.

[349] Martin, With God, 355.

[350] Martin, With God, 355.

[351] Time, 14 June 1993, 48-51, quoted in Jill Smolowe, "New, Improved and Ready for Battle," in Human Sexuality 94/95, 19th ed., ed. Ollie Pocs (Guilford, CT: The Dushkin Publishing Group, 1994), 116.

[352] Martin, With God, 355-56.

[353] Conway, Holy Terror, 109.

[354] Swomley, Abortion, 419.

[355] Wright, The New York, 480.

[356] Bill Baird and Joni Scott, "A Test of our resolve: the religious right's attack on freedom," The Humanist, September/October 2000, 14-21, cited in WilsonSelect Plus_FT [database online] [cited 4 June 2001.

[357] David C. Trosch, "Has Rome Become the Seat of the Anti-Christ?" Most Holy Family Monastery [online] [cited 6 May 2002]; available at http://www.trosch.org/jpi/history-ref-jp2.htm.

[358] American Civil Liberties Union, 2001 Workplan, 3.

[359] American Civil Liberties Union, 4.

[360] American Civil Liberties Union, 4.

[361] Swomley, Abortion, 416.

[362] John M. Swomley, "The Pope Versus the Bible," The Humanist November/December 1997, 36.

[363] "Republican Platform Puts Fetus Before Mother," New York Times, 27 September 1988, A34 quoted in John Swomley, Abortion and Public Policy, 417.

[364] Swomley, Abortion, 417.

[365] Conway, Holy Terror, 111.

[366] "Church, Medicine and Women," CBS Health Watch by Medscape [database online] [cited 15 June 2001]; available at http://cbshealthwatch.medscape.com/cx/viewarticle/231433.

[367] John M. Swomley, "The 'Partial-Birth' Debate in 1998," The Humanist March/April 1998, 7.

[368] Swomley, "The Partial-Birth."

[369] Wright, The New York, 370.

[370] Percentage based on 320 to 600 abortions performed per year as reported in Swomley, "The 'Partial-Birth,' Debate in 1998," The Humanist, March/April 1998, pages 6-7 and the 1,184,758 total abortions reported in the United States in 1997 as reported in John W. Wright, The New York Times Almanac 2001, 371.

[371] John M. Swomley, "The Population Wars," The Humanist July/August 1998, 26.

[372] Swomley, "The Partial-Birth," 5.

[373] Swomley, "The Partial-Birth," 5.

[374] Swomley, "The Partial-Birth," 6.

[375] Swomley, "The Partial-Birth," 6.

[376] Linda Rocawich, "Desperation: Before Roe v. Wade, After Roe is Reversed" in Human Sexuality 94/95, 19th ed., ed. Ollie Pocs (Guilford, CT: The Dushkin Publishing Group, 1994), 119.

[377] Vandana Shiva, Third World Network Features, 1 September 1994 [online] [cited 20 October 2002]; available at http://www.iisd.ca/linkages/Cairo/twnpop.txt citing Flora Davis, Moving the Mountain: the Women's Movement in America since 1960.

[378] Shiva, Third World.

[379] Rocawich, "Desperation,: 119.

[380] Baird and Scott, "A Test," 2.

[381] Rocawich, "Desperation," 119.

[382] Wright, The New York, 480.

[383] Rocawich, "Desperation," 121-22.

[384] Swomley, Abortion, 423.

385 Swomley, "The Population," 25.

386 "It's Time for a Change – A 'See Change,'" Catholics for a Free Choice website [online] [cited 7 May 2002]; available at http://www.seechange.org/.

387 Swomley, "The Population," 25.

388 American Civil Liberties Union, 3.

389 Baird and Scott, "A Test," 8.

390 Baird and Scott, "A Test," 8.

391 Swomley, Abortion, 420.

Chapter 5 Notes

392 Christian Arsenal, 2001. "Archive Quotes: Week of November 25, 2001." (Memphis, Tennessee: ChristianArsenal.com [cited 29 May 2002]); available from http://www.christianarsenal.com/ArchivesQuotes.htm.

393 Promise Keepers Annual Conference, 1993.

394 John M. Swomley, "War and the Population Explosion: Some Ethical Implications," Christian Ethics Today: Journal of Christian Ethics online June 2002 [online] [cited 25 June 2002]; available at http://www.christianethicstoday.com/Issue/016/War%20and%20the%20Population%20Explosion%20-%20Some%20Ethical%20Implications%20By%20John%20M%20Swomley_016_16_.htm.

395 Swomley, "War and the Population."

396 "Low-income Children in the United States: A Brief Demographic Profile," National Center for Children in Poverty website [online] [cited 24 June 2002]; available at http://cpmcnet.columbia.edu/dept/nccp/ycpf.html.

397 "Poverty Rates for Children by Family Type," Luvenberg Income Study [online] [cited 24 June 2002]; available at http://www.lisproject.org/keyfigures/childpovrates.htm.

398 Based on data from the self-reported enrollment of churches as listed in the 2001 Yearbook of American and Canadian Churches, published on the American Religion Data Archive (www.arda.org), and data obtained from U.S. Census Bureau, Poverty in the United States 2000. Figures are for 1998 to 1999 averages.

399 Charles Zastrow and Karen K. Kirst-Ashman, Understanding Human Behavior and the Social Environment, Third ed., (Chicago: Nelson-Hall Publishers, 1994), 492-93.

400 Zastrow, Understanding Human, 492-93.

401 Zastrow, Understanding Human, 492-93.

402 Zastrow, Understanding Human, 492-93.

403 Zastrow, Understanding Human, 492-93.

404 General Social Survey.

405 Shawna Vogel, "Teen Pregnancy Worldwide," ABC News, 2000 [online] [cited 19 March 2002]; available at http://abcnews.go.com/sections/living/DailyNews/pregrates000224.html.

406 Vogel, "Teen Pregnancy."

407 Data obtained for the Morality Weekly Report 1997, except California, Iowa, New Hampshire, Oklahoma, and Florida from the Alan Guttmacher Institute (1999) "Teenage Pregnancy: Overall Trends and State-by-State Information."

408 Tim Stafford, "Inside Crisis Pregnancy Centers," Christianity Today 17 August 1992, 20-23.

409 Stafford, "Inside Crisis," 20-23.

410 Stafford, "Inside Crisis," 20-23.

411 Stafford, "Inside Crisis," 20-23.

256   *The Fundamentals of Extremism*

[412] George Brown Tindall, America: A Narrative History vol. 1 (New York: W.W. Norton & Company, 1984), 568.
[413] William Martin, With God on Our Side: The Rise of the Religious Right in America (New York: Broadway Books, 1996), 4.
[414] Alan Brinkley, American History: A Survey, Volume I: To 1877, 9th ed. (New York: McGraw-Hill, Inc., 1995), 373.
[415] Tindall, America, 568.
[416] Brinkley, American History, 373.
[417] Kimberly Blaker, "African-Americans Who Took a Stand."
[418] Forrest G. Wood, The Arrogance of Faith: Christianity and Race in America from the Colonial Era to the Twentieth Century (New York: Alfred A. Knopf, 1990), 106-7.
[419] "Inerrancy as Defined by: Conservative Protestants, Catholics & Liberal Christians," Religious Tolerance website [online] [cited 30 June 2002]; available at http://www.religioustolerance.org/inerran1.htm.
[420] "Inerrancy as Defined."
[421] Wood, The Arrogance, 107.
[422] B.A. Robinson, "Christian Reconstructionism, Dominion Theology, and Theonomy," Ontario Consultants on Religious Tolerance [online] [cited 14 June 2002]; available at http://www.sullivan-county.com/nf0/fundienazis/cr.htm.
[423] Robinson, "Christian Reconstructionism."
[424] God's Order Affirmed in Love website [online] [cited 30 June 30, 2002]; available at http://www.melvig.org/.
[425] God's Order
[426] Patricia Lines, "Private Edication Alternatives and State Regulation," Journal of Law and Education 12, no.2 Spring 1983, 191, found in Susan Rose, "Christian Fundamentalism and Education in the United States," Fundamentalisms and Society (Chicago: University of Chicago Press, 1993), 462.
[427] "Characteristics of Private Schools:1987-1988," p. 2, found in Susan Rose, "Christian Fundamentalism and Education in the United States," Fundamentalisms and Society (Chicago: University of Chicago Press, 1993), 462.
[428] Nancy Ammerman, Bible Believers, 177 found in Susan Rose, "Christian Fundamentalism and Education in the United States," Fundamentalisms and Society (Chicago: University of Chicago Press, 1993), 462.
[429] Susan Rose, "Christian Fundamentalism and Education in the United States," Fundamentalisms and Society (Chicago: University of Chicago Press, 1993), 462.
[430] "Religious Private Schools Most Segregated in U.S.," 25 June 2002, Research Matters at Harvard University website [online] [cited 20 October 2002]; available at http://www.law.harvard.edu/groups/civilrights/press_releases/private_schools.html.
[431] Rose, "Christian Fundamentalism," 462.
[432] Kimberly Hohman, "Bob Jones Bends," About.com [online] [cited 30 June 2002]; available at http://racerelations.about.com/library/weekly/aa030600a.htm.
[433] Jay Reeves, Associated Press, "Book Links found of Bob Jones University with Alabama Klan," [online] [cited 14 June 2002]; available at http://www.geocities.com/hylesjack/bjuklan.htm.
[434] "A look inside the wacky world of Bob Jones University," [online] [cited 14 June 2002]; available at http://www.nobojo.com/minorities.html.
[435] "A look inside."
[436] Jonathan Paite, "Letter from Bob Jones University," The Multiracial Activist, link found at Kimberly Hohman, "Bob Jones Bends," About.com [online] [cited 30 June 2002]; available at http://racerelations.about.com/library/weekly/aa030600a.htm.
[437] Paite, "Letter from."
[438] "BoJo and Politics," [online] [cited 14 June 2002]; available at http://www.nobojo.com/politics.html.

[439] General Social Survey, 2000.

[440] "News in Brief," Freethought Today April 2001, 11.

[441] "News in Brief."

[442] Allie Martin and Jody Brown, "Lesbian-Raised Daughter Rebuts Doctors' Stance on Same-Sex Parenting," Agape Press, 13 February 2002 [online] [cited 24 June 2002]; available at http://headlines.agapepress.org/archive/2/132002a.asp.

[443] Dennis Coon, Introduction to Psychology: Exploration and Application (Minneapolis/St. Paul: West Publishing Company, 1995), 615.

[444] American Civil Liberties Union, 2001 Workplan.

[445] Peter Hanson, "The Hatred Behind the Defense of Marriage Act," The Online Daily of the University of Washington, [online] [cited 28 June 2002]; available at http://archives.thedaily.washington.edu/1996/093096/hanson93096.html.

[446] Del Stover, "The At-Risk Students Schools Continue to Ignore," in Oppression and Social Justice: Critical Frameworks 4th ed., ed. Julie Andrzejewski (Needham Heights, MA: Ginn Press, 1993), 261. Reprinted from The Education Digest, May 1992, vol. 57, no. 9, 36-40.

[447] Stover, "The At-risk," This 30% figure is widely quoted from Paul Gibson's section of Report of the Secretary's Task Force on Youth Suicide, entitled "Gay Male and Lesbian Youth Suicide." This report was commissioned and published by the U.S. Department of Health and Human Services in 1989. The statistic was later repudiated and removed, but it is unclear if this was due to any reason besides pressure from the Religious Right (since the statistic gave schools strong motivation to provide counseling and resources for gay and lesbian students).

[448] Stover, "The At-Risk," 262.

[449] Stover, "The At-Risk," 261.

[450] Stanton L. Jones, "The Loving Opposition," Christianity Today 19 July 1993: 19-25.

[451] Jones, "The Loving," 19-25.

[452] Julie Cart, "Wyoming Campus Mourns Slaying of Gay Student," Los Angeles Times, 13 October 1998, A-1.

[453] Julie Cart, "Killer of Gay Student Is Spared Death Penalty -- Courts: Matthew Shepard's father says life in prison shows 'mercy to someone who refused to show any mercy.'" Los Angeles Times, 5 November 1999, A-1.

[454] Based on the Federal Bureau of Investigation Uniform Crime Reporting Program statistics on hate crimes for 1999 and US Census statistics on minority population for 2000. Gay, lesbian, and bisexual population is estimated liberally at 10%. As the actual population of active gays and lesbians is probably quite a bit smaller, they are statistically even more likely to be targeted for hate crimes than ethnic minorities.

[455] David Doege, "Anger at his homosexuality led Dahmer to kill, psychiatrist says," Milwaukee Sentinel, 7 February 1992.

[456] Gerald C. Davison and John M. Neale, Abnormal Psychology, 7th ed. (New York: John Wiley & Sons, Inc.), 382.

[457] Davison, Abnormal Psychology, 382.

[458] General Social Survey, 1984 and 2000.

[459] Ethics and Religious Liberty Commission, "The Case Against Disney: Twenty-three reasons (and counting) to beware of the 'Magic Kingdom,'" Ethics and Religious Liberty Commission 2002 [online] [cited 3 May 2002]; available at http://www.erlc.com/Culture/Disney/1997/case.htm.

[460] Concerned Women for America, "In Defense of Marriage," CWFA.org, 29 February 2000 [online] [cited 2 June 2002]; available at http://www.cwfa.org/library/family/2000-01-31_ca-prop-22.shtml.

[461] Bruce Hunsberger, "Religion and Prejudice: The Role of Religious Fundamentalism, Quest, and Right-wing Authoritarianism," Journal of Social Issues, 51 (1995): 118.

[462] Michael Franklin and Marian Hetherly, "How Fundamentalism Affects Society," The Humanist, 1 September 1997, 26.

[463] Franklin, "How Fundamentalism," 26.

[464] A review of studies was conducted by Batson, Schoenrade, and Ventis (1993) cited in Hunsberger, "Religion," 114-16.

[465] Hunsberger, "Religion," 114-16.

[466] Hunsberger, "Religion,"113.

[467] Hunsberger, "Religion," 118.

[468] Hunsberger, "Religion," 121.

[469] Hunsberger, "Religion," 123.

[470] Hunsberger, "Religion," 123.

[471] Hunsberger, "Religion," 126.

[472] C.D. Batson, W.L. Ventis, and P. Schoenrade, Religion and the individual: A social-psychological perspective (New York: Oxford University Press, 1993), referenced in Bruce Hunsberger, "Religion and Prejudice: The Role of Religious Fundamentalism, Quest, and Right-wing Authoritarianism," Journal of Social Issues, 51 (1995): 122.

[473] Hunsberger, "Religion," 122.

[474] Allport, 1954, cited in Hunsberger, "Religion," 124.

[475] Glock & Stark, 1966, cited in Hunsberger, "Religion," 124.

[476] Eisinga et al., 1990, cited in Hunsberger, "Religion," 124.

[477] Adorno et al., 1950; Altemeyer, 1988, cited in Hunsberger, "Religion," 124.

[478] Rokeach, 1960, cited in Hunsberger, "Religion," 124.

[479] Altemeyer, 1981, cited in Hunsberger, "Religion," 124.

[480] Mark Nathan Cohen, Culture of Intolerance: Chauvinism, Class, and Racism in the United States (New Haven: Yale University Press, 1998), 299.

[481] Cohen, Culture, 299.

[482] Cohen, Culture, 297.

[483] Cohen, Culture, 297.

[484] Cohen, Culture, 299-300.

[485] Richard J. Gelles and Ann Levine, Sociology: An Introduction 5th. Ed. (New York: McGraw-Hill, Inc., 1995), 453.

[486] Rodney Stark, Sociology, 7th ed. (Belmont, CA: Wadsworth Publishing Company, 1998), 391.

[487] Gelles, Sociology, 453.

[488] Stark, Sociology, 391.

[489] Stark, Sociology, 391.

[490] Stark, Sociology, 394.

[491] Stark, Sociology, 392.

[492] Stark, Sociology, 394-95.

[493] Stark, Sociology, 394-95.

[494] Gelles, Sociology, 456.

[495] Flo Conway and Jim Siegelman, Holy Terror: The Fundamentalist War of America's Freedoms in Religion, Politics and Our Private Lives (Garden City: Doubleday, 1982), 5.

[496] Conway, Holy Terror, 5.

[497] Conway, Holy Terror, 5.

[498] Doni P. Whitsett, "A Self Psychological Approach to the Cult Phenomenon," Clinical Social Work Journal vol. 20, no. 4, Winter 1992, 369.

[499] Whitsett, "A Self Psychological."

[500] Whitsett, "A Self Psychological," 363.

[501] Donald C. Swift, "A Short History of Cults in America," in Cults, ed. Jill Karson (San Diego: Greenhaven Press, Inc., 2000), 29.

[502] Johan D. Vander Vyver, "Religious Fundamentalism and Human Rights," Journal of International Affairs, 50 (1996): 29.

[503] "An Overview of the ICC/ICOC." REVEAL.org, 2002 [online] [cited 10 March 2002]; available at http://www.reveal.org/abouticc/overview.html.

[504] Daily Bruin, UCLA publication, date unknown

[505] Whitsett, "A Self Psychological," 365.

[506] Whitsett, "A Self Psychological," 371-72.

[507] Whitsett, "A Self Psychological," 371-72.

[508] Whitsett, "A Self Psychological," 371-72.

[509] Based on data obtained from the U.S. Bureau of Justice statistics, 1999 violent crime rates and data obtained from American Religion Data Archive, 1990 Church and Church Membership State Report.

[510] Steve Chapman, "Praise the Lord, Pass the Ammo," Chicago Tribune [online] [cited 4 July 2000]; available at www.losingmyreligion.com/articlesl/passtheammo/html.

[511] E. Currie, "Fighting Crime," Working Papers 9 (May/June 1982): 26-35, found in D. Stanley Eitzen and Doug A. Timmer, Criminology: Crime and Criminal Justice (New York: MacMillan Publishing Company, 1985), 571.

[512] Marguerite Holloway, "The Aborted Crime Wave?" Scientific American, December 1999.

[513] David Minzey in a letter addressed to Gael Parr, reprinted by Libertus.net, Brisbane, Australia [online] [cited 24 June 2002]; available at http://libertus.net/censor/docarchive/920820-398az.html#michigansp.

[514] Coon, Introduction.

[515] Coon, Introduction, 523.

[516] Christine E. Gudorf, "The worst sexual sin: Sexual violence and the church," Christian Century, 6-13 January 1993, 21.

[517] Gudorf, "The worst," 21.

[518] Tom Economus, "Catholic Pedophile Priests: The Effect on U.S. Society," The Linkup website [online] [cited 21 February 2000]; available at http://www.thelinkup.com/stats.html.

[519] Economus, "Catholic Pedophile."

[520] Coon, Introduction, 522.

[521] Paul O'Brien, letter to Kimberly Blaker, 7 September 1997

[522] O'Brien, letter.

[523] O'Brien, letter.

[524] O'Brien, letter.

[525] O'Brien, letter.

[526] O'Brien, letter.

[527] "What Makes Serial Killers Tick?" The Crime Library website [online] [cited 20 June 2002]; available at http://www.crimelibrary.com/serials/what/whatabuse.htm.

[528] Franklin, "How Fundamentalism," 27.

[529] Franklin, "How Fundamentalism," 27 cited as the conclusion of Ryan W. LaMothe, Ph.D.,

[530] Martin E. Marty, "Crime Data," The Christian Century, in WilsonSelectPlus_FT [database online] (117, no. 4 2000-[cited 5 June 2001]) p. 167.

[531] "Pharmacist at center of cancer drug scare was innovative, driven by desire to succeed," Jefferson City News-Tribune 5 September 2001 Online Edition.

[532] "Pharmacist."

[533] Freethought Today, September 1991, 12.

[534] Marty, "Crime Data."

[535] Karen Armstrong, The Battle for God (New York: Alfred A. Knopf, 2000), 364.

[536] Charles B. Strozier, Apocalypse on the Psychology of Fundamentalism in America (Boston: Beacon Press, 1994) cited in Don Lattin, "Apocalypse Now?" Common Boundary May/June 1996, 32-38. Replicated in SIRS CD-ROM, 4.

[537] Charles B. Strozier, Apocalypse on the Psychology of Fundamentalism in America (Boston: Beacon Press, 1994), 72.

[538] Strozier, Apocalypse.

[539] Scott R. Appleby, "The God Squads," Notre Dame Magazine summer 1995, 33-38. Replicated in SIRS CD-ROM, 9.

[540] Appleby, "The God Squads."

[541] Skipp Porteous, "Olson calls militia to Montana," [online] [cited 19 October 2001]; available at http://www.ifas.org/fw/9605/militia.html.

[542] Skipp Porteous, "Field Manual of the Free Militia: Foreword," January 1996, [online] [cited 19 October 2001]; available at http://www.rickross.com/reference/militia9.html.

[543] Kenneth Stern, A Force Upon the Plain: The American Militia Movement and the Politics of Hate (Simon & Schuster, 1996) quoted at "Armed & Dangerous: Militias Take Aim in Virginia and North Carolina" Eye on the Christian Right website [online] [cited 18 June 2002]; available at http://www.sullivan-county.com/news/mine/militia.htm.

[544] Stern, A Force.

[545] Porteous, "Field Manual."

[546] Larry Pratt, "What Does the Bible Say About Gun Control?" Chalcedon Report February 2000 [online] [cited 24 June 2002]; available at http://www.chalcedon.edu/report/2000feb/pratt.shtml.

[547] Pratt, "What Does."

[548] Pratt, "What Does."

[549] Pratt, "What Does."

[550] John Anderson, "Itching for a Fight," About.com, [online] [cited 19 October 2001]; available at http://pirateradio.about.com/library/weekly/aa052901b.htm.

[551] "Summer Camps," Camp Peniel website [online] [cited 28 May 2001]; available at http://www.camppeniel.org/scamp.htm.

[552] "Thoughts," Camp Peniel website [online] [cited 28 May 2002]; available at http://www.camppeniel.org/thoughts.htm.

[553] "Thoughts."

[554] "Summer Camps."

[555] "Summer Camps."

[556] "Thoughts."

[557] "Thoughts."

[558] "Picture Gallery," Camp Peniel website [online] [cited 28 May 2002]; available at http://www.camppeniel.org/pg1.htm.

[559] "High Court Pops Floating Bubble Zones," Christianity Today 28 April 1997, 84.

[560] "Violence Continues: Links Between Militants and Militia," Westchester Coalition for Legal Abortion, Inc. Coalition Online [online] [cited 24 June 2002]; available at http://www.wcla.org/97-spring/sp97-06.html.

[561] Tom Burghardt, "Gods, Guns, & Terror: Missionaries to the Preborn" [online] [cited 15 November 2002]; available at http://www.webcom.com/~pinknoiz/right/bacorr1.html.

[562] "Violence Continues."

[563] "Violence Continues."

[564] Adam Hochschild, "Changing Colors," Mojo Wire [online] [cited 21 October 2002]; available at http://www.motherjones.com/mother_jones/MJ94/hochschild.html.

[565] Don Lattin, "Apocalypse Now?" Common Boundary May/June 1996, 32-38. Replicated in SIRS CD-ROM, 1.

[566] Lattin, "Apocalypse," 1.

[567] Swift, "A Short," 29.

[568] Lattin, "Apocalypse," 1.

[569] Strozier, Apocalypse, 253.

[570] Lattin, "Apocalypse," 6.

[571] Strozier, Apocalypse, 90-91.

[572] Strozier, Apocalypse, 91.

[573] Armstrong, The Battle, 362.

[574] Armstrong, The Battle, 362.

[575] Porteous, "Olson calls."

[576] John M. Swomley, "The Population Wars," The Humanist, July/August 1998, 24.

[577] Information combined from two sources: Coon, Introduction, 397 and Robert N. Barger, Ph.D., 2000. "A Summary of Lawrence Kohlberg's Stages of Moral Development" University of Notre Dame [online] [cited 2 June 2002]; available at http://www.nd.edu/~rbarger/kohlberg.html.

[578] Information combined.

[579] Coon, Introduction, 397.

[580] Emile Durkheim, On Morality and Society (Chicago, Illinois: The University of Chicago Press, 1973).

[581] Durkheim, On Morality, 145-146.

[582] Durkheim, On Morality, 145-146.

[583] "Social Theory Reading Notes" [online] [cited 24 June 2002]; available at http://www.belmont.edu/sociology/classes/theories.htm.

[584] David Riesman, The Lonely Crowd (Binghamton, New York: Yale University Press, 1961), 9-17.

[585] "Social Theory."

[586] "Social Theory."

[587] "Social Theory."

[588] "The Book of Genesis," book 1 of The Holy Bible, King James Version, University of Michigan Humanities Text Initiative, 1996 [online] [cited 29 May 2002]; available at http://www.hti.umich.edu/k/kjv. chapters 1-48.

[589] "The Hang Ten Campaign," The Interfaith Alliance [online] [cited 31 May 2002]; available at www.interfaithalliance.org/Resources/tenc.pdf.

[590] "The Hang Ten."

[591] American Civil Liberties Union, "Posting of the Ten Commandments: Quick Takes" American Civil Liberties Union [online] [cited 31 May 2002]; available at http://www.aclu.org/clis/tencommandments.html.

[592] Associated Press, "Ten Commandments Take Center Stage," 7 January 2000 [online] [cited 31 May 2002]; available at http://www.aclu.org/news/2000/w010700b.html.

[593] "The Book of Exodus," book 2 The Holy Bible, King James Version, University of Michigan Humanities Text Initiative, 1996 [online] [cited 29 May 2002]; available at http://www.hti.umich.edu/k/kjv. chapter 20, verse 12.

[594] "The Book of Exodus," verse 13.

[595] Department of Health and Human Services, Accountability Report, 1999 Department of Health and Human Services [online] [cited 14 June 2002]; available at http://www.hhs.gov/of/reports/account/acct99/misc/century.html.

[596] "The Book of Exodus," ch. 20 v. 14.

[597] Ian Robertson, Sociology, 3rd ed. (New York, New York: Worth Publishers, Inc. 1987), 225.

[598] "Grounds for Divorce FAQ," Nolo Press, 2002 [online] [cited 2 March 2002]; available at http://www.nolo.com/lawcenter/faqs/detail.cfm/objectID/6191B9DC-00BF-42CA-A5ADA95C2AEC5196.

[599] US Census Bureau, Number, Timing, and Duration of Marriages and Divorces: 1996 (Washington, D.C.: US Census Bureau, 1996) 6-7.

[600] J. Hare, "Long-lasting Marriages: Why Do They Survive?" Oregon State University Extension Service 2002 [online] [cited 11 February 2002]; available at http://eesc.orst.edu/agcomwebfile/edmat/html/ec/ec1460/ec1460.html.

[601] US Census Bureau, Number.

[602] "The Book of Exodus," ch. 20 v. 15.

[603] "The Book of Exodus," ch. 20 v. 16.

[604] David R. Weissbard, "Bearing Witness: True and False." The Unitarian Universalist Church, [online] [cited 11 February 2002]; available at http://members.aol.com/uurockford/s96-11rpt.htm.

[605] "The Book of Exodus," ch. 20 v. 17.

Chapter 6 Notes

[606] Wallace v. Jaffree,105 U.S. 2479 (1985).

[607] First Amendment, Bill of Rights, United State Constitution.

[608] Religious Freedom Amendment, H.J.Res 78, 8 May 1997.

[609] Robert Boston, Why The Religious Right Is Wrong (Buffalo: Prometheus Books, 1993), 50.

[610] Boston, 51.

[611] Boston, 55.

[612] Boston, 53.

[613] Boston, 56.

[614] John M. Swomley, Religious Liberty and the Secular State (Buffalo: Prometheus Books, 1987), 18.

[615] Boston, 60.

[616] Boston, 61.

[617] Boston, 65.

[618] Boston, 65.

[619] Letter to the Danbury Baptists (1802).

[620] Wallace v. Jaffree.

[621] Boston, 223.

[622] Boston, 223.

[623] Boston, 224.

[624] Robert S. Alley, The Supreme Court on Church and State (New York: Oxford University Press, 1988), 3.

[625] Alley, 6.

[626] Boston, 96.

[627] Boston, 97.

[628] Everson v. Board of Education, 330 U.S. 1 (1947).

[629] Everson.

[630] McCollum v. Board of Education, 333 U.S. 203 (1948).

[631] Zorach v. Clauson, 343 U.S. 306 (1952).

[632] Engel v. Vitale, 370 U.S. 421 (1962).

[633] School District of Abbington Township v. Schempp, 374 U.S. 203 (1963).

[634] Lemon v. Kurtzman, 403 U.S. 602 (1971).

[635] Stone v. Graham, 449 U.S. 39 (1981).

[636] Wallace v. Jaffree.

[637] Lee v. Weisman, 505 U.S. 577 (1992).

[638] Santa Fe Independent School District v. Doe, 530 U.S. 290 (2000).

[639] Board of Education v. Mergens, 496 U.S. 226 (1990).

[640] Good News Club v. Milford Central School, 553 U.S. 98 (2001).

[641] Epperson v. Arkansas, 393 U.S. 97 (1968).

[642] Edwards v. Aguillard, 482 U.S. 578 (1987).

[643] Employment Division v. Smith, 496 U.S. 913 (1990).

[644] Rob Boston, "Evangelism, Public Schools and The Supreme Court," Church & State, January 2001, 8.

[645] Rob Boston, "In Don We Trust?," Church & State, May 2001, 8.

[646] Steve Benen, "Monumental Mistake," Church & State, December 2001, 4.

[647] Steve Benen, "Leap of Faith," Church & State, March 2001, 4.

[648] Rob Boston, "Faith –Based Backlash," Church & State, April 2001, 4.

[649] Joseph Conn, "DiIulio Departs," Church & State, October 2001, 13.

[650] "Should You Pay Taxes to Support Religious Schools?," Faith and Freedom Series, Americans United for Separation of Church and State.

[651] John M. Suarez, "School Vouchers – Yesterday, Today and Forever." Secular Humanist Bulletin, 14 no.2 (1998), 8.

[652] David C. Berliner and Bruce J. Biddle, The Manufactured Crisis (Reading: Addison-Wesley Publishing Company, 1995).

[653] Suarez, 9.

[654] Zelman v. Simmons-Harris, 122 S. Ct. 2460 (2002).

[655] Rob Boston, "Supreme Mistake," Church & State, July/August, 2002, 4.

[656] Rob Boston, "Voucher Victory," Church & State, September, 2002, 7.

[657] Committee for Public Education and Religious Liberty v. Nyquist, 413 U.S. 756 (1973).

[658] Sloan v. Lemon, 413 U.S. 825 (1973).

[659] Rob Boston, "The Blaine Game," Church & State, September, 2002, 4.

[660] Bush v. Holmes, 767 So. 2nd 668 (Fla. App. 2000), review denied, 790 So. 2nd 1104 (2001), opinion on remand (Fla. Cir. Ct., Aug. 5, 2002).

[661] Edd Doerr, Albert J. Menendez, and John M. Swomley, The Case Against School Vouchers (Americans For Religious Liberty, 1995) and Albert J. Menendez, Visions of Reality: What Fundamentalist Schools Teach (Buffalo: Prometheus Books, 1993).

[662] "Foundation's 'Scopes II' Victory Halts Illegal Bible Instruction." Freethought Today, March 2002.

Chapter 7 Notes

[663] "I do guerilla warfare": Norfolk Virginian-Pilot, 9, November 9, 1991.

[664] Frederick Clarkson, Eternal Hostility: The Struggle Between Theocracy and Democracy (Monroe, Maine: Common Courage Press, 1997), 84.

[665] Mark Silk, Spiritual Politics: Religion and America Since World War II (New York: Simon and Schuster, 1988), 99-100.

[666] "The Candidates, the platforms, and Church State-Issues," Church & State, 33 (September 1980), 6-10.

[667] John M. Swomley, "Neo-fascism and the religious right," The Humanist January/February 1995, 3-6.

[668] Swomley, "Neo-fascism," 3-6.

[669] Oklahoma City, World, Nov. 16, 1999.

[670] Scott Appleby, "The God Squads," Notre Dame Magazine summer 1995, 33-38.

[671] Appleby, "The God," 33-38.

[672] William Martin, With God on Our Side (New York: Broadway Books, 1996), 353.

[673] Martin, With God, 353.

[674] Martin, With God, 353.

[675] Martin, With God, 353.

[676] Rodney Clapp, "Democracy as Heresy," Christianity Today, 20 February 1987.

[677] Martin, With God, 354.

[678] Martin, With God, 354.

[679] Jerry Falwell, Listen America! (New York: Doubleday-Galilee, 1980).

[680] Falwell, Listen America!, 202.

[681] Falwell, Listen America!,205.

[682] Falwell, Listen America!

[683] Rob Boston, Close Encounters with the Religious Right (New York: Prometheus, 2000), 107.

[684] Stephen L. Carter, God's Name in Vain (New York: Basic Books, 2000), 45.

[685] Rob Boston, Why the Religious Right is Wrong, (New York: Prometheus, 1993), 234.

[686] Richard Swift, "Fundamentalism Reaching for Certainty," New Internationalist, August 1990.

[687] Martin, With God, 317.

[688] Martin, With God, 317.

[689] Ralph Reed, Active Faith, (New York: Free Press, 1996), 140.

[690] Sidney Blumenthal, "Christian Soldiers," The New Yorker, 18 July 1994.

[691] Reed, "I do guerilla," Norfolk Virginian-Pilot, 9, November 9, 1991.

[692] Joseph L. Conn, "Judgement Day," Church & State, September 1996.

[693] Martin, With God, 318.

[694] Joe Conason, "Christian Coalition Enters New York City," The Freedom Writer, May/June 1992.

[695] Tanya Melich, The Republican War Against Women (New York: Bantam Books, 1996), 291.

[696] Reed, Active Faith, 200-207.

[697] Joseph L.Conn, "Power Trip," Church & State, October 1995.

[698] Boston, Close Encounters, 68.

[699] Boston, Close Encounters, 71.

[700] Boston, Close Encounters, 72.

[701] Pat Robertson, "Message from the President," Christian Coalition of America website [online] [cited 13 June 2001]; available at http://www.cc.org/aboutcca/patmessage1.html.

[702] Charleston Gazette, July 5, 2000

[703] Sonja Barisic, "Falwell Says Antichrist Probably on Earth Now," Associated Press dispatch, 16 January 1999.

[704] Barisic, "Falwell Says."

[705] John Harris, "God Gave U.S. 'What We deserve,' Falwell says," Washington Post, 14 September 2001.

[706] Skip Porteus, Freedom Writer, December 1995.

[707] Boston, Close Encounters, 190.

[708] Martin, With God, 341-42.

[709] Rob Boston, "Family Feud," Church & State , May 1998.

[710] Boston, Close Encounters, 186.

[711] John M. Swomley, "Right-Wing Strong-Arming," The Humanist, September/October 1998, 40.

[712] Boston, Close Encounters, 189.

[713] Martin, With God, 355.

[714] Scott DeNicola, "Girl Scouts Lose their Way," Citizen, 21 February 1994.

[715] Boston, Why the Religious, 98.

[716] Boston, Why the Religious, 99.

[717] John Swomley, "One Nation Under God," The Humanist, May/June 1998, 6.

[718] Swomley, "One Nation," 6.

[719] John Swomley, "A League of the Pope's Own," The Humanist January/February 1998, 32.

[720] Swomley, "A League," 32.

[721] Swomley, "A League," 32.

[722] Swomley, "A League," 32.

[723] Swomley, "A League," 32.

[724] Boston, Close Encounters, 236.

[725] Neal Tannahill, American Government: Policy and Politics, 4th ed. (New York: HarperCollins, 1995), 110.

[726] Flo Conway and Jim Siegelman, Holy Terror: The Fundamentalist War on America's Freedoms in Religion, Politics and Our Private Lives, (New York: Dell, 1984), 143.

[727] Conway, Holy Terror, 144.

[728] Mike Phillips, "Tet offensive: Attack stunned American public" The Cincinnati Post, April 26, 2000.

[729] Boston, Why the Religious, 135.

[730] Rob Boston, "Operation Precinct," Church & State, July/August 1994.

[731] Gary North, Political Polytheism, 601.

[732] Martin, With God, 325.

[733] Martin, With God, 340.

[734] Boston, Why the Religious, 114.

[735] "School Bible Reading Survey," Church & State 13 (January 1960): 5.

[736] Joseph L. Conn, "Reagan Backs Government Sponsored School Prayer," Church & State 35 (June 1982): 3.

[737] Swomley, "Right Wing," 40.

[738] Boston, Close Encounters, 108.

[739] Boston, Why the Religious, 121.

[740] Boston, Why the Religious, 121

[741] Boston, Why the Religious, 52.

[742] Boston, Close Encounters, 17.

[743] "Statement on Teaching Evolution," National Association of Biology Teacher [online] [cited 21 October 2002]; available at http://www.nabt.org/sub/position_statements/evolution.asp.

[744] Boston, Close Encounters, 110.

[745] Carter, God's Name, 152.

[746] Jonathan Sarfati, "Refuting Evolution," Answers in Genesis Ministries website 1998 [online] [cited 14 April 2002]; available at http://answersingenesis.org/docs/1341.asp.

[747] Nicholas Humphrey, "What Shall We Tell the Children?" from Amnesty Lecture, Oxford, 21 February 1997 printed in Edge [online] [cited 14 November 2002]; available at http://www.edge.org/3rd_culture/humphrey/amnesty.html.

[748] "The Righteous Empire: A Short History of the End of History and Maybe Even of the GOP," The New Republic, 22 October 1984, 18-24.

[749] Martin, With God, 234.

[750] Appleby, "The God Squads," 33-38.

[751] Martin, With God, 217

[752] Martin, With God, 217.

[753] Martin, With God, 217.

[754] "Whose Prayer Does God Hear?" Ecumenical Trends, Graymore Ecumenical Institute, vol. 10, no. 1, January 1981, 12.

[755] Martin, With God, 221.

[756] Martin, With God, 222.

[757] Martin, With God, 222.

[758] Martin, With God, 225.

[759] Thomas, Cal (with Dobson, Ed) Blinded by the Might (Grand Rapidsm MI, Zenderrman Publishing House 1999)

[760] Boston, Close Encounters, 37.

[761] Hanna Rosin, "The Moral Minority: Thomas Was Among the Right, Now They Find Him Wrong," Washington Post, 18 March 1999.

[762] Herb Silverman "Indoctrination," Charleston Post and Courier, January 8, 1995, Letter to the Editor.

[763] D. James Kennedy and Jim Nelson Black, Character and Destiny: A Nation in Search of its Soul (Grand Rapids, Michigan: Zondervan Publishing House, 1994), 76.

[764] Martin, With God, 325
[765] Martin, With God, 366.
[766] http://www.bju.edu/
[767] Jake Tapper, "Jonesing For Votes," Salon.com, 3 February 2000 [online].
[768] Bill Baird and Joni Scott, "A test of our resolve: the religious right's attack on freedom," The Humanist, September/October 2000, 14-21 cited in WilsonSelect Plus_FT [database online] [cited 4 June 2001], 5.
[769] American Civil Liberties Union, 2001 work plan, 6-7.
[770] American Civil Liberties Union, 6-7
[771] American Civil Liberties Union, 5.
[772] American Civil Liberties Union, 7.
[773] "Candidate says there are probably still closet atheists," A.P. Charleston News & Courier, May 3, 1990.
[774] "Avoiding professor's legal trap," Charleston News & Courier, May 16, 1990, editorial.
[775] John Whitehead, The Second American Revolution, (Elgin, Illinois: David C. Cook, 1982).
[776] Deposition of Carroll A. Campbell, Jr., March 3, 1995, Case no. 94-CP-40-3594
[777] "Atheists have rights, too," Spartanburg Herald-Journal, August 13, 1995, editorial.
[778] "Gov. David Beasley wants…," Charleston Post and Courier, October 31, 1995.
[779] Heather Campbell "Professor still fighting for his religious rights," Cougar Pause. April 16, 1997.
[780] "Freedom for all," Herald-Journal, Spartanburg, SC,May 30, 1996, editorial.
[781] Conway, Holy Terror, 338.
[782] Gary North, Tools of Dominion (Tyler, Texas: Institute for Christian Economics, 1990), 1190-1216.
[783] Clarkson, Eternal Hostility, 10.
[784] Clarkson, Eternal Hostility, 10.
[785] Federal News Service, 3 February 1994.
[786] Michael Kinsley, "Martyr Complex," The New Republic, 13 September 1993.
[787] Mallica Dutt, "God's Guerrillas," New Internationalist , August 1999, 17.
[788] Appleby, "The God Squads," 10.
[789] Michael Lienesch, Redeeming America Piety & Politics in the New Christian Right (Chapel Hill, NC:Unversity of North Carolina Press, 1993), 249-52.
[790] Lienesch, Redeeming, 249.
[791] Richard J. Gelles and Ann Levine, Sociology: an Introduction 5th ed. (New York: McGraw-Hill, 1995), 472.
[792] Curt Sytsma, "A Humanist Manifesto," cited in Corliss Lamont, The Philosophy of Humanism (Amherst, New York: Half-Moon Foundation 8th ed., 1997), xv.

Chapter 8 Notes

[793] Curtis Lee Lawes, "Convention Side Lights," The Watchman Examiner, 1 July 1920, 834.
[794] Interfaith Alliance Foundation and Americans United for Separation of Church and State, "The Christian Coalition's 'Road to Victory' Conference: Warning: Hazards Ahead," September, 1995, 8-11, http://www.interfaithalliance.org/tia/final.rtf [online] [cited 28 April 2002].
[795] See, for example, Adib Rashad, "Fundamentalism: A Christian Word," http://www.escape.ca/~dkost/fundamentalism.htm
[796] Maureen Dowd, "Sacred Cruelties," New York Times, 7 April 2002, section 4, 15.
[797] Harish Desai, "Religious strife in India: Attack, more deaths bring clampdown," Atlanta Journal and Constitution, 17 March 2002, C-4; and Barry Bearak, "Angry and ashamed, Indian Prime Minister tours riot-torn state," New York Times, 5 April 2002, A-3.
[798] Michael Casey, "Attackers kill 14 in Indonesia massacre," Associated Press, Atlanta Journal and Constitution, 29 April 2002, A-5.

[799] D'Arcy Doran, "Miss World leaves, but unrest continues," Associated Press, Buffalo News, 24 November 2002, A-3.

[800] See, for an example of this, Nicholas D. Kristof, "Stoning and Scripture," New York Times, 30 April 2002, A-31.

[801] The Qur'an and Traditions, VIII. 39-42.

[802] The Qur'an and Traditions, IX. 5-6.

[803] See, for example, these books by Ibn Warraq: Why I Am Not A Muslim (Amherst, NY: Prometheus Books, 1995); The Quest for the Historical Muhammad (Amherst, NY: Prometheus Books, 2000); and What the Koran Really Says: Language, Text, and Commentary (Amherst, NY: Prometheus Books, 2002); also see Parvin Darabi and Romin P. Thomson, Rage Against Evil: The Courageous Life and Death of an Islamic Dissident (Amherst, NY: Prometheus Books, 2000); and Paul Fregosi, Jihad in the West: Muslim Conquests from the 7th to the 21st Centuries (Amherst, NY: Prometheus Books, 1999).

[804] Lawrence Davidson, Islamic Fundamentalism (Westport, Connecticut: Greenwood Press, 1998), 85.

[805] Bernard Lewis, "What Went Wrong," The Atlantic Monthly, January 2002, 43.

[806] Lewis, "What Went," 45.

[807] Lewis, "What Went," 45.

[808] Ibn Warraq, Why I Am Not a Muslim (Amherst, NY: Prometheus Books, 1995), 359.

[809] Warraq, Why I Am, 360.

[810] Gregory J. Rummo, "Calling Christians 'Taliban' is Slander," 14 March 2002, American Family Association Online [online] [cited 16 June 2002]; available at http://www.afa.net/culture/gr031402.asp in partially quoting Daniel Pipes, The Record, 10 January 2002.

[811] Richard Swift, "Fundamentalism: Reaching for Certainty," New Internationalist 4 August 1990 reprinted in SIRS CD-ROM 1997.

[812] Microsoft Encarta Encyclopedia 2000.

[813] Takbeer (Karachi), 23 November 1989, found in Mumtaz Ahmad, "Islamic Fundamentalism in South Asia: The Jamaat-I-Islami and the Tablighi Jamaat of South Asia," in Martin E. Marty and R. Scott Appleby Fundamentalisms Observed (University of Chicago Press: Chicago, 1991), 457-58.

[814] Mashriq (Lahore), 6 November 1989, found in Mumtaz Ahmad, "Islamic Fundamentalism in South Asia: The Jamaat-I-Islami and the Tablighi Jamaat of South Asia," in Martin E. Marty and R. Scott Appleby Fundamentalisms Observed (University of Chicago Press: Chicago, 1991), 458.

[815] Mumtaz Ahmad, "Islamic Fundamentalism in South Asia: The Jamaat-I-Islami and the Tablighi Jamaat of South Asia," in Martin E. Marty and R. Scott Appleby Fundamentalisms Observed (University of Chicago Press: Chicago, 1991), 458.

[816] Abul Ala Maududi, The Islamic Law and Constitution (Lahore: Islamic Publications, 1980), p. 263, quoted in Ann Elizabeth Mayer, "The Fundamentalist Impact on Law, Politics, and Constitutions in Iran, Pakistan, and the Sudan," Fundamentalisms and the State, eds. Martin E. Marty and R. Scott Appleby (Chicago: The University of Chicago Press, 1993), 113-14.

[817] Homa Hoodfar, "Bargaining with Fundamentalism: Women and the Politics of Population Control in Iran," Global Reproductive Health Forum [online] [cited 30 May 2002]; available at http://www.hsph.harvard.edu/Organizations/healthnet/gender/docs/hoodfar.html.

[818] Richard Swift, "Fundamentalism: Reaching for Certainty," New Internationalist 4 August 1990 reprinted in SIRS CD-ROM 1997.

[819] "Pakistan: Insufficient Protection of Women," Amnesty International, [online] [cited 6 June 2002]; available at

http://web.amnesty.org/802568F7005C4453/0/B681F17BF82BE7BE80256B8100631267?Open
&Highlight=2,women,Islam,beating.
[820] "Pakistan: Insufficient Protection."
[821] "Pakistan: Insufficient Protection."
[822] Azam Kamguian, "Crimes of Honour," Institute for the Secularisation of Islamic Society
[online] [cited 27 May 2002]; available at http://www.secularislam.org/women/honor.htm.
[823] Richard Lacayo, "About face," Time 3 December 2001.
[824] "What is Female Genital Mutilation?" Amnesty International, [online] [cited 6 June 2002];
available at
http://web.amnesty.org/802568F7005C4453/0/3B10EA18B5DF096E802569A5007186E4?Ope
n.
[825] "What is Female."
[826] Philip Smucker and Michael Satchell, "Hearts and Minds," U.S. News 15 October 2001
[online] [cited 15 October 2001]; available at
http://www.usnews.com/usnews/issue/011015/ideas/taliban.htm.
[827] O. N. Trisal, "Islamic Fundamentalism in Kashmir," Kashmir Information Network website
[online] [cited 8 June 2002]; available at http://www.kashmir-
information.com/Miscellaneous/trisal.html.
[828] Trisal, "Islamic Fundamentalism."
[829] "Sudan: Suppression of Information," News from Africa Watch, 30 August 1990, 23-24,
quoted in Ann Elizabeth Mayer, "The Fundamentalist Impact on Law, Politics, and
Constitutions in Iran, Pakistan, and the Sudan," Fundamentalisms and the State, eds. Martin E.
Marty and R. Scott Appleby (Chicago: The University of Chicago Press, 1993), 113-14.
[830] "Sudan: Suppression," 23-24.
[831] Akbar S. Ahmed, "Pakistan's Blasphemy Law: Words Fail Me," Washington Post, 17 May
2002.
[832] "Malaysia: Christian Persecution in Malaysia," International Christian Concern website
[online] [cited 7 June 2002]; available at
http://www.persecution.org/humanrights/malaysia.html.
[833] "Bosnia and Herzegovina--Christian Persecution in Bosnia and Herzegovina," International
Christian Concern website [online] [cited 7 June 2002]; available at
http://www.persecution.org/humanrights/bosnia.html.
[834] "Middle East," Microsoft Encarta Encyclopedia 2000.
[835] James A. Haught, Holy Hatred: Religious Conflicts of the '90s (Amherst, NY: Prometheus
Books), 124-25.
[836] Haught, Holy Hatred, 129.
[837] Albert J. Menendez, Visions of Reality: What Fundamentalist Schools Teach (Buffalo:
Prometheus Books, 1993), 8-9.
[838] See, for example, Randall Balmer, Blessed Assurance: A History of Evangelicalism in
America (Boston: Beacon Press, 1999), 28-30.
[839] Colin Campbell, "Faith Seems Increasingly Linked with Killing Others," Atlanta Journal and
Constitution, 14 March 2002, A-14.
[840] Miroslav Hroch and Anna Skybova, Ecclesia Miltans: The Inquisition, translated by Janet
Fraser (Germany: Edition Leipzig, 1988).
[841] Leonard W. Levy, Blasphemy: Verbal Offense Against the Sacred, from Moses to Salman
Rushdie, (New York: Alfred A. Knopf, 1993), 65-69.
[842] The widespread use of the Bible by clergymen in the American South to support slavery
(and, later, segregation and racial discrimination) is well-documented. See, for example, Edward
T. Babinski, Leaving the Fold: Testimonies of Former Fundamentalists (Amherst, NY:
Prometheus Books, 1995), 35-39; "Alabama candidate for U.S. House says Bible justifies
slavery," Dallas Morning News, 10 May 1996, 7-A; E.N. Elliott, Cotton is King and Pro-
Slavery Arguments (Augusta, GA: Pritchard, Abbott, & Loomis, 1860); E. W. Heaton,
Everyday Life in Old Testament Times (NY: Charles Scribner's Sons, 1956), 142-143; and Judy

Elliott, "Author takes fresh look at the Good Book—and slavery," Marietta (Georgia) Daily Journal, 7 June 1998.

[843] See for example, Daniel Jonah Goldhagen, Hitler's Willing Executioners: Ordinary Germans and the Holocaust (New York: Alfred A. Knopf, 1996); or Robert P. Ericksen and Susannah Heschel, eds., Betrayal—German Churches and the Holocaust (Minneapolis: Fortress Press, 1999).

[844] Dayton (Tennessee) Herald-News, 15 February 2002.

[845] Rod L. Evans and Irwin M. Berent, Fundamentalism: Hazards and Heartbreaks (LaSalle, Illinois: Open Court, 1988), 153.

[846] Evans, Fundamentalism, 154.

[847] Marlene Winell, Leaving the Fold: A Guide for Former Fundamentalists and Others Leaving Their Religion (Oakland, CA: New Harbinger Publications, Inc., 1993).

[848] Kimberly Blaker, "Christian Fundamentalism: A Growing Danger," first-place research paper in the category of philosophy/religious studies in the Student Scholars at Michigan's Two-Year Colleges 1998 conference.

[849] Frederick Clarkson, Eternal Hostility: The Struggle Between Theocracy and Democracy (Monroe, Maine: Common Courage Press, 1997), 203.

[850] Clarkson, Eternal Hostility, 203-216.

[851] Robert Boston, Close Encounters with the Religious Right: Journeys Into the Twilight Zone of Religion and Politics (Amherst, NY: Prometheus Books, 2000), 261-270.

[852] Karen Armstrong, A History of God: The 4000-Year Quest of Judaism, Christianity and Islam (New York: Alfred A. Knopf, 1994), 391.

[853] Armstrong, A History, 399.

[854] Karen Armstrong, The Battle for God, (New York: Alfred A. Knopf, 2000), 364.

[855] Armstrong, The Battle, 368.

[856] Armstrong, The Battle, 368.

[857] Armstrong, The Battle, 368.

[858] Armstrong, A History.

[859] Balmer, Blessed Assurance, 140.

[860] Randall Balmer, Mine Eyes Have Seen the Glory: A Journey into the Evangelical Subculture in America, Expanded Edition (New York: Oxford University Press, 1993), 277.

[861] Balmer, Blessed Assurance, 101.

[862] John Shelby Spong, Rescuing the Bible from Fundamentalism: A Bishop Rethinks the Meaning of Scripture (San Francisco: Harper San Francisco/Harper Collins Paperback, 1992), 247.

[863] Spong, Rescuing, 5.

[864] Lloyd J. Averill, Religious Right, Religious Wrong: A Critique of the Fundamentalist Phenomenon (New York: The Pilgrim Press, 1990), 12.

[865] Averill, Religious, 103.

[866] Averill, Religious, 157-175.

[867] Bruce Bawer, Stealing Jesus: How Fundamentalism Betrays Christianity (New York: Crown Publishers, 1997), 307

[868] Bawer, Stealing Jesus, 326-327.

[869] Lorene Hanley Duquin, When a Loved One Leaves the Church (Huntington, Indiana: Our Sunday Visitor, Inc., 2001) 152-153.

[870] Duquin, When a Loved, 152.

[871] The Academy of Humanism, Neo-Fundamentalism: The Humanist Response (Buffalo: Prometheus Books, 1988).

[872] Vern Bullough, "The Return to Islamic Fundamentalism," The Academy of Humanism, Neo-Fundamentalism: The Humanist Response (Buffalo: Prometheus Books, 1988), 51.

[873] Alberto Hidalgo Tuñon, "The Dilemma of Fundamentalism," The Academy of Humanism, Neo-Fundamentalism: The Humanist Response (Buffalo: Prometheus Books, 1988), 91.

[874] Paul Kurtz, "The Growth of Fundamentalism Worldwide," The Academy of Humanism, Neo-Fundamentalism: The Humanist Response (Buffalo: Prometheus Books, 1988), 20.

[875] Kurtz, "The Growth," 21.

[876] Kurtz, "The Growth," 24.

[877] Gerald LaRue, "The Threat of Neo-Fundamentalism," The Academy of Humanism, Neo-Fundamentalism: The Humanist Response (Buffalo: Prometheus Books, 1988), 38.

[878] Paul Kurtz, personal interview, October 2001.

[879] Marvin Harris, Our Kind: Who We Are, Where We Came From, Where We Are Going (New York: Harper & Row, Publishers, 1989), 401.

[880] Harris, Our Kind, 414.

[881] Keith M. Parsons (editor: Edward M. Buckner), Why I Am Not a Christian (Roswell, Georgia: The Freethought Press, Atlanta Freethought Society, 2000), 1.

[882] Parsons (editor: Edward M. Buckner), Why I Am Not.

[883] Toby Lester, "Oh Gods!," The Atlantic Monthly, February 2002, 37.

[884] Lester, "Oh Gods!" 38.

[885] Lester, "Oh Gods!" 39.

[886] Barry A. Kosmin, Egon Mayer, and Ariela Keysar, American Religious Identification Survey, 2001 (New York: Graduate Center of the City University of New York, 2001), 17.

[887] Kosmin, American, 19.

[888] Kosmin, American, 13.

[889] Dan Barker, Losing Faith in Faith: From Preacher to Atheist (Madison, Wisconsin: Freedom From Religion Foundation, Inc., 1992).

[890] Edward T. Babinski, ed., Leaving the Fold: Testimonies of Former Fundamentalists (Amherst, NY: Prometheus Books, 1995).

[891] Bob Altemeyer and Bruce Hunsberger, Amazing Conversions: Why Some Turn to Faith and Others Abandon Religion (Amherst, NY: Prometheus Books, 1997).

[892] Altemeyer, Amazing, 212-13.

[893] Babinski, Leaving the Fold: Testimonies of Former Fundamentalists, throughout, but especially in the "Introduction," 15-17.

[894] David Montoya, "The Political Disease Known as Fundamentalism," in Babinski, Leaving the Fold: Testimonies of Former Fundamentalists, 132.

[895] Farrell Till, "From Preacher to Skeptic," in Babinski, Leaving the Fold: Testimonies of Former Fundamentalists, 294.

[896] Maxine Parshall, Email Correspondence to Kimberly Blaker, May 2002.

[897] Thomas Jefferson, letter to Benjamin Rush, April 21, 1803; from Daniel B. Baker, ed., Political Quotations (Detroit: Gale Research, Inc., 1990), 189.

[898] John Adams, "A Defence of the Constitutions of Government of the United States of America" [1787-1788]; from Adrienne Koch, ed., The American Enlightenment: The Shaping of the American Experiment and a Free Society (New York: George Braziller, 1965), 258.

[899] Notes on the State of Virginia, Query XVII, Torchbook Edition, (New York: Harper & Row Publishers, 1964,) 152.

[900] Michael E. Buckner, "The UnChristian Roots of the Fourth of July," Secular Web [online] [cited 8 March 2002]; available at http://www.infidels.org/library/modern/features/2000/buckner1.html.

Permissions Acknowledgments

The following have granted permission to reprint or paraphrase previously published material from the titles listed.

Appleby, R. Scott: "The God Squads" by R. Scott Appleby appearing in *Notre Dame Magazine* Summer 1995.

Baker House Book Company: *Women, Abuse, and the Bible: How Scripture Can Be Used to Hurt or Heal* by Catherine Clark Kroeger and James R. Beck (contributors cited: Shirley Gillett, Carolyn Holderread Heggen, Jackie J. Hudson, Alice P. Mathews, and David M. Scholer), Baker Book House, a division of Baker Book House Company ©1996.

Barna Research Group, LTD.: "Christians Are More Likely to Experience Divorce Than Are Non-Christians," The Barna Research Group Online, Ventura, CA, www.barna.org, 21 December 1999.

Blackwell Publishing: "Religion and Prejudice: the Role of Religious Fundamentalism, Quest, and Right-Wing Authoritarianism," by Bruce Hunsberger *Journal of Social Issues* vol. 51, No. 2, 1995.

Broadway Books: *With God on Our Side: The Rise of the Religious Right* by William Martin and Lumiere Production, Inc. Copyright ©1996 by William Martin and Lumiere Productions, Inc. Used by permission of Broadway Books, a division of Random House, Inc.

Doyle, Rodger: "Down with Evolution" by Rodger Doyle, *Scientific American* March 2002.

Human Sciences Press: "A Self-Psychological Approach to the Cult Phenomenon," by Doni P. Whitsett *Clinical Social Work Journal* vol. 20, No. 4, Winter 1992.

Lattin, Don: "Apocalypse Now?" by Don Lattin, *Common Boundary* May/June 1996.

Prometheus Books: *Close Encounters with the Religious Right by Robert Boston*, extracts from pp. 37, 52, 68, 71, 72, 107, 108, 186, 189, 190, 236 (Amherst, NY: Prometheus Books). Copyright ©2000 by Robert Boston. Reprinted with permission of the publisher.

Prometheus Books: *Why the Religious Right is Wrong* by Robert Boston (Amherst, NY: Prometheus Books). Copyright ©1993 Robert Boston. Reprinted with permission.

Ontario Consultants on Religious Tolerance: "Millennialism: Competing Theories" by B.A. Robinson copyright © 1996 to 2001 incl. By Ontario Consultants on Religious Tolerance.

Sterling Lord Literistic, Inc.: *Holy Terror: the Fundamentalist War on Religion, Politics and Our Private Lives* by Flo Conway and Jim Siegelman copyright ©1983 by Flo Conway. Reprinted by permission of Sterling Lord Literistic, Inc.

Swomley, John M.: "The 'Partial-birth' Debate in 1998" by John M. Swomley, *The Humanist* March/April1998.

Sytsma, Curt: "A Humanist Manifesto" by Curt Sytsma published in *The Philosophy of Humanism* by Corliss Lamont.

Time Inc.: "Letting God Back In" by Jodie Morse, *Time* 22 October 2001. Copyright ©2001 TIME Inc. excerpts reprinted by permission.

Westchester Coalition for Legal Abortion: "Violence Continues: Links Between Militants and Militia.

Suggestions for Further Reading

Altemeyer, Bob, and Bruce Hunsberger, *Amazing Conversions: Why Some Turn to Faith and Others Abandon Religion* (Prometheus Books, 1997).

Armstrong, Karen, *A History of God: The 4,000 Year Quest of Judaism, Christianity and Islam* (Ballantine Books, 1994).

Armstrong, Karen, *The Battle for God* (Alfred A. Knopf, 2000).

Askin, Steve, *A New Rite: Conservative Catholic Organizations and Their Allies* (Catholics for a Free Choice).

Averill, Lloyd J., *Religious Right, Religious Wrong: A Critique of the Fundamentalist Phenomenon* (The Pilgrim Press, 1990).

Babinski, Edward T., ed., *Leaving the Fold: Testimonies of Former Fundamentalists* (Prometheus Books, 1995).

Balmer, Randall, *Mine Eyes Have Seen the Glory: A Journey into the Evangelical Subculture in America* (Oxford University Press, 1989).

Barkun, Michael, *Religion and the Racist Right: The Origins of the Christian Identity Movement* (University of North Carolina Press, 1996).

Bawer, Bruce, *Stealing Jesus: How Fundamentalism Betrays Christianity* (Crown Publishers, 1997).

Bellant, Russ, *The Coors Connection: How Coors Family Philanthropy Undermines Democratic Pluralism* (South End Press, 1991).

Bellant, Russ, *The Religious Right in Michigan Politics* (Americans for Religious Liberty, 1996).

Blanchard, Dallas, *The Anti-Abortion Movement and the Rise of the Religious Right: From Polite to Fiery Protest* (Twayne Publishers, 1994).

Boston, Robert, *Close Encounters with the Religious Right* (Prometheus Books, 2000).

Boston, Robert, *The Most Dangerous Man in America?: Pat Robertson and the Rise of the Christian Coalition* (Prometheus Books, 1996).

Boston, Robert, *Why the Religious Right Is Wrong about Separation of Church and State* (Prometheus Books, 1993).

Buckner, Edward M., and Michael E. Buckner, eds., *Quotations That Support the Separation of State and Church* 2d ed. (Atlanta Freethought Society, Inc., 1995).

Clarkson, Frederick, and Skipp Porteous, *Challenging the Christian Right: The Activists Handbook* (Institute for First Amendment Studies, Ms. Foundation, 1992).

Clarkson, Frederick, *Eternal Hostility: The Struggle Between Theocracy and Democracy* (Common Courage Press, 1997).

Conway, Flo and Jim Siegelman, *Holy Terror: The Fundamentalist War on America's Freedoms in Religion, Politics and Our Private Lives* (Doubleday, 1982).

Detwiler, Fritz, *Standing on the Premises of God: The Christian Right's Fight to Redefine America's Public Schools* (New York University Press, 1999).

Sara Diamond, *Roads to Dominion: Right-Wing Movements and Political Power in the United States* (The Guilford Press, 1995).

Doerr, Edd, *Catholic Schools: The Facts.*

Doerr, Edd, Albert J. Menendez, and John Swomley, *The Case Against School Vouchers* (Prometheus Books, 1996).

Faludi, Susan, *Backlash: The Undeclared War Against Women* (Anchor \Books-Doubleday, 1991).

Haught, James A., *Holy Hatred: Religious Conflicts of the '90s* (Prometheus Books).

Kitcher, Philip, *Abusing Science: The Case Against Creationism* (The MIT Press, 1993).

Kroeger, Catherine Clark and James R. Beck, *Women, Abuse, and the Bible: How Scripture Can Be Used to Hurt or Heal* (Baker, 1996).

La Piana, Fr. George, John W. Swomley, and Herbert F. Vetter ed., *Catholic Power Vs. American Freedom* (Prometheus Books, 2002).

Larue, Gerald, *Playing God: 50 Religions' Views on Your Right to Die* (1996).

Levy, Leonard W., *Blasphemy: Verbal Offense Against the Sacred, from Moses to Salman Rushdie* (Alfred A. Knopf, 1993).

Martin, William, *With God on Our Side: The Rise of the Religious Right in America* (Broadway Books, 1996).

Marty, Martin E. and R. Scott Appleby, ed., *Fundamentalisms Observed* (University of Chicago Press, 1991).

Marty, Martin E. and R. Scott Appleby, ed., *Fundamentalisms and theState: Remaking Polities, Economies, and Militance* (University of Chicago Press, 1997).

Marty, Martin E., R. Scott Appleby, and Scott R. Appleby, ed., *Fundamentalisms and Society: Reclaiming the Sciences, the Family, and Educatio* (University of Chicago Press, 1997).

Marty, Martin E. and R. Scott Appleby, ed., *Accounting for Fundamentalisms: The Dynamic Character of Movements* (University of Chicago Press, 1994).

Marty, Martin E. and R. Scott Appleby, ed., *Fundamentalisms Comprehended* (University of Chicago Press, 1997).

Melich, Tanya, *The Republican War Against Women: An Insider's Report from Behind the Lines* (Bantam Doubleday, 1996).

Menendez, Albert J., *Evangelicals at the Ballot Box*, (Prometheus Books, 1996).

Menendez, Albert J., *Three Voices of Extremism: Charles Colson, James Dobson, D. James Kennedy* (Americans for Religious Liberty, 1997).

Menendez, Albert J., *Visions of Reality: What Fundamentalist Schools Teach* (Prometheus Books, 1993).

Reiter, Jerry, *Live From the Gates of Hell: An Insider's Look at the Antiabortion Underground* (Prometheus Books, 2000).

Spong, John Shelby, *Rescuing the Bible From Fundamentalism: A BishopRethinks the Meaning of Scripture* (HarperCollins, 1992).

Spong, John Shelby, *Why Christianity Must Change or Die: A Bishop Speaks to Believers in Exile* (Harper SanFrancisco, 1999).

Strozier, Charles B., *Apocalypse: On the Psychology of Fundamentalism in America* (Beacon, 1994).

Strozier, Charles B. and Michael Flynn, eds., *The Year 2000: Essays on the End* (New York University Press, 1997).

Swomley, John M., *Religious Liberty and the Secular State*, (Prometheus Books, 1992).

Index

Editor and Contributors

Kimberly Blaker, of Michigan, is a syndicated writer and columnist, social advocate, and staunch supporter of the separation of church and state. Her column, The Wall™, covering issues pertaining to the religious right and civil liberties, appears regularly in news publications around the country. Her commentaries have also appeared in the *Detroit Free Press*, *Detroit News*, *San Francisco Examiner*, and *Los Angeles Daily Journal*. Her syndicated articles have appeared in more than 90 regional magazines. She has also been published several times in the national *Complete Woman Magazine*. *The Fundamentals of Extremism* was inspired by her award-winning research paper, "Christian Fundamentalism: A Growing Danger."

Edward M. Buckner, Ph. D. of New York, is Executive Director of the Council for Secular Humanism and editor of the *Secular Humanist Bulletin*. He received his B.A. in English from Rice University in 1967 and his Ph. D. in Educational Leadership from Georgia State University in 1983. He is former Director of planning, research, and development for Atlanta Technical Institute. Formerly he also served as Vice President of Communications for Americans United for Separation of Church and State, Georgia Chapter, and as chair of the 7th U.S. Congressional District Democratic Party. He is co-editor of *Quotations that Support the Separation of State and Church*.

Edwin Frederick Kagin, J.D., of Kentucky, is an attorney and the son of a Presbyterian minister. He received his B.A. degree in English Language and Literature from University of Missouri at Kansas City in 1964 and his J.D. degree from the School of Law of the University of Louisville in 1971. He is an Eagle Scout, former college English Instructor, U.S. Air Force veteran, and a founding board member of Recover Resources Center, an alternative to Alcoholics Anonymous. In 1996, he founded Camp Quest, the first residential summer camp in the U.S. for children of atheists and other freethinkers, which he directs. He is a speaker, debater, and outspoken critic of violations of church and state.

Bobbie Kirkhart, of California, is a retired teacher. She earned her B.A. in journalism from University of Oklahoma in 1965. Her first national article appeared in *Christianity Today*, while teaching Sunday school during her academic career. She then spent five years as a social worker in South Central Los Angeles working with abused children, ultimately leading to an alteration in her beliefs. She is president of Atheist Alliance International, the nation's only national (and international) democratic atheist organization. She has been published in *Secular Nation* and has made several radio and television appearances including *To The Point*, syndicated on National Public Radio.

Herb Silverman, Ph. D. of South Carolina, is Distinguished Professor of Mathematics at the College of Charleston, which he joined in 1976, and is a National Board Member of the American Humanist Association. He received his Ph.D. in Mathematics from Syracuse University in 1968. He is the author of over 100 research articles and recipient of the Outstanding Research Award at the College of Charleston. He attained the office of notary public in 1997 when the South Carolina Supreme Court ruled unconstitutional the state law that prohibited nonbelievers from holding public office. For his successful constitutional challenge, he was recognized by the *Wall Street Journal* and placed in their winners' column.

John M. Suarez, M.D., of California, is formerly Associate Professor of Psychiatry at the University of California, Los Angeles and is on the Board of Trustees for Americans United for Separation of Church and State. He received his M.D. from Columbia University School of Medicine in 1960 and his M.S. from UCLA in 1964. During his career, he specialized in legal psychiatry. He has had forty-one articles published in professional journals, including the *Journal of Forensic Sciences* and *Bulletin American Academy of Psychiatry and The Law*. He also serves as Chairman of the Committee on Education for Americans United and Vice Chairman of Development at the Center for Inquiry West and has been a long time social activist.

The Fundamentals of Extremism "deserves all the attention it can get, whether or not you agree with its premise, its assertions or its conclusions. It is scrupulously researched by a team of veteran Christian Right critics who know the game and the players. The subtleties this movement uses to push its political agenda are sophisticated and scary. And they're worth knowing in full detail."
-- *Blue Ridge Business Journal,* Dan Smith

"Though *Fundamentals* doesn't focus on gun-toting, overtly racist goose-stepping Nazi flag-waving curiosities, it isn't any less disturbing than James Ridgeway's pivotal work *Blood in the Face*, or equally scholarly studies on the Christian Identity. This book's authority hinges on meticulous documentation of a slow but tangible national shift from a constitutionally based, secular democracy to an unabashedly apostolic theocracy. . . None of the arguments presented in Fundamentals are radical . . ."
-- *San Antonio Current*, Anjali Gupta

"[*The Fundamentals of Extremism*] is filled with astonishing citations that demonstrate the virulence of the Christian fundamentalists and the negative and destructive character of their agenda. Some come from unsuspected quarters. . . . It is worth reading for anyone who wishes to understand one of the constituencies Mr. Bush relies upon to stay in power for another four-year term. That one or more Supreme Court Justices may be in the balance should send people to read this book, talk to their friends and neighbors and run to the polls in November 2004."
--*Swans,* Gilles d'Aymery

"This book is an encyclopedic indictment of the extreme Christian right, but its content can be applied to any extremist belief system. It and the current world situation can help awaken us to the need to consider and better understand all sides of religious differences and see them in total and true perspective. The book is recommended for what it is: a well-articulated informative secular presentation in the debate between liberal and conservative views of religion and the danger in extremes."
-- *Cultic Studies Review*, Frank MacHovec, Ph.D.